modern
defence

by Jon Speelman & Neil McDonald

EVERYMAN CHESS

Published by Everyman Publishers plc, London

First published in 2000 by Gloucester Publishers plc, (formerly Everyman Publishers plc), Northburgh House, 10 Northburgh Street, London, EC1V 0AT

Reprinted 2004, 2005

British Library Cataloguing-in-Publication Data
A catalogue record for this book is available from the British Library.

ISBN 1 85744 281 4

Distributed in North America by The Globe Pequot Press, P.O Box 480, 246 Goose Lane, Guilford, CT 06437-0480.

All other sales enquiries should be directed to Gloucester Publishers plc, Northburgh House, 10 Northburgh Street, London, EC1V 0AT
tel: 020 7253 7887 fax: 020 7490 3708
email: info@everymanchess.com
website: www.everymanchess.com

Everyman is the registered trade mark of Random House Inc. and is used in this work under license from Random House Inc.

EVERYMAN CHESS SERIES (formerly Cadogan Chess)

Chief Advisor: Garry Kasparov
Commissioning Editor: Byron Jacobs
Typeset and edited by First Rank Publishing, Brighton.
Production by Navigator Guides.
Cover Design by Horatio Monteverde.
Printed in the U.K. by Lightning Source

CONTENTS

BIBLIOGRAPHY

Books

Encyclopaedia of Chess Openings volume B, third edition (Sahovski Informator, 1997)

Nunn's Chess Openings, Nunn, Burgess, Emms and Gallagher (Everyman, 1999)

The Modern Defence, Keene and Botterill (Batsford, 1972)

Winning with the Modern, Norwood (Batsford, 1994)

Fire on Board, Shirov (Cadogan/Everyman, 1997)

Periodicals

Informator

New in Chess Yearbooks

New in Chess Magazine

Chess Monthly

British Chess Magazine

ChessBase MegaBase CD-ROM

INTRODUCTION

When Byron Jacobs originally asked me (Jon Speelman) if I was interested in writing a book on the Modern, I was both somewhat apprehensive and rather pleased: apprehensive, because I thought it might entail an inordinate amount of work; and pleased, because my opening repertoire has for some time been crying out for redevelopment – and it's always nice to be paid for essential work.

Although I used to play the Pirc/Modern complex at the end of the eighties and start of the 1990s, in recent years I've drifted towards light-square systems: the French and Caro-Kann against 1 e4, with a very occasional Centre-Counter chucked in; and far too many outings with the English Defence starting 1 d4 e6 2 c4 b6 or 1 c4 b6 against queen's pawn players. While the latter in particular has maintained my appreciation of the virtues of cramped but potentially dynamic positions, it was nevertheless evidently high time for a visit to the bowyer in order to add another (somewhat stretched) string to my rather decrepit bow.

The present work is the result of these labours, an attempt to explain that extremely slippery but plucky and resilient customer the Modern Defence, ably assisted by Neil McDonald, who has written the 1 e4 sections.

What is the Modern Defence?

Whereas most openings are extremely easy to define, one of the greatest virtues of the Modern Defence is its extreme mutability and fickleness. All the games in this book could have started either 1 e4 g6 or 1 d4 g6, but of course, many began 1 e4/1 d4 d6 or 1 c4 g6 or indeed 1 d4 ♘f6 2 ♘f3 g6 3 ♗g5 (which transposes into Chapter 4, notes to Game 20, after 3...♗g7 4 ♘bd2 0-0 5 c3 d6 6 e4). Rather then, than defining the opening by the very first moves, it seems more sensible to consider the family it is part of and what it is *not*.

The Dark-Square Family

The Modern is one member of a family of openings in which Black fianchettoes his king's bishop and usually initially plays his d-pawn to d6 rather than d5. His counterplay will then normally be based on this bishop either along the long diagonal after ...c7-c5, d4-d5 – a 'Benoni-type' pawn structure – or on the kingside after ...e7-e5, d4-d5 or sometimes against the enemy centre after either ...e5xd4 or ...c5xd4 – the 'Maroczy Bind' pawn structure, which usually stems from the Sicilian – 1 e4 c5 2 ♘f3 ♘c6 3 d4 cxd4 4 ♘xd4 g6 5 c4. All of these structures, already familiar in other contexts, arise in the course of this book.

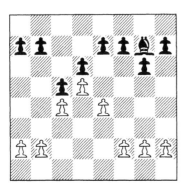

A 'Benoni-type' pawn structure.

Typical King's Indian pawn structure – also very common in Chapter 6.

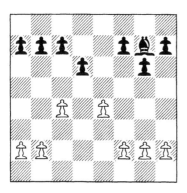

Another typical King's Indian pawn structure – often Black's c-pawn is on c6.

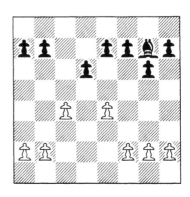

A 'Maroczy Bind' pawn structure

What Black is avoiding
Pre-eminent in this dark-square group are the King's Indian which normally starts 1 d4 ♘f6 2 c4 g6 and the Pirc after 1 e4 d6 2 d4 ♘f6 3 ♘c3 g6. Perhaps the Modern Defence is best defined by the fact that by delaying the development of his king's knight Black attempts either to avoid the main lines of these – or perhaps to transpose back into them at his own convenience into (favourable) lines of his choosing.

In particular, when he plays the Modern, Black is definitely avoiding the various main lines of the King's Indian after 1 d4 ♘f6 2 c4 g6 3 ♘c3 ♗g7 4 e4 d6 and the Austrian Attack against the Pirc after 1 e4 d6 2 d4 ♘f6 3 ♘c3 g6 4 f4 ♗g7.

Eccentric Relatives
If White attempts to set up these systems then the Modern player can employ one of a variety of cunning move orders to thwart him. Some of these 'eccentric relatives' remain most uncommon, but others have been played thousands of times, setting up independent lines of considerable theoretical importance.

I realise that this plethora of lines may

be rather disconcerting and in the discussion below we have concentrated on the most important, hoping to spare the reader too complex a maze of ideas. But if as one of the (I presume) majority of readers who intend to play the Modern as Black, you are at first sight confused then consider how much more worrisome the matter is for White: for usually it is Black who chooses which particular side line to go down and (s)he is likely to be much more familiar with the matter in the first place.

The 1 e4 Modern

In the first part of this book (Chapters 1-4, written by Neil McDonald) we are concerned with variations in which c2-c4 isn't played by White in the opening. These games tend to start 1 e4 rather than 1 d4. Many die-hard 1 e4 players regard c2-c4 as a alien move, something quite beyond the ken and mysterious; they instinctively avoid it, especially if Black is also bluffing them with the threat of a transposition to a King's Indian and thirty moves of main line theory. Of course, in some cases this isn't a bluff: Botvinnik was one of the first players to play the Pirc against 1 e4 and transpose to the King's Indian after c2-c4.

One of the things we love about the Modern is its flexibility. This, however, causes problems when we try to divide the material into meaningful chapters. Perhaps it is a good time to recall an amusing, and probably apocryphal, story about an attempt by Janos Flesch, the late Hungarian Grandmaster, to beat the World Blindfold simultaneous record. His opponents, who all belonged to the same club, played a really dirty trick on him! Half of them answered Flesch's 1 d4 or 1 e4 with 1...g6, while the other half played 1...d6; then on the second move half of those who had played 1...g6 played 2...♗g7, while the other half played 2...d6; meanwhile the

1...d6 players were choosing between 2...g6 and 2...c6 and 2...♘d7. By the third move Black was announcing moves like 3...g6, 3...c6, 3...♗g7, 3...d6 or 3...♘d7 and poor Flesch, who of course had no sight of the boards, couldn't remember which moves had been played in each individual game. One version of the story has him escaping through a toilet window.

We hope things aren't so desperate for our readers, but they should be aware of the enormous transpositional possibilities in the Modern. We are especially keen to offer our apologies to any player of White who finds that his or her favourite line against the Modern has been torn to shreds and the entrails cheerfully scattered at random throughout the remaining chapters.

Any division of material in the Modern is fairly arbitrary, but we have decided on the following approach. Note that in general we regard an early ...♘f6 by Black as anathema, since that infringes upon Pirc territory.

In Chapter 1 we cover the Gurgenidze main line. This includes all games beginning 1 e4 g6 2 d4 ♗g7 3 ♘c3 c6 4 f4 d5 5 e5 or 1 e4 d6 2 d4 g6 3 ♘c3 c6 4 f4 d5. We also look at 4 f4 d6 and 4...♕b6, where Black turns down the chance for the Gurgenidze. So far, so simple...

In Chapter 2 we consider lines where White avoids the Gurgenidze by answering 1 e4 g6 2 d4 ♗g7 3 ♘c3 c6 with 4 ♘f3 or 4 ♗e3. Black may reply with either 4...d6 or 4...d5.

In Chapter 3 we look at lines beginning 1 e4 g6 2 d4 ♗g7 3 ♘c3 d6, where after 4 f4 or 4 ♘f3 or 4 ♗e3 Black plays 4...a6 rather than 4...♘f6 (really a Pirc Defence) or 4...c6, which would transpose to Chapter 2, or in the case of 4 f4, possibly Chapter 1, or the 'Pirc-ish' 4...♘f6.

Finally, in Chapter 4, we consider 1 e4 g6 2 d4 ♗g7 3 ♘c3 d6 (or 3...c6) 4 ♗c4 and (after 3...d6) 4 ♗g5, as well as two quieter systems for White: firstly, the fianchetto with g2-g3 and secondly, the solid c2-c3.

We should like to remind the reader that 3...c6 can lead to a pawn structure significantly different to that reached after 3...d6, assuming that Black strikes immediately at White's centre with ...d7-d5. In fact, *Informator*, as well as *ECO*, categorises the positions after ....d7-d5 as a hybrid of the Caro-Kann (it is often reached via the move order 1 e4 c6 2 d4 d5 3 ♘c3 g6 etc.). So if you want to find examples from this hallowed journal you should look under the code B15 as well as B06!

The 1 d4 Modern

If White aims directly for the King's Indian, then Black may co-operate to the point of reaching this position, e.g. via 1 d4 g6 2 c4 ♗g7 3 e4 d6 4 ♘c3 – what Keene and Botterill in their seminal work the Modern Defence, term the starting point of the Averbakh variation.

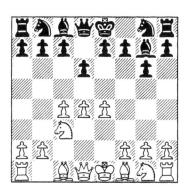

The Averbakh variation

Here Black has a variety of independent options.

4...♘c6 is very active and most popular – Chapters 5 and 6, but he can also play 4...♘d7 (Chapter 7) or a rarer move such as 4...c6, 4...e5 or even the rather dubious

4...f5 (all Chapter 8).

If White is more subtle in his attempts to foist the King's Indian on Black, then there are also several other lines which we can try. For instance if 1 d4 g6 2 c4 ♗g7 3 ♘c3 d6 4 ♘f3.

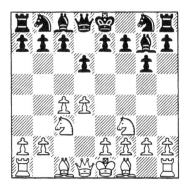

Then there are several important lines, particularly 4...♗g4 and 4...♘d7 5 g3 e5 (Chapter 9, Games 52-56).

Under the move order above – 1 d4 g6 2 c4 ♗g7 3 ♘c3 Black also has an opportunity to muddy the waters with 3...c5.

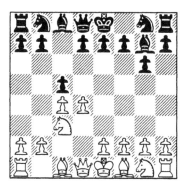

Now if 4 d5 he can avoid a normal Benoni with either 4...f5 or first 4...♗xc3+ 5 bxc3 f5 (Chapter 9, Game 59).

White can of course play 4 ♘f3 but after 4...cxd4 5 ♘xd4 ♘c6 6 ♘c2 (6 e3 is playable but slightly passive) again 6...♗xc3+ is possible while there are other playable independent lines with 6...d6 in which Black takes advantage of the fact that he hasn't played ...♞f6 to exert immediate pressure against the queenside.

However White can second guess us by playing ♞f3 first – 1 d4 g6 2 c4 ♝g7 3 ♞f3.

Now if we want to avoid the lines with 3...d6 4 ♞c3 then we can again try 3...c5 but after 4 e4 White has almost tricked us into a normal Maroczy Bind since 4...cxd4 5 ♞xd4 seems most 'normal'. However, we can wriggle out with 4...♛a5+ when all of 5 ♝d2 ♛b6, 5 ♞c3 ♞c6 and 5 ♞c3 ♞f6 have independent significance (Chapter 9 Game 58).

To round off, if you don't see the move or idea you want to study, look at the nearest variation you can find to it, and there will be something about it (we hope), though on the question of specific moves, we should point out that the aim of our book is to explain ideas in a friendly way, and not to burden the reader with an exhaustive mass of variations. That would defeat the primary purpose of the Modern, which is to escape from the clutches of theory. A knowledge of some key variations, plus an understanding of the strategical motifs behind the moves, will allow the reader to go out and conquer the chess world with spontaneous and original chess.

Neil McDonald, Jon Speelman
England
May 2000

CHAPTER ONE

Black plays 3...c6 and 4...d5 (Gurgenidze Main Line)

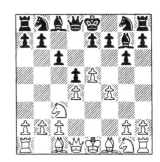

1 e4 g6 2 d4 ♗g7 3 ♘c3 c6 4 f4 d5 5 e5

At first glance, 3...c6 seems a less than impressive move. After all, a subsequent ...c6-c5, which is the natural way to attack the d4-square and so increase the strength of the fianchettoed bishop, will now lose a tempo. Furthermore, the knight on b8 is denied its most active post on c6, where it could also put pressure on d4.

However, in the Gurgenidze Black rejects the plan of a concerted attack on d4 and instead stakes an immediate claim for space in the centre with ...d7-d5. He aims for a blockade on the light squares after 4 f4 d5 5 e5. This offers him a very solid position which is safe from tactical threats.

In fact, as far as opening traps, sharp attacking variations and nasty novelties are concerned, Black's pawn centre affords him a virtually 'bomb proof' shelter. This doesn't mean, of course, that Black never suffers any quick defeats in this opening, as the games below will prove. However, his reverses generally occur when he deliberately loosens his pawn centre in search of counterplay at the wrong time. The Gurgenidze remains an excellent choice for players who have the patience to nurse a cramped position until the correct moment to break out arrives.

After 4 f4 d5 5 e5 White is committed to maintaining a big centre. Objectively, this should give him the slightly better long-term chances; other things being equal a space advantage must be worth something. However, the blocked positions that necessarily results aren't to everyone's taste. Those who prefer active piece play to slow manoeuvring are better advised to simply develop with 4 ♘f3 or one of the other moves analysed in Chapter 2.

In Game 1 we examine Black's traditional set-up in the Gurgenidze with 4 f4 d5 5 e5 h5!? Black entrenches himself on the kingside and prepares for a war of attrition. An attempt to improve on this basic design by avoiding ...♗g7 is examined in Game 2, with the distinctive move order 1 e4 g6 2 d4 d6!? 3 ♘c3 c6 4 f4 d5!? 5 e5 h5. The reasoning behind this is explained in the preamble to Game 2. In Game 3 we turn our attention to an early ...♕b6 by Black, with the move order 2 d4 ♗g7 3 ♘c3 c6 4 f4 ♕b6 5 ♘f3 d5 6 e5 ♗g4. Instead of 4...♕b6, 4...d5 5 e5 ♘h6!? is one of Black's most active ways of handling the position. After 6 ♘f3 Black can either choose 6...♗g4 (Game 4) or delay this move with 6...f6!? (Game 5).

Finally, we should mention that White has ways to side-step the lines in this chapter, notably with 3 ♘f3, when 3...c6 4 c3 (also 4 c4 may be an unwelcome variation, depending on the reader's preparation; you may prefer 3...d6) 4...d5?! 5 e5 is a favourable version of the Gurgenidze for White, as it is better to have played c2-c3, consolidating the pawn structure, than ♘c3. However, this is something of a Pyrrhic victory for White, as his opponent can always play 4...d6, when White has achieved no more than a quiet variation of lines with c2-c3 (see Chapter 4). Or a move earlier, he can switch to 3...d6, when the early 3 ♘f3 restricts White's choice of opening plans.

Game 1
Hellers-Petursson
Malmo 1993

---

1 e4 g6 2 d4 ♗g7

The so-called Accelerated Gurgenidze 2...d6!? 3 ♘c3 c6 4 f4 d5!? is an important alternative (see Game 2). It is recommended that the reader study these two games together as they contain many common ideas.

3 ♘c3 c6

This move is the subject of Chapters 1 and 2, while 3...d6 is considered in Chapter 3.

4 f4

White seizes more space in the centre. Alternatives involving piece play are to be found in Chapter 2.

4...d5

Black can also keep the position more fluid with 4...d6. However, this seems to give White a promising position after 5 ♘f3 ♗g4 (the alternative plan of 5...b5 left Black passively placed after 6 ♗d3 ♗g4 7 e5! dxe5 8 dxe5 ♘h6 9 0-0 0-0 10 h3 ♗f5 11 ♘e4 in Anand-Norwood, Oakham

1990, mainly because his bishop on g7 is shut out of the game) 6 ♗e3 ♕b6 7 ♕d2 ♗xf3 8 gxf3 ♘d7 9 0-0-0 ♕a5 10 ♔b1, when White's potential attack on the kingside is stronger than anything Black can muster on the queenside. For example, 10...b5 11 f5 (11 h4 is also good) 11...♘gf6 12 ♗d3 b4 13 ♘e2 c5 14 ♗h6 0-0 (it was better for the king to stay in the centre) 15 ♗xg7 ♔xg7 16 h4 ♖fc8 17 h5! c4 18 hxg6 cxd3 19 ♕h6+ ♔h8 20 cxd3 and White, who intends 21 gxf7 followed by 22 ♘f4 and 23 ♘g6 mate, had a decisive attack in Franzen-McAlpine, correspondence 1991. Of course, this short analysis doesn't cover all of Black's options after 4...d6, but it does seem to indicate why blocking the centre with 4...d5 is considered by most players to be Black's best plan.

5 e5

White sets up a huge pawn chain in the centre which shuts out the bishop on g7 and deprives the knight on g8 of its natural square on f6. Players of the 1920s would have been aghast at Black's neglect of the basic principles of space and development, but his next move would have completely confounded them!

5...h5

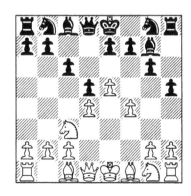

In fact, once it is accepted that the centre is closed and therefore rapid mobilisation of the pieces is of secondary importance, this move is easily justifiable in strategic terms. Black prevents, or at least seriously hinders, a g2-g4 advance by White and therefore makes f5 an attractive outpost for his knight, which normally arrives there via h6. Black is also waiting for White to play ♘f3 so that he can pin it with ...♗g4.

For a long time ...h7-h5 was the standard move in this position. However, at the time of writing Black's interest has switched to ideas of ...♘h6, planning ...f7-f6 or ...♕b6 (see Games 3-5 below). Possibly the system with ...h7-h5, though solid, is regarded as a little too passive and inflexible for modern taste. This is somewhat ironic as it would have been hailed as the apotheosis of 'modern enterprise' when the Gurgenidze was developed in the 1960s. Clearly chess has come a long way when the formerly 'avant-garde' can be considered as lacking vitality! Or has it only gone full circle?

6 ♘f3

Also possible is 6 ♗e3 ♘h6 7 ♘f3 ♗g4 8 h3 ♗xf3 9 ♕xf3 ♘f5 10 ♗f2 h4 11 ♗d3 e6 12 ♘e2 ♘a6 13 c3 ♘c7 14 0-0 with a comfortable edge for White in De Firmian-Rashkovsky, Reykjavik 1994. The merit or otherwise of the ...h5-h4 plan by Black, as seen in this sequence, is considered at move 10 below. Perhaps Black should have tried ...♕b6!? at move six or seven to disrupt the smooth build up of White's game. Compare this with Game 3 below.

6...♗g4

In view of the blocked nature of the centre, Black is happy to exchange his bishop for the knight. After all, he is getting rid of his so-called 'bad' bishop before completing his central blockade of the light squares with ...e7-e6. Surely the exchange must be in his favour? However, things aren't so strategically simple as this. The problem is that closed positions do tend to become open positions at some

point. The dilemma for Black is that if he tries for counterplay with a later ...c6-c5 or ...f7-f6, the position will open up and the white bishops may become dangerously potent. If on the other hand, Black sits back in his solid shelter, then White can try to encroach further on the centre with the pawn advances b2-b3 and c2-c4 on the queenside or h2-h3 and g2-g4 on the kingside (after of course a great deal of preparation). Black would remain well entrenched and it would be by no means easy for White to exploit his space advantage without losing control of the position. In fact a purely passive approach for Black may work well at club and intermediate levels where White often runs out of patience and self-destructs. But at the highest levels, where players have a greater positional aptitude, Black is in danger of being gradually constricted until his carapace of pawns turns into his coffin. That is why, after establishing his centre, Black looks for counterplay either with ...f7-f6 or ...c6-c5, even if opening the position poses some risks.

7 h3!

It makes sense for White to provoke the exchange, as the queen will be well placed on f3. In contrast, after 7 ♗e2 (answered by 7...♘h6 etc.), an eventual ...♗xf3 will force the white bishop to recapture on f3 and sit on a blocked diagonal.

7...♗xf3 8 ♕xf3 ♕b6

The development of the queen to this square is a very important idea that will be further discussed in the Game 3 below. Here it obliges the white queen to defend the d-pawn, which rules out a quick g2-g4, and also deters any idea White may have had of preparing to castle queenside, as 9 ♗e3? drops the b2-pawn.

9 ♕f2 e6 10 ♗d3

see following diagram

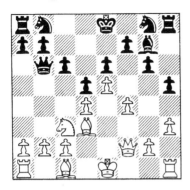

Here an important strategical question arises. It seems that Black has the chance to rule out White's g2-g4 advance for ever by playing ...h5-h4. Then he can follow up with ...♞e7 and ...♞f5, when the knight is cemented on the f5-square and free from pawn attack. In the game Mas-Kasimdzhanov, Malaysia 1998, White was anxious to prevent this possibility and so played the immediate 10 g3?!, whereupon 10...♞e7 11 ♗d3 ♞f5 12 ♞e2 ♗f8! (the reader should note the effectiveness of the 12...♗f8! retreat, preparing ...c6-c5) 13 c3 c5 14 dxc5 ♗xc5 15 ♕f3 ♞c6 was at least okay for Black. As a rule, White shouldn't worry about ...h5-h4 disabling his kingside. The h4-pawn will more often than not turn out to be weak, and may even be captured, for example after ♗d3x♞f5 followed by ♕xh4. Black can leave his rook on h8 guarding the pawn, but in that case how is he ever going to castle kingside or bring that piece into active play? Therefore, although it is strategically desirable to hobble the white g-pawn, other positional considerations normally render this move dubious. However, in quite a number of cases, especially when Black has played the Accelerated Gurgenidze and so can add to the pawn's support with ...♗e7, the advance *may* be attractive. A good example is given in the note to Game 2 at move 19.

10...♞e7 11 0-0 ♞d7 12 b3 ♞f5 13 ♞e2 c5?

The fundamental question for Black in the Gurgenidze concerns the timing of his bid for activity. We have already touched on this subject in the note to Black's sixth move above. Black needs to undermine the white centre in order to achieve counterplay, but in so doing he may be cutting his own throat by opening up lines for his opponent's pieces. In the Mas-Kasimdzhanov extract above at move 10, Black achieved ...c6-c5 under favourable circumstances. His bishop was on f8 to support the advance, which seems more useful than having the knight on d7 in our present game, and White had made the pointless and weakening move g2-g3. In contrast, in our main game Hellers has played b2-b3!, a much more valuable move which supports the c2-c4 breakthrough that every Gurgenidze player fears. This comparison suggests that Black should play 13...♗f8! here. White can try to gun him down with 14 g4, but 14...hxg4 15 hxg4 ♞h4, when the knight can be supported with ...♗e7 if necessary, looks unclear. For example, if 16 c4 Black already has the cheapo 16...♞c5!? lined up, or if 16 f5? then 16...♞xe5! etc., in both cases exploiting the potential pin of the queen against the king with ...♗c5.

Instead, Hellers recommends the more cautious 13...h4, when 14 c4 ♗f8 leaves White with a slight edge.

14 c4!

White rips open the centre. We don't need to talk about the two bishops to realise this is White's best strategy: it is self-evident that a switch from a war of attrition to a pitched battle must favour him, as the black king is still in the centre and the idle bishop on g7 is taking no part in the action.

14...dxc4

If Black captures on d4 then ♗b2 at

some point will recover the pawn with the advantage.

15 ♗xf5!

This eliminates Black's best minor piece and forces him to compromise his pawn structure.

15...gxf5?

Hellers rightly gives this a question mark and recommends 15...exf5, which he says gives White only a slight advantage. After 16 bxc4 cxd4 (or else 17 d5) 17 ♘xd4 (with the idea of ♗e3 or maybe ♗a3, combined with ♘b5 and ♘d6 and ♖ab1), Black can still defend with 17...a6! 18 ♗e3 ♛c7, the same plan that he adopts in the game, when 19 e6 ♘f6 is none too clear. After the game move Black's king can never be castled into safety on the kingside, which also means that the king's rook cannot be brought into the centre to join the struggle. It is therefore possible to conclude that Black is positionally lost.

16 bxc4 cxd4 17 ♘xd4 a6

A necessary precaution against ♘b5 following 18 ♗e3.

18 ♗e3 ♛c7

If Black succeeds in playing ...♘c5 and ...♘e4 (after a preparatory ...♗f8 to rule out ♘xf5 in reply) then things look okay for him. White's next move scotches this hope.

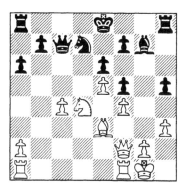

19 c5!

Pawns are almost always needed to carry through an attack, even if most of the work is done by the pieces. Black is now in a strategically hopeless situation, as he cannot allow the position to become open after 19...♘xc5 20 ♖ac1 b6 21 ♘b3 followed by a capture on c5. Nor can his king escape its fate in the centre, as 19...0-0 20 ♛h4 intends a massacre with ♛xh5, ♖f3 and ♖g3, or ♘f3 and ♘g5.

19...♘f8 20 ♖ab1

White plans 21 ♖b6 followed by doubling rooks and ♛f3 to win the b-pawn. Black therefore makes a pitiful bid for activity which spells instant doom.

20...f6 21 ♛f3 ♖b8 22 ♖b6 fxe5 23 ♘xe6 ♘xe6 24 ♖xe6+ ♔f8 25 fxe5 ♔g8 26 ♛d5 1-0

Game 2
Sepp-M.Gurevich
Bruges 1995

The reader who has played through Game 1 will have noticed that the bishop on g7, to use Nimzowitsch's evocative expression, was 'biting on granite'. In the Gurgenidze, the white pawn on e5 is solidly supported by its colleagues on f4 and d4; it can no longer be undermined by ...d7-d6, while the attack with ...f7-f6 (of which more in Games 4 and 5 below) seldom removes the e-pawn. It is chiefly valuable for opening the f-file for the rook rather than increasing the scope of the bishop. Therefore, in order to activate the bishop, Black sometimes tries ...♗h6, but more often he retreats the bishop back to f8. One advantage of ...♗f8 is that the bishop supports the ...c6-c5 advance, which is Black's main source of counterplay, assuming he has avoided the ...f7-f6 line. The d4-pawn is the most vulnerable point in the white centre, as it is the 'base' of White's pawn chain and cannot easily be defended by a pawn, unless White has found time to move his knight from c3 and play c2-c3. A good example of the effectiveness of the bishop retreat was seen in the extract from Mas-Kasimdzhanov given at move 10 in Game 1 above.

The desirability of the bishop retreat begs the question: if Black is intending to allow his opponent to set up a pawn mass on d4, e5 and f4 which blots out his bishop, why ever should he play the bishop to g7 in the first place? Why not leave the bishop on f8 and develop something else? This is good reasoning, and it would seem that by a judicious choice of moves Black can save a tempo by keeping the bishop on f8. Or rather *two* tempi, since it takes no moves to leave the bishop on f8, while it takes two moves to move it to g7 and then back to f8!

Unfortunately, we will search in vain for the ideal choice of moves. For example, let's try the sequence of moves 1 e4 g6 2 d4 c6 3 ♘c3 d5 4 e5. What should Black play now, assuming he wishes to avoid playing his bishop to g7? The advance 4...h5?! is decidedly inferior here as White hasn't yet committed himself to f2-f4. White could try to exploit the weakened g5-square by playing ♘g5 at some point combined with ♗d3, ♕f3 and even e5-e6 if Black lets him. An alternative for Black is 4...♗f5, but he may want to play ...♗g4 to pin the knight later on, so this would probably waste the tempo we were trying to save. A third try is 4...♘h6, but this blocks the h-pawn, so Black would have to switch to the plan of ...f7-f6, which requires ...♗g7. The avant-garde 4...♕b6 is the most intriguing option for Black, but of course White is by no means obliged to continue 5 f4.

Another practical objection to this move order is that not everyone wishes to allow White to play c2-c4 without having the option of transposing to the King's Indian Defence (after say 1 e4 g6 2 d4 ♗g7 3 c4 d6 4 ♘c3 ♘f6). As soon as Black

plays 2...c6 he is committed to the Modern set-up, even if White plays 3 c4. We hope that the first four chapters of this book prove that there is nothing wrong with this for Black, but fans of the King's Indian Defence are hereby warned!

Therefore, the attempt to save time by omitting ...♗g7 sounds like a great idea until you try to implement it in practice. But remember that we are talking about a saving of potentially two tempi. If Black is less greedy he has a surprising move which saves him *one* tempo, which is illustrated in our present game.

1 e4 d6 2 d4 g6 3 ♘c3 c6 4 f4 d5!?

This is the idea. Black has spent one extra move playing ...d6-d5, but he could claim to have saved two moves by not putting his bishop on g7 and then moving it back again to f8. So overall he is one tempo to the good. And what's more, White has already blocked the position with 4 f4, so he cannot really hope to exploit Black's multiple pawn moves with a direct attack.

5 e5 h5 6 ♘f3 ♘h6

Of course 6...♗g4 is also quite reasonable.

7 ♗e3 ♕b6

The familiar queen sortie, which hopes to create confusion by attacking b2.

8 ♘a4

White tries to combine 'business' (the

necessity of defending b2) with 'pleasure' (the clearance of the c-file to make way for space gaining pawn advances). The tepid 8 ♖b1 would at least be a moral victory for Black, who would know that White could never castle queenside.

8...♕a5+ 9 c3 ♕c7!?

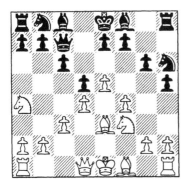

Black seems bent on flouting every opening rule in the book. He began with five consecutive pawn moves, including moving his d-pawn twice and the wing advance ...h7-h5; he developed his knight to the edge of the board; and now he moves his queen three times in a row. How can you tell a novice that the queen shouldn't be brought out early in a game or recite aphorisms like 'a knight on the rim is dim' when a former Russian champion can play in this style?

Of course, Gurevich doesn't move his queen around the board aimlessly, as many beginners would do. The check on a5 provoked 9 c3, which cut off the retreat square of the knight on a4. This may or may not cause the horse some discomfort later on; in any case, no harm is done by the check, as White's natural plan to increase his advantage involves playing b2-b3 and c2-c4 (or in this case c3-c4). Also, provoking c3-c3 can be regarded as a canny psychological move, as it encourages White to follow up with the incorrect plan b2-b4? rather than b2-b3 and c2-c4.

Nor is the queen retreat to c7 made on a whim. It was based on a concrete appraisal of the position. According to his notes in *Informator 65*, Gurevich was afraid of the variation 9...♗g4 10 ♘c5 ♘f5 11 ♗f2 e6 12 ♕b3!? (but not 12 ♘xb7?! ♕b6 13 ♕b3 ♗xf3 14 gxf3 ♘d7, intending 15...♖b8, with advantage to Black) 12...♕b6 13 ♘d2!? and White has the edge. Therefore he prefers to bolster c7 immediately.

10 ♗e2 ♗g4 11 0-0 ♘f5 12 ♗f2 e6 13 b4?

As usual in the Gurgenidze, the best idea for White is to increase the pressure on Black's centre with 13 b3! followed by c3-c4. If White succeeds in opening the c-file after a subsequent c4xd5 and the recapture ...c6xd5, then he can embarrass the black queen with ♖c1, answering ...♘c6 with ♗b5.

The plan White actually adopts is not just inferior but positively harmful as it leaves a hole on c4 and exposes his queenside to the undermining flank attack ...a7-a5. However, things only begin to get serious when White makes a further inaccuracy on the next move.

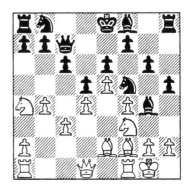

13...♘d7 14 ♘c5

White carries on playing aggressive-looking moves, but his knight achieves nothing on this square and will soon be evicted. In contrast, the black knight on d7 will find an excellent outpost on c4 where it is safe from pawn attack. This being the case, White shouldn't let the black knight cross the b6-square. Gurevich assesses 14 ♖b1 ♘b6 15 ♘xb6! axb6 16 a4 as unclear. Black's pawns are more compact (the white a-pawn is slightly weak) but White can still trust in his space advantage. It is never pleasant to play an anti-positional looking move like 15 ♘xb6, strengthening Black's pawns, but safety comes before pride.

14...♘b6!

Heading for c4 after the inevitable capture on f3.

15 ♖b1

White could keep the knight out of c4 with 15 ♘d2, but 15...♗xe2 16 ♕xe2 is a favourable exchange for Black

15...♗xf3 16 ♗xf3 ♘c4

The knight achieves its objective, with the threat of a fork on e3. The next stage in Black's plan is to drive back the impostor on c5 and begin the process of undermining White's queenside pawns.

17 ♕e2 b6 18 ♘d3 a5 19 g3!

Not 19 b5? ♘a3. Having been positionally routed on the queenside, White's only remaining chance for activity is to force through g3-g4. Of course, after Black responds ...h5xg4 White wants to be able to recapture on g4 with a pawn, in order to oust the black knight from f5. However, the immediate 19 h3, preparing 20 g4, allows 19...h4! when the pawn never reaches g4. In this instance, it would be difficult for White to prove that the h4-pawn is vulnerable, as it can be further defended by ...♗e7. Black meanwhile could play his king to g7 via f8, where it looks very safe, and then concentrate his fire on White's weakened queenside pawns. With no pawn breaks available to White, he would face a miserable defensive task.

Therefore, White advances g2-g3-g4 in 'two goes'.

19...♗e7 20 h3! axb4 21 ♘xb4

The alternative 21 cxb4 ♕a7 22 ♖a1 ♕a3 is also uncomfortable for White.

21...♔d7!

An excellent positional move. The black king is safest in the centre, hiding behind the barrier of pawns, both White and Black! On d7 the king defends the c6-pawn, which frees the queen for active duty along the a-file. It also clears the way for the rook on h8 to enter the fray, e.g. after ...♖a3 and...♖ha8. Therefore it becomes imperative for White to begin his kingside counterplay. In positions of this sort passivity means death.

22 g4 hxg4 23 hxg4 ♘h4 24 ♗xh4 ♖xh4 25 ♗g2

White clears the way for f4-f5. Of course, these intemperate pawn advances, which are aimed at exposing the enemy monarch to attack, are also denuding his own king, but White really must strike a blow before his queenside crumbles.

25...♖a3 26 ♖b3 ♕a7 27 f5!

This is the culmination of White's determined fight-back. In contrast, 27 ♘xc6, hoping for 27...♔xc6? 28 ♕xc4+, proves a mirage after 27...♖xa2.

27...gxf5 28 gxf5 ♕a8!

The bishop is needed to defend the king, so 28...♗xb4 would be a highly risky venture. One possible variation is 29 fxe6+ fxe6 30 cxb4 ♖xa2 31 ♖f7+ ♔e8 32

罝xa7 罝xe2 33 罝g3, when the threat of mate guarantees White at least a draw after 33...含f8 34 罝a8+ etc.

Instead, Black brings his queen over to the kingside both to repel White's insurgency on the f-file and also to begin his own attack against White's exposed king.

29 fxe6+ fxe6 30 罝f7 豐g8 31 罝xa3 ②xa3 32 豐f2?

After exploiting his chances to the full on the kingside, White finally goes wrong. According to Gurevich he should have given up the exchange to discomfort the black king: 32 罝xe7+! 含xe7 33 豐a6!, when 33...②c4 34 ②xc6+ 含f8 35 豐c8+ 含g7 36 ②d8! 罝h6 37 豐d7+ 含f8 is unclear. Taking this a little further, after 38 含f2 (with the idea of 39 ②xe6+ 豐xe6 40 豐xe6 盒xd5, impaling two black pieces) 38...②b2 39 豐d6+ 含e8 40 豐c6+ forces a draw after 40...含f8 41 豐d6+, but not 40...含xd8? 41 豐a8+. So a draw seems a legitimate result. From this we can conclude that White's inaccurate opening play cost him the advantage, but still left him the chance to save himself with sufficiently resolute play.

32...罝g4

Now the threat of 33...罝xg2+ forces the white rook to retreat, after which his counterplay fizzles out. This leaves the white king facing a dangerous attack while his counterpart is snugly placed on d7.

33 罝f3 ②c4 34 ②d3 豐g6 35 含h2 豐h6+ 36 盒h3 ②d2 37 罝f4

White's last chance was 37 罝f6! when 37...盒xf6 38 exf6 罝g8 (the only move according to Gurevich, but see below!) 39 ②e5+ 含c7 is only slightly better for Black. However, a Silicon friend called Crafty suggests 38...罝g3!!, planning a knight fork on e4 or f1 according to how White plays.

37...②e4

The agile knight runs rings around the white pieces.

38 豐f1 罝g5!

Now there is no good answer to the threat of 39...罝h5 and 40...②g5. White gives up the exchange immediately, after which his desperate attack is easily defeated.

39 罝f3 ②d2 40 豐e2 ②xf3+ 41 豐xf3 罝g7 42 ②f2 盒g5 43 ②g4 盒f4+ 44 含g2 豐g5 45 c4 含c7 46 cxd5 exd5 47 豐a3 含b7 48 豐f8 盒e3 49 e6 盒xd4 50 含f3 盒c5 51 豐h8 豐f5+ 0-1

Although White made things much easier for his opponent by choosing the wrong plan in the opening, this was an interesting battle which shows the value of the Accelerated Gurgenidze.

Incidentally, we have borrowed the speedy adjective in the name of this line from David Norwood's book. But if the Gurgenidze is defined by the pawn structure d4/e5/f4 versus c6/d5/g6, rather than by the bishop on g7, isn't this line better described as the 'Delayed' rather than 'Accelerated' Gurgenidze, since it takes an extra move to set it up?

Game 3
Tzermiadianos-Norwood
Isle of Man 1996

---

1 e4 g6 2 d4 盒g7 3 ②c3 c6 4 f4 豐b6!?

This is an extremely clever move order, which is what you would expect of someone who has played the Modern for more than a decade!

The queen is often deployed on this square in the main line Gurgenidze, so it makes sense to play it there immediately. A 'trick' next move ensures that Black can still play 5...d5, despite the queen's abandonment of the pawn's defence. This means that the standard pawn structure of the line is reached, whilst cutting out some of White's options, as will be seen.

5 ♘f3 d5

This is an essential part of Black's plan. Instead 5...d6 6 ♗c4 ♘h6 7 ♗b3! ♗g4 8 ♗e3 d5 9 ♕d2!? dxe4 10 ♘e5 proved strong for White in Kovacevic-Barlov, Igalo 1994.

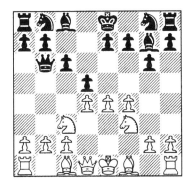

6 e5

6 exd5 ♗g4 is awkward for White since the d4-pawn cannot be conveniently defended. Therefore he closes the centre and directs play along typical Gurgenidze lines.

6...♗g4

Here we begin to see the effect of Black's unusual move order. After the standard 4...d5 5 e5 h5, White can avoid having his knight pinned immediately by playing 6 ♗e3 rather than 6 ♘f3. In contrast, 4...♕b6 gives White no choice but to defend d4 with his knight, as 5 ♗e3 drops the b2-pawn, and Black can now pin the knight at once. There is a significant ad-

vantage to Black in combining an early ...♕b6 with ...♗g4. If you put the black queen back on d8 and move up the h7-pawn to h5, then we have the position in Game 1 in which White gained some advantage with 7 h3 ♗xf3 8 ♕xf3. But with the black queen on b6 this simply allows 8...♕xd4 winning a pawn. White has nothing better than to meet the positional threat of 7...♗xf3, which would force the gruesome recapture 8 gxf3, with....

7 ♗e2

This is a small victory for Black, since the white bishop will be much less powerful than the queen on f3 after a subsequent ...♗xf3; ♗xf3 exchange (compare this with the note to White's seventh move in Game 1).

7...e6

This is an important moment. If 7...♘h6 then 8 ♘g5 ♗xe2 9 ♘xe2 looks a bit better for White, but the immediate exchange 7...♗xf3 8 ♗xf3 is critical.

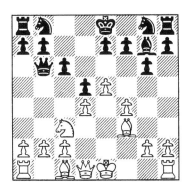

Now 8...♘d7 was played in Z.Almasi-Hodgson, Horgen 1995. If White continues with the casual 9 0-0, Black will achieve counterplay with ...♘h6 and ...♘f5. So Almasi preferred 9 ♕d3!, keeping the option of queenside castling and planning to answer 9...♘h6 with 10 g4!, which leaves the knight uselessly placed on h6. There followed 9...e6 10 ♗d2 ♘e7 11 g4 (still denying the knight the f5-

square) 11...c5 (the logical bid for counter-play against the under-defended d4-point) 12 ♘a4 ♕c7 13 ♘xc5 ♘xc5 14 dxc5 g5! (this is the culmination of Black's strategy; the white centre looks like it is about to collapse, but remember that the white bishops have been eagerly awaiting the opening of lines!) 15 ♕b5+! ♘c6 16 c4! (Black's centre also begins to crumble) 16...0-0-0 17 cxd5 exd5 18 0-0-0. Now Almasi gives as best play 18...gxf4 19 ♗xf4 ♗xe5 20 ♗xe5 ♕xe5 21 ♖hf1 with a slight edge for White. This looks eminently survivable for Black.

Returning to the last diagram, in the later game Cherniaev-Hodgson, Blackpool 1998, Hodgson diverged with 8...e6, when play went 9 ♘a4 (9 ♕d3 ♘d7 would transpose to the Almasi game above, but perhaps Hodgson was hoping to molest the white queen with 9...♕a6; Black would be very happy to exchange queens and so avoid the danger of a direct attack on his king) 9...♕c7 10 b3 ♘d7 11 0-0 ♘e7 12 ♗a3 ♘f5 13 ♕d2 h5 14 c4 dxc4 15 bxc4 ♘b6 16 ♘xb6 axb6 17 ♗b2 with a slight edge to White according to Cherniaev. White's plans include ♗e4, when if the knight stands its ground on f5 the exchange ♗xf5 and recapture ...e6xf5 allows White to create a passed pawn with d5. On the other hand retreating the knight would leave Black rather passively placed.

8 0-0 ♘e7 9 ♘a4!

We have already discussed the merits of ...♕b6, but the downside of the queen deployment is always apparent: White gains a tempo to clear the way for his c-pawn to advance. White already has a space advantage in the centre and on the kingside; now he wants to gain territory on the queenside.

9...♕c7

In *Informator 68*, Tzermiadianos says he intended to answer 9...♕a5 with 10 c3, aiming for 11 b4 and 12 ♘c5, but this was

the plan which worked out none too well for White in Game 2. There seems nothing wrong with the standard 10 b3, e.g. 10...♘d7 11 c4 and if 11...b5? 12 ♗d2 etc.

10 ♗e3

Instead 10 b3 with the added option of 11 ♗a3!? was worth considering, as long as White watches out for a ...♘f5 and ...♘e3 fork.

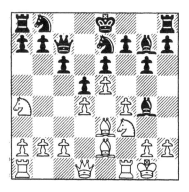

10...♘d7 11 b3 h5?!

At first glance pre-emptive action on the queenside with 11...b5 12 ♘b2 a5 looks as if it just exposes Black's pawns to attack. However, White will only be able to advance c2-c4 at the cost of ceding the d5-square to a black knight after a double exchange on c4. So this attempt to escape from his positional straitjacket was certainly worth considering. Instead, Black prefers to await his opponent's queenside advance and takes a preventive measure against a future g2-g4.

12 c4

Tzermiadianos was later critical of his decision here. Instead, he says he should have played 12 h3 when 12...♗xf3?! 13 ♖xf3!, planning c2-c4, ♖c1, ♗f2 and ♖fc3, is very nice for White. However, he also points out that Black can improve with the *zwischenzug* 12...♘f5!, when 13 ♗f2 ♗xf3 14 ♗xf3 is much less good for White: his rook is left sitting passively on f1 while the bishop has no desire to be on the blocked a8-h1 diagonal. Still, White would have had a comfortable position due to his space advantage.

12...♘b6!? 13 c5?!

A dubious decision. The Greek player rejected 13 ♘xb6 because of 13...axb6 14 h3 ♘f5 15 ♗f2 ♗xf3 16 ♗xf3 dxc4 17 bxc4 ♖d8 with counterplay for Black against d4. However, 18 d5! cxd5 19 cxd5 exd5 20 ♖c1 followed by ♗xb6 looks very strong for White. So Black would have to play with greater vigilance, e.g. he could leave his knight on e7 and try 14...♗xf3 15 ♗xf3 0-0, though 16 g4 may then be good for White.

13...♘xa4 14 bxa4 b6

Instead 11...♗h6 was worth considering, when the bishop is a bit more active. The immediate follow-up idea would be 12...♘f5, when the white bishop can't retreat to f2 without dropping the f-pawn.

15 ♖c1 0-0 16 h3 ♘f5!

Compare this with the note at White's 12th move. Black forces his opponent to recapture on f3 with the bishop rather than the rook, as 16...♗xf3 17 ♖xf3 followed by ♗f2 and ♖fc3 would increase White's advantage.

17 ♗f2 ♗xf3 18 ♗xf3 ♖ab8

Black hopes to generate counterplay along the b-file.

19 g4

Having been stymied on the queenside, White turns his attention to the alternative plan of gaining space on the kingside as a prelude to a direct attack on the enemy monarch.

19...hxg4 20 hxg4 ♘e7 21 ♕d2!

White plans to manoeuvre his bishop to b3 via d1 to block the b-file and so rule out any black counterplay there.

21...f5?

This looks like a great move, as it seems to give White three unpalatable alternatives:

a) He can block the kingside with 22

g5?, when 22...♔f7! with the idea of ...♖h8 is by no means worse for Black.

b) He can play 22 exf6?, but this breaks up his proud centre. After 22...♖xf6 he already has to think about defending the f4-pawn.

c) He can try 22 gxf5?, or a quiet move which allows Black to play 22...fxg4. This cedes the f5-square to the black knight, where it is magnificently placed. The only way to dislodge it would be by arranging ♗xf5, but this would deprive White of his excellent bishop and leave many light-square holes in his position.

However, there is a fourth alternative which ensures that White retains a strong initiative.

22 ♗h4!!

White eliminates the knight with his 'bad' bishop before it gets the chance to go to f5. In view of the strength of this move, Black should have played 21...f6! when Tzermiadianos intended to answer 22 ♗d1. Then 22...fxe5 23 fxe5 (if 23 dxe5 g5!? might be good) 23...♖f7, planning ...♖bf8, looks unclear. In that case, White maintains his space advantage, but if Black succeeds in breaking out it could all fall to pieces for him.

22...fxg4 23 ♗xe7! ♕xe7 24 ♗xg4

White now has good winning chances because of the difference in strength between the opposing bishops. Black's bishop is shut in whereas White's has the freedom of action to direct its fire at either the weak point on e6 or g6.

24...♗h6?!

Perhaps 24...b5 was better. As played, the black queen's rook is forced to a passive square where it can no longer assist in the defence of the kingside.

25 cxb6 ♖xb6 26 a5! ♖a6 27 ♖c3 c5

Not 27...♖xa5 28 ♖xc6 winning e6 (less clear is 28 ♖h3 ♖a3! because of 29 ♖xh6 ♖g3+). Black finds a use for his isolated rook: it now defends e6 and so frees the queen to go to h4. Black is fighting very hard, and it demands great care from White to press home the victory.

28 ♖g3!

Better than 28 ♖xc5 ♕h4.

28...♔g7 29 ♗e2 c4

Ironically, Black now has an excellent pawn structure on the queenside. The problem is that White's attack on the kingside is about to become irresistible. The absence of the rook on a6 proves decisive.

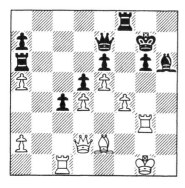

30 ♗d1! ♖g8 31 ♗c2 ♔f8 32 ♕h2 ♕h7 33 ♖b1

Now Black is completely encircled.

33...♖g7 34 ♖b8+ 1-0

Black resigned as 34....♔f7 (34...♔e7 35 ♕h4+) 35 ♗xg6+ ♖xg6 36 ♖b7+ wins his queen. Of course, White also has other ways to win.

> ### Game 4
> ## Almasi-Hodgson
> *Groningen 1994*

1 e4 g6 2 d4 ♗g7 3 ♘c3 c6 4 f4 d5 5 e5 ♘h6!?

This is a completely different, and much more aggressive approach than 5...h5. Black mobilises his knight immediately and plans to strike out at the white centre with ...f7-f6.

6 ♘f3

White can also delay this move with 6 ♗e2!?, when after 6...f6 7 ♗e3 0-0 8 ♕d2 ♘f5 (Black doesn't really want to be playing this with the bishop still on c8, but 8...♗g4 9 f5!? looks awkward) 9 ♗f2 ♕b6 10 ♘a4 ♕c7 11 ♘f3 fxe5 12 fxe5 White was ready to drive back the knight with 13 g4 in Morozevich-Iordachescu, Zagan 1997. Nunn and McNab suggest 6...♕b6!? which would hinder White's plan of 7 ♗e3 by attacking b2. If White reverted to 7 ♘f3 then 7...♗g4 follows and White won't get to activate his game by recapturing with his queen after a later ...♗xf3.

6...♗g4

The alternative 6...f6!? is examined in Game 5 below.

7 h3 ♗xf3 8 ♕xf3 f6

If 8...♕b6 9 ♘e2 f6 (as in Belotti-Krasenkov, Reggio Emilia 1996/97) 10 e6!?, planning 11 g4, is recommended by Mirkovic as good for White. The idea of restricting the knight on h6 is almost identical to that explained in the note to the next move.

9 g4!? fxe5

Instead 9...♕b6 was tried in Illescas-Shirov, Dos Hermanas 1996, but this rather missed its mark as White ignored the attack on d4 with 10 e6!, whereby White is willing to sacrifice a pawn in order to ensure that the knight on h6 is completely entombed. Thus after 10...♕xd4 11 ♗e3 ♕b4 12 0-0-0, the knight can retreat to g8 at some point, but then how does it re-enter the game if White answers a subsequent ...f6-f5 or ...h7-h5 with g4-g5, guarding the f6- and h6-squares? In the actual game, Shirov tried to solve the problem by sacrificing the knight: 10...f5 11 g5 ♕xd4!? 12 gxh6 ♗xh6 13 ♗e3 ♕f6 14 0-0-0 ♕xe6, when Black had three pawns for the piece. Nevertheless, 15 h4! would have given White the makings of a dangerous attack.

10 dxe5

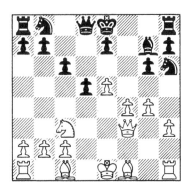

10...e6?!

White's plan is to maintain a massive clump of pawns on the kingside in order to restrict the black pieces. Thus, the e5-spearhead shuts the bishop on g7 out of the game, while the g4-pawn deprives the knight on h6 of the f5-square. If Black were to achieve freedom of action for his pieces, it is reasonable to suppose that he would have good chances, as by recapturing on e5 with the d-pawn White has weakened himself along the a7-g1 diagonal. White has also compromised his development somewhat in order to set up his pawn centre, so it would be good if Black could find a way to strike immediately. The Achilles heel of the pawn mass is Black's ability to undermine the f4-pawn with ...g6-g5. Almasi, writing in *Informator 62*, says that after 10...0-0 he intended 11 ♕g3 and then h2-h4-h5 'with a clear advantage to White'. However, Black could try 11...g5, e.g. 12 fxg5 (12 f5 ♕c7 wins the e5-pawn) 12...♘f7 13 ♗f4 (if 13 e6 ♘e5 and then 14...♕d6) 13...e6!?, planning 14...♘d7 and perhaps ...♕c7 to win the e5-pawn. Play might continue 14 ♗d3 ♘d7 15 g6 (15 ♕h4? h6!) 15...hxg6 17 ♗xg6 ♘dxe5 with unclear play. The immediate 10...g5 also needs investigation.

Black's quiet game move allows his opponent to rule out the advance ...g6-g5 at once.

11 h4! ♖f8

If 11...0-0 then 12 ♕g3, when White would develop, castle queenside and have a readymade pawn roller against the black king.

12 ♕g3 ♕b6 13 ♗d2!

If now 13...♕xb2 14 ♖b1 ♕a3 (14...♕xc2?? 15 ♗d3) 15 ♖xb7 favours White as his pieces as his pieces have greater mobility to respond to the opening of the queenside, e.g. 15...♘d7 16 ♖h3!?

13...♘d7 14 0-0-0

see following diagram

White completes his development smoothly, whilst maintaining his bind on the kingside. This shows the bankruptcy of Black's opening plan: he needed to find a way to disrupt White's slow build-up.

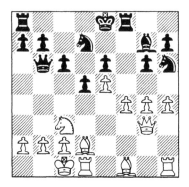

14...0-0-0 15 ♗e2

But not 15 h5 g5! White's correct strategy is to try to exploit the greater flexibility and manoeuvrability of his pieces by beginning a direct attack on the queenside. He should maintain the status quo on the kingside where the black bishop and knight on h6 remain at least temporarily shut out of the game.

15...♘g8

The knight hobbles back to the central zone.

16 ♖h3 ♘c5?!

True to his inventive style, Hodgson raises the stakes by attempting a freeing manoeuvre. Unfortunately for him this fails against White's coldly exact play. In any case, Black's position was already very unpleasant as if left in peace White would prepare a build-up such as ♘a4, ♕a3 followed by ♖b3 or perhaps ♗b4 angling for ♗d6.

17 ♗e3 d4

If 17...♕a5 18 ♔b1, with ideas such as 19 ♖d4 threatening 20 b4 ♕a3 21 ♗c1 would be strong.

18 ♖xd4 ♖xd4 19 ♗xd4 ♘b3+ 20 axb3 ♕xd4 21 ♗c4!

Black's activity has exposed the soft under belly of his position on e6.

21...♖xf4 22 ♗xe6+ ♔c7

Slightly better was 22...♔b8, but 23 ♕d3! should win for White according to

Almasi.

23 ♕e1! ♖f8

This is the only answer to the threats of 24 ♗xg8 and 24 ♖d3.

24 ♖e3 ♘e7 25 ♖d3 ♕f4+ 26 ♔b1 ♗xe5

There was no good answer to the threat of 27 ♖d7+, as 27...♖d8 28 ♖xd8 ♔xd8 29 ♕d1+ would be fatal.

27 ♖d7+ ♔b8 28 ♖xe7 ♗d6 29 ♖g7 ♖e8 30 ♖g8 ♗f8 31 ♕d1 ♕f6 32 ♕d7 ♖xe6 33 ♖xf8+ ♕xf8 34 ♕xe6 ♕f1+ 35 ♔a2 ♕a6+ 36 ♘a4 b5 37 ♕g8+ ♔c7 38 ♕xh7+ 1-0

Game 5
Al.Sokolov-Komliakov
Novgorod 1998

---

1 e4 g6 2 d4 ♗g7 3 ♘c3 c6 4 f4 d5 5 e5 ♘h6 6 ♘f3 f6

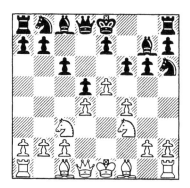

A clever move order. Black doesn't want the white queen on f3 after the standard 6...♗g4 7 h3 ♗xf3 8 ♕xf3, and so he delays putting his bishop on g4 until White has played ♗e2.

7 ♗e2

If 7 ♗e3 Black can play 7...♗g4 or maybe 7...0-0, waiting for White to commit his bishop to e2 before playing ...♗g4.

7...♗g4 8 ♗e3 0-0 9 h3?

Since Black is planning a quick assault against White's kingside, it seems highly dubious to spend a move forcing him to make an exchange that he no doubt intends anyway. Furthermore, the white centre pawns, though exerting a strong cramping influence on Black's pieces, are somewhat fragile and vulnerable to attack. The last thing White should do is weaken his dark squares by leaving a hole on g3.

White could try 9 ♕d2, when 9...♘f5 10 ♗f2 fxe5?! 11 ♘xe5! ♗xe2 12 ♕xe2 looks good for him. However, Black can improve in this sequence with 10...♗h6!, when the pin on the f4-pawn could become annoying. Perhaps White's best move is the subtle 9 ♗f2!?, which anticipates ...♘f5. Then 9...♘f5 (not 9...fxe5 10 fxe5 ♘f5?! 11 ♘g5! etc.) 10 0-0 ♗h6 (10...♗xf3 11 ♗xf3 ♗h6 12 ♘e2 is probably a small advantage for White) 11 ♘h4! ♗xe2 12 ♕xe2 ♗xf4?! (12...♘xh4 13 ♗xh4 slightly favours White) 13 ♘xf5 gxf5 14 e6! looks good for White.

9...♗xf3 10 ♗xf3 ♘f5 11 ♗f2 fxe5 12 fxe5

As will be seen, this gives away the g5-square to the black queen and further weakens White's control of the dark squares. In all probability 12 dxe5 was better, when 12...e6 13 h4 or 12...♗h6?! 13 g4 d4 (retreating the knight loses a piece to 14 g5) 14 ♘e4 ♕a5+ 15 c3!? both favour White. However, Black can play the ultra-sharp 12...g5!?, when 13 g4 ♘h6 14 fxg5 ♘f7 gives him considerable counterplay.

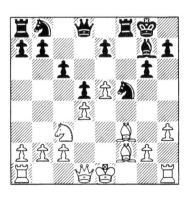

12...e6 13 0-0 h5?

Black should have continued the process of undermining White's dark squares with 13...c5!

14 ♕d3?

White misses the chance to play 14 g4! with double-edged play. Now Black finds the correct plan.

14...c5! 15 ♖ae1 ♘c6 16 ♘e2 ♕g5 17 c4

The last chance was 17 c3, when 17...♗xe5? hoping for 18 dxe5 ♘xe5 winning the bishop on f3, fails to 18 h4! However, Black could keep up the pressure with 17...♖f7.

17...cxd4 18 ♘xd4 ♘cxd4 19 ♗xd4 ♘h4 20 ♕e2

If 20 cxd5 ♖xf3! wins instantly. Note how the weakening of his dark squares is causing severe problems for White on the light squares. The bishop on f3 is a wretched piece.

20...♖ac8!

Black could also have played 20...♕g3!, threatening to pick up the rook on e1 after a double capture on f3. Then 21 ♖d1 ♘xf3+ 22 ♖xf3 ♖xf3 23 ♕xf3 ♕xf3 24 gxf3 dxc4 leaves him a pawn up in the endgame. However, his initiative is so strong that he aims to finish the game by direct attack.

21 c5

After 21 cxd5 Black can play 21...♖xf3 22 ♖xf3 ♖c2! 23 ♕xc2 ♘xf3+ 24 ♔f1 ♘xd4 with two pieces for a rook and an attack.

21...♖f7 22 g4?!

Losing at once, but there was little to be done against the threat of 22...♖cf8, putting more pressure on the paralysed bishop on f3.

22...♕f4 0-1

Black's system of development in this game was very interesting, and deserves to be further explored.

Summary

In the Gurgenidze main line White's large phalanx of pawns in the centre gives him a space advantage. However, Black is safe from immediate attack and the closed nature of the position normally leads to heavyweight positional manoeuvring. The more skilful strategist should therefore come out on top. If Black is careful in the timing of his bid for activity (usually with ...c6-c5) he can maintain the balance; however, a premature opening of the centre can be disastrous. Black's most interesting response is 4...d5 5 e5 ♘h6 6 ♘f3 f6 (Game 5) which tries to achieve counterplay by a direct attack on White's centre.

1 e4 g6 2 d4 ♗g7 3 ♘c3 c6 4 f4 *(D)*

4...d5
> 4...♕b6 – *Game 3*

5 e5 *(D)* **♘h6**
> 5...h5 – *Game 1*
> (1 e4 d6 2 d4 g6 3 ♘c3 c6 4 f4 d5 5 e5) 5...h5 – *Game 2*

6 ♘f3 *(D)* **f6**
> 6...♗g4 – *Game 4*

7 ♗e2 ♗g4 – *Game 5*

4 f4

5 e5

6 ♘f3

CHAPTER TWO

Black plays 3...c6 and 4...d5 (Gurgenidze Odds and Ends)

1 e4 g6 2 d4 ♗g7 3 ♘c3 c6

Although, theoretically at least, White has a slight advantage in the main line Gurgenidze, the prospect of a blocked position doesn't appeal to everyone. Hence White often declines the chance to set up a big centre and instead develops his pieces. In this chapter we discuss lines where White avoids the Gurgenidze by answering 1 e4 g6 2 d4 ♗g7 3 ♘c3 c6 with 4 ♘f3 or 4 ♗e3 (the alternative 4 ♗c4 is seen in Chapter 4). In each case, Black may reply with either 4...d6 or 4...d5.

In Games 6-8 we examine 4 ♘f3 d5. Black seeks to negate his opponent's space advantage at once. After 5 h3 both 5...♘f6 (Game 6) and 5...♘h6 (Game 7) seem satisfactory. Meanwhile, the more direct 5 ♗f4 (Game 8) shouldn't trouble Black so long as he knows the correct idea at move seven! In Game 9 we deal with all 'Pseudo-Classical' lines after 4 ♘f3 d6. None of these should cause Black too much trouble either. Much more challenging is White's system with an early ♗e3, as in Games 10 and 11, which feature 4 ♘f3 d6 5 h3 b5 6 ♗d3 and 4 ♗e3 respectively. Black's principal method of counterplay is by expanding on the queenside with ...b7-b5, but other methods also deserve consideration,

e.g. 4 ♗e3 d5 (mentioned in the notes to Game 11) and the rapid preparation of ...e7-e5.

Game 6
Delchev-Rey
Val Thorens 1996

---

1 e4 g6 2 d4 ♗g7 3 ♘c3 c6 4 ♘f3

White's most restrained reply here.

4...d5

Black is eager to attack the white centre quickly in order to cancel out some of his opponent's space advantage. The alternative 4...d6, which invites either the 'Pseudo-Classical' or the ♗e3 system from White, is seen in Games 9 and 10 below.

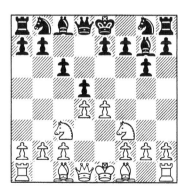

5 h3

The black bishop on c8 has few attractive-looking squares, while the knight on f3 is performing a valuable service in defending the d4-point. Thus it is logical to prevent the exchange of bishop for knight which will occur if Black is permitted to play ...♗g4, even if it costs White a tempo. Sometimes undoing the work of the opponent's pieces is more valuable than increasing the activity of one's own pieces.

Nevertheless, rapid development with 5 ♗f4 also has its virtues, as will be seen in Game 8 below.

5...♘f6!?

A highly provocative move, after which White (despite his modest play so far) allows himself to be tempted forwards. The alternative 5...♘h6 is seen in the next main game.

6 e5

The more solid 6 ♗d3 allowed Black to equalise after 6...dxe4 7 ♘xe4 ♘bd7 (or 7...♘xe4 8 ♗xe4 0-0) 8 0-0 ♘xe4 9 ♗xe4 ♘f6 10 ♗d3 ♕c7 (stopping 11 ♗f4) 11 ♖e1 0-0 12 ♗g5 e6 13 ♕d2 b6 followed by ...♗b7 with the idea of ...c6-c5 in Stefanova-Istratescu, Krynica 1998.

6...♘e4

More or less forced.

7 ♘xe4 dxe4 8 ♘g5 c5

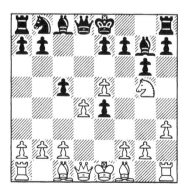

Black has to attack d4 else the e4-pawn will be lost for no real compensation.

Both sides have changed their plans. White began in a very solid style, declining the opportunity to seize the space offered to him with f2-f4 and e4-e5, but then the sight of the knight on f6 caused his e-pawn to break ranks and rush forwards. Black, for his part, initially chose a light-square strategy aimed at gaining a foothold in the centre and a quiet life, but then seemed to decide he wanted a tactical battle after all. The result is that he has been compelled to move his c-pawn a second time and switch to the dark-square strategy of putting pressure on d4 in order to soften up the diagonal for his bishop. The critical question now is: Has White over-extended himself in the centre or will the weakness of the e4-pawn seal Black's fate?

9 d5

In this game the above question remains unanswered, as White makes no attempt to directly refute Black's play, but he simply ensures that he maintains a space advantage. Instead 9 dxc5 ♕a5+ 10 ♗d2 ♕xc5 11 ♗c3 ♘c6! 12 ♘xe4 ♕b6 13 ♗c4 0-0 14 0-0 ♗xe5 is harmless (Dvoretsky-Zilberstein, USSR 1973). This leaves White with two aggressive options:

a) 9 ♗c4 0-0 10 c3 ♘c6 11 ♗e3 cxd4 12 cxd4 ♕a5+ 13 ♔f1 h6 14 ♘xe4 ♖d8 when Black's pressure on d4 gave him enough compensation for the pawn in Ibragimov-Stangl, Dortmund 1992.

b) 9 e6 f6 (Black is more or less forced to sacrifice the exchange, but in return he gains a pawn and a big centre) 10 ♘f7 ♕xd4 11 ♘xh8 ♗xe6 (11...♗xh8 12 ♕xd4 cxd4 13 ♗c4 is a little better for White) 12 ♘xg6 hxg6 13 ♗b5+ ♘d7 14 0-0 a6! (this is Bogdan Lalic's suggested improvement on his game with Andrew Webster at Jersey 1997) 15 ♗xd7+ ♗xd7 16 ♗e3 ♕e5 and although White maintains a slight edge, Black is very solidly placed.

9...♗xe5 10 ♘xe4 0-0 11 c3

This curtails the black bishop and

threatens 12 ♘xc5.

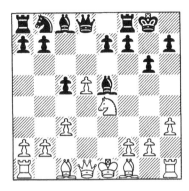

11...b6??

It is incredible that such an apparently innocuous move can do so much damage to Black's chances, both structurally and tempo wise. The two question marks are justified, as will be seen.

It is always difficult to judge the time factor in the Modern Defence. It looks as if Black can afford the luxury of this leisurely move as he is ahead in development; in fact White only has one piece developed. But over the next five moves every other white piece, including the rooks, is brought into action. The astonishing speed of this mobilisation leaves Black facing a dangerous attack. Delchev recommends 11...♘d7, when 12...♘f6 next move should force either the exchange of knights or the exchange of the d5-pawn for the c5-pawn. Then most of the danger would evaporate. A more ambitious idea would be 11...♕c7 to answer 12 ♗h6 with 12...♖d8, when Black is trying to prove that the d5-pawn is weak.

12 ♗h6 ♖e8

After 12...♗g7, Delchev gives the variation 13 ♕d2 ♗xh6? 14 ♕xh6 ♕xd5 15 ♘g5 ♕e5+ 16 ♗e2 ♕g7 17 ♕xg7+ ♔xg7 18 ♗f3 which shows that 12...b6 has created a weakness on the a8-h1 diagonal.

13 ♕f3 ♘d7 14 ♗b5

And here we see that 12...b6 has also se-

riously weakened Black's resistance on the a4-e8 diagonal. If we imagine that Black had chosen 12...♕c7 instead, then he could now play 14...a6 15 ♗a4 b5 to break the annoying pin of the bishop on his knight. But here 14...a6 would be answered by 15 ♗c6, when the bishop remains menacing.

14...♗b7 15 0-0-0 ♕c7 16 ♖he1 ♖ed8 17 d6!

As we have seen so many times before, when all the pieces are mobilised it is a pawn that provides the breakthrough (for example, compare this with the first game in Chapter 1, when 19 c5! was the killer move). However, in this case White's offer of a pawn is the prelude to a much more spectacular clearance sacrifice!

17...♗xd6

Black faces a strong attack after 17...exd6 18 ♗c4 d5 19 ♖xd5! (Delchev).

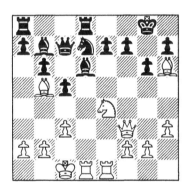

18 ♕xf7+!!

A beautiful move. White gives up his queen to open the a2-g8 diagonal. The interesting variations that follow are based on Delchev's comments in *Informator 68*.

18...♔xf7 19 ♗c4+ ♗d5

The only move, as returning the queen with 19...♔e8 20 ♘xd6+ ♕xd6 21 ♖xd6 still leaves Black facing a decisive attack, while he is devastated by a typical windmill combination after 19...e6 20 ♘xd6+ ♔g8 21 ♗xe6+ ♔h8 22 ♘f7+ ♔g8 23 ♘xd8+ ♔h8 24 ♘f7+ ♔g8 25 ♘e5+ ♔h8

26 ♖xd7 etc.

20 ♘xd6+

Not giving Black any respite with 20 ♖xd5? ♗f4+.

20...♛xd6 21 ♖xd5 ♛e6?

Here Black should have played 21...♛f6!, when 22 ♗g5 ♔f8!! 23 ♗xf6 ♘xf6 24 ♖de5 is strong for White but probably not decisive. This is a bit sad, as it would be nice to be able to say that White's brilliant queen sacrifice won by force. But then, as aesthetic consolation, there is something quite special about the supremely nonchalant 22...♔f8!!, replying to the attack on the queen by calmly retreating the king one square. How often is a queen sacrificed in such a quiet style? Alas, Black failed to find this resource.

The game continuation demonstrates the enormous power of the two bishops against an exposed king. The black monarch is driven all the way from the centre to the far corner of the board, where pins and skewers make huge material losses inevitable.

22 ♖xe6 ♔xe6 23 ♖d3+ ♔e5 24 ♖e3+ ♔d6 25 ♖e6+ ♔c7 26 ♗f4+ ♔b7 27 ♖xe7 ♔c6 28 a4! a6 29 ♗e2! ♔b7 30 ♗f3+ ♔a7 31 ♗xa8 ♔xa8 32 ♗c7 1-0

Game 7
Topalov-Shirov
Linares 1994

---

1 e4 g6 2 d4 ♗g7 3 ♘c3 c6 4 ♘f3 d5 5 h3 ♘h6

In contrast to the previous game, where the black knight was buffeted after 5...♘f6 6 e5, Black plan here is to play ...f7-f6 and provide his horse with a peaceful haven at f7.

6 ♗f4

This logical reply forces Black's hand in view of the threat of 7 ♕d2, when the knight would have to go back to g8. However, a possible drawback to this

move is that the bishop could become exposed on f4 to a space gaining ...e7-e5 advance. White therefore has to make sure that he keeps the black centre restrained.

After the alternative 6 ♗d3 0-0 7 0-0 f6 8 ♘e2 ♘a6! (planning to meet the attack on his centre after 9 exd5 cxd5 10 c4 with 10...♘b4) 9 a3 ♘f7 10 exd5 cxd5 11 c4 ♘c7 Black had a solid position in Wolff-Minasian, Glendale 1994.

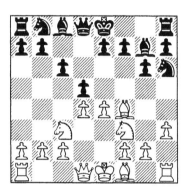

6...f6 7 ♗e2

Instead White could speculate with the immediate 7 exd5 cxd5 8 ♘b5, when 8...♘a6 is solid, but looks somewhat worse for Black. Critical is 8...0-0 (Shirov's recommendation in *Informator 60*) which looks unclear in view of 9 ♘c7 e5! This is still unknown territory, so the reader is advised to investigate the line thoroughly before playing it with either White or Black. However, the indirect evidence suggests that Black is okay after 8 ♘b5, as Topalov avoided the possibility with White and Shirov allowed it as Black!

With his modest game move White makes no attempt at a tactical refutation of Black's set-up, merely trying to exploit the very slight structural weakness in Black's kingside. However, Topalov has seen that Black will be forced to compromise his pawn structure on the queenside as well in order to complete his development. This provides White with more targets.

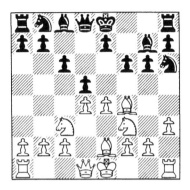

7...♘f7 8 ♗h2!

A precaution against ...e7-e5.

8...0-0 9 0-0 b6

How else is Black to develop his bishop? Freeing the f5-square for it by giving up the centre with 9...dxe4 10 ♘xe4 looks positionally awful, while 9...♗e6 10 ♖e1 leaves the bishop uncomfortably placed after 11 ♗f1 etc. (there should be a pawn on f7 defending the bishop, not a knight!), so the only reasonable way to bring it out is via b7. This exposes the b6-pawn to a later a2-a4-a5 advance, as occurs in the game. It also means that Black is weakening even further his control of the e6-square by moving his bishop away from c8. However, modern players aren't as squeamish as their classical forebears about leaving holes in their pawn structure, as long as they have active pieces. Hence Shirov judges that his almost systematic weakening of the e6-square is a price worth paying in order to have his knight ensconced on f7 and his bishop bolstering the d5-centre point. Topalov seeks to prove him wrong.

10 ♖e1 ♗b7 11 ♗f1 ♘d7 12 a4

Having restrained Black in the centre, White now attempts to soften up him up on the queenside. His immediate intention is 13 a5!?, even as a pawn sacrifice, in order to break up Black's pawns.

Not so good is direct action in the centre with 12 exd5 cxd5 13 ♗e6, as after 13...♖e8 14 ♘b5, planning a fork on c7, 14...♘f8 15 ♖e1 e5! allows Black to break out with a fine game.

12...a6 13 a5 b5

Black keeps his pawns intact.

14 exd5 cxd5 15 ♗e6

A white piece finally lands on the hole in Black's centre.

15...♖c8

According to Shirov, correct was 15...♖e8! when 16 ♘e1 ♘g5 17 ♖e2 ♘e4, plugging the e-file, is unclear. In fact, this looks perfectly okay for Black, which seems to vindicate Shirov's judgement when he conceded the e6-square. Or maybe Topalov's play can be improved somewhere?

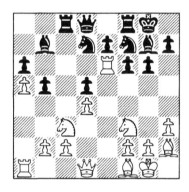

16 ♘xb5?!

Black's last move was inaccurate, but at least it has the virtue of provoking a speculative sacrifice. It seems that Topalov's patience finally ran out. Instead he should have played the calm 16 ♘e2! when 16...♖e8 17 ♘f4 gives him some advantage according to Shirov. Nevertheless, the sacrifice is very dangerous and it requires all of Shirov's renowned resourcefulness to achieve counterplay before the white passed pawns destroy him.

16...axb5 17 ♗xb5 f5!

Black clears the f6-square for his knight.

18 ♕e2?!

Better was 18 ♕e1 when 18...♘f6 19 ♖xe7 ♗a8 is unclear (Shirov). White's natural move allows Black to ease his game by forcing the exchange of a pair of rooks, as will be seen at move 20.

18...♘f6 19 a6

Perhaps the best way to keep fighting chances was the positional queen sacrifice 19 ♖xe7 ♖xc2 20 ♖xb7!? ♖xe2 21 ♗xe2. Then Shirov assesses 21...♕a8 22 a6 ♘e4 23 ♖c1 ♘d8 as slightly better for Black. White has only a rook for the queen which is a terrible material deficit, but on the other hand the passed pawn on a6 gives him dynamic play. Furthermore, his kingside is solidly defended, which is of great importance as the natural way for Black to exploit his advantage in firepower is by beginning a direct attack on the white king. I'm sure that with roles reversed Shirov would have played the queen sacrifice!

19...♗a8 20 ♖xe7 ♖xc2! 21 ♕xc2 ♕xe7

The bishop on a8 proves an excellent blockader of the a-pawn. Meanwhile, the b-pawn is too far back to cause Black any immediate problems. White begins to advance this pawn, but before it can become dangerous, his opponent is able to develop a strong offensive on the kingside.

22 ♕a4

The best way to force through b2-b4.

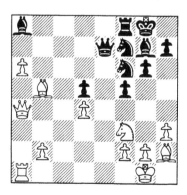

22...♕e6!

Black prevents his opponent from exchanging bishops with 23 ♗c6, when the blockade of the a-pawn would be considerably loosened.

23 b4

A better try was 23 a7 with the idea of 24 ♕a6 to blunt Black's coming attack by offering the exchange of queens. However, 23...g5 (Shirov) is still very strong.

23...♘e4 24 ♗f1 g5

Now Black develops a deadly attack.

25 b5 g4 26 ♘e1 ♕b6 27 ♘c2 ♖c8 28 ♗f4 ♗h6!

The exchange of bishops destroys White's resistance on the dark squares, after which f2 becomes fatally weak.

29 ♗xh6 ♕xh6 30 hxg4 ♕d2 31 f3 ♕f2+ 32 ♔h2 ♘fg5 33 ♘e1

Or 33 fxe4 ♘f3+ with mate next move.

33...♕h4+ 34 ♔g1 ♘h3+ 0-1

White resigned as 35 gxh3 ♕f2+ 36 ♔h1 ♘g3 is mate.

Game 8
Schaefer-Novik
Sofia 1994

---

1 e4 g6 2 d4 ♗g7 3 ♘c3 c6 4 ♘f3 d5

Where appropriate, we have chosen to standardise the move order of games for the sake of clarity. The previous game actually began with the very non-Modern looking sequence of moves: 1 e4 c6 2 d4 d5 3 ♘c3 g6 4 ♘f3 ♗g7. Incidentally, books on the Caro-Kann normally give 3 ♘d2 as more accurate than 3 ♘c3, so that if Black persists with the plan of 3...g6 White can support his centre with c2-c3 more conveniently.

5 ♗f4

In contrast to the games above, White decides that he doesn't need to play the preventive 5 h3. The straightforward development of the bishop dissuades Black from adventures with 5...♘f6 or 5...♘h6, as White will have gained a useful tempo by avoiding the 'superfluous' h2-h3. Of course, whether or not White should want to dissuade his opponent from playing these risky moves is open to debate! However, it is clear that Black's next move is the key test of White's idea (though 5...dxe4 also looks playable).

5...♗g4 6 exd5

White must force things as otherwise Black will achieve the strategically desirable exchange of bishop for knight with impunity.

6...cxd5 7 ♘b5

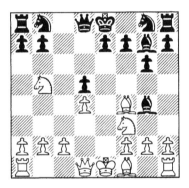

7...♘a6?

This is a perfectly natural response to the attack on c7. Indeed, it looks forced and it is doubtful that many players reaching this position over the board as Black would spend much time looking at alternative ideas. However, Black needed to show some finesse. A year after this game, Komliakov came up with 7...♔f8! which aims to answer 8 ♘c7? with 8...e5! winning material after 9 ♘xa8 exf4 by later trapping the knight in the corner. So 8 h3 ♗xf3 9 ♕xf3 ♘c6 was played in Vorobiov-Komliakov, Moscow 1995. Black's king is displaced, but then so is the white knight on b5. (In our main game, Novik plays his knight to a6 and then has to spend three whole tempi re-routing it to a decent square: firstly, ...♖fc8 - not a good

square for the rook, but he has to guard c7 - secondly ...♘b8 and finally ...♘c6. So assuming that the king is safe on f8, Black is gaining at least two moves - arguably three moves as the rook on c8 will have to be moved again - by playing 7...♔f8 rather than 7...♘a6.) Let's see some further moves in the Komliakov game: 10 c3 ♖c8 11 ♗d3 a6 12 ♘a3 ♗h6! (again Black avoids a stereotyped approach such as 12...♘f6, preferring instead to clear g7 for his king) 13 ♘c2 (if White plays 13 ♗h2 then there will be no future ideas of ♗g5 or ♕e3, combined with ♗h6, to bother Black) 13...♗xf4 14 ♕xf4 ♔g7 15 ♘e3 e6 16 0-0 (16 ♘g4 to occupy e5 looks better, e.g. 16...h5 [or 16...♕c7 17 ♕e3] 17 ♘e5 ♕f6 18 ♕e3!) 16...h5! (ruling out 17 ♘g4, after which it's difficult to find a constructive plan for White) 17 ♖fe1 ♕f6 18 ♕xf6+ ♘xf6 19 ♘f1 h4! and Black, who has nothing to fear on the kingside, later won by beginning a minority attack against the c3-pawn with ...b7-b5, ...a7-a5, ...b5-b4 etc., which led to the collapse of White's queenside pawn structure. Of course, in this extract White's play was very compliant with his opponent's wishes, but it is still useful to see what Black planned against zero resistance.

Things are very different in our main game, where Black's opening inaccuracy forever blights his middlegame chances.

8 h3 ♗xf3 9 ♕xf3 ♘f6 10 c3 0-0 11 ♗d3 ♕d7

As explained in the last note, the only way for Black to unwind his position is to put his king's rook on c8 and play the knight from a6 via b8 to c6. Of course, this takes a long time and White can simply continue to build up pressure on the kingside.

12 0-0 ♖fc8 13 ♖fe1 ♘b8 14 ♖e2 ♘c6 15 ♖ae1

see following diagram

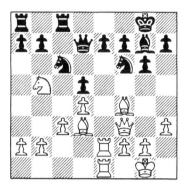

15...e6

Why does White double rooks on the e-file when there is no chance of a break-through there? We could talk about Nimzowitschian ideas of overprotection: the e5-square is a key centre point and any pieces controlling this square will find themselves well placed 'by accident' when the game opens up and the real battle begins. At a less abstract level, we could say that White has successfully provoked a positional concession from his opponent, as follows: Black plans to start queenside counterplay with ...a7-a6 and ...b7-b5 followed by ....♘a5 and ...♘c4, so his knight doesn't want to be tied down to the task of defending the pawn on e7. After White has doubled rooks his opponent decides to play 15...e6 to release the knight from guard duty. But this creates a secondary problem for Black by undermining the knight on f6, as will be seen. Perhaps in the long run Black cannot avoid ...e7-e6, but maybe he shouldn't play it so casually, as it makes a pawn storm by White on the kingside more plausible by ruling out defences such as ...♕g4. It may have been better to play 15...a6, e.g. 16 ♘a3 b5 17 ♘c2 ♖e8 18 ♗g5 (18 ♘e3 e5!?) 18...♖ab8, refusing to play ...e7-e6. Of course, it is psychologically difficult for Black to play 15...a6 as he appears to be spending a tempo chasing the white knight where it

wants to go (see White's next move). However, 15...a6 is preparatory to 16...b5; the attack on the white knight is purely coincidental.

16 ♘a3 ♘a5 17 ♗g5 ♘e8 18 h4!

Black's kingside structure is extremely solid, but enormous pressure is beginning to build up against it. His own counter-play on the queenside is painfully slow.

18...♘d6 19 h5 b5 20 hxg6 hxg6 21 ♘c2 ♖ab8 22 ♕f4!

It seems that Nimzowitsch was right (see the note at move 15). The white rook on e2, which seemed condemned to star-ing at the 'brick wall' on e6, suddenly has the chance to swing to the h-file via e3 and join in the attack on Black's king.

22...♘ac4

Novik and Nesis, writing in *Informator 61*, claim that Black can defend success-fully with 22...♖e8, but 23 ♖e3 and 24 ♖h3 looks very frightening.

23 ♘e3

This knight threatens to jump into g4 and then f6 and so forces Black to clear the way for the rook.

23...♘xe3 24 ♖xe3 b4

Black's counterattack finally hits home after a laborious build-up, but things have become critical on the kingside.

25 ♖h3 bxc3 26 bxc3 ♖xc3 27 ♕h4

With threats such as 28 ♗f6 planning 29 ♕h8+! ♗xh8 30 ♖xh8 mate. Black therefore offers the exchange but his opponent isn't to be deflected from his assault on the king.

27...♖xd3 28 ♕h7+ ♔f8 29 ♗h6! ♗xh6 30 ♕xh6+ ♔e7 31 ♕g5+ ♔f8 32 ♕h6+ ♔e7 33 ♕g5+ ♔f8 34 ♖h8+ ♔g7 35 ♕h6+ ♔f6 36 ♖xb8?

Finally White gives into the temptation to win material. Instead he could have finished the game with 36 ♕h4+! ♔g7 (if 36...g5 37 ♖h6+ mates in a few moves) 37 ♖h7+ ♔f8 (37...♔g8 38 ♕h6! wins) 38 ♕f6! and mate follows on h8. Evidently White was in time pressure here. Fortunately for him, the black king still proves fatally exposed.

36...♘f5 37 ♕h8+ ♔g5 38 ♖b3 ♖xd4 39 ♕e5 ♕d8 40 ♖h3 ♖c4 41 ♖ee3! ♖g4

The defenders and attackers struggle desperately around the hapless monarch.

42 ♖eg3 ♖xg3 43 ♖xg3+ ♔h6 44 ♖h3+ ♔g5 45 ♔h2!

The white king and his 'bodyguard' – the kingside pawns – also become involved in regicide. Now the attempt to exchange queens with 45...♕d6 allows the nice finish 46 f4+ ♔g4 47 ♖h4+!! ♔xh4 (47...♘xh4 48 ♕g5 mate) 48 ♕f6+ and mate on g5. This variation, and the even prettier one that follows in the next note, are given by Novik and Nesis. It seems that despite losing the game in what must have been an excruciating style, Novik

was still impressed enough by the aesthetic beauty of White's mating variations to want to annotate the game. Such a noble gesture deserves praise, since most players would only consider writing notes to their losses to prove how extraordinarily unjust chess can be.

45...d4 46 f3! f6

If 46...d3 47 ♖h4!! ♔xh4 (47...d2 48 ♔h3!! ♕d3 49 ♖g4+ ♔h5 50 ♕h8+ ♘h6 51 ♕f6) 48 ♕f4+ ♔h5 49 g4+ ♔h4 50 g5+ ♔h5 51 ♕g4 mate! The actual finish is slightly more prosaic.

47 f4+ ♔g4 48 ♕e2+ ♔xf4 49 ♖f3+ ♔g5 50 ♕d2+ ♔h5 51 g4+ ♔h4 52 ♕f4! 1-0

Mate with ♖h3 follows.

Game 9
J.Polgar-Shirov
Linares 1994

---

1 e4 g6 2 d4 ♗g7 3 ♘c3 c6 4 ♘f3 d6

Black avoids the 4...d5 lines above. In what follows we have chosen in principle not to give variations in which Black plays a quick ...♘f6, as this results in a direct transposition to the Pirc Defence, which is outside the scope of this book. Nevertheless, it is inadvisable to stick to this 'rule' too religiously. Sometimes ...♘f6 is clearly the best move and it is foolish to forbid it! A good example is if White now plays 5 a4, a standard move in the Classical. Since this rules out 5...b5, virtually the only 'Modern' move left is 5...♘d7. However, this allows White's bishop to get to a good diagonal after 6 ♗c4!, when 6...e6 7 0-0 ♘gf6 8 ♖e1 0-0 9 ♗b3 ♕c7 10 h3 a6?! (better is 10...e5 but 11 a5 is still favourable for White – Nunn and McNab) 11 ♗f4 e5 12 ♗h2 gave White an irritating edge in Barua-Petursson, Novi Sad 1990. Therefore, in this instance we recommend 5...♘f6!, when 6 ♗c4 can now be answered by 6...d5 with good chances to equalise. Instead the game Leko-Shirov, Dortmund 1996, went 6 ♗e2 0-0 7 0-0 ♘bd7 8 ♗f4 (not letting Black play 8...e5 with impunity) 8...♖e8!? (Shirov says he didn't like the variation 8...♕c7 9 e5 ♘h5 10 ♗g5 dxe5 11 ♗xe7 ♖e8, when after 12 d5! Black is committed to 12...♖xe7 13 d6 ♕d8 14 dxe7 ♕xe7. Black may well have adequate compensation for the exchange here, but if a cheerful sacrificer like Shirov refuses to play it then perhaps we should also think twice!) 9 ♖e1 (9 ♘d2 has also been suggested, but 9...e5 surely equalises) 9...♕c7 10 e5 ♘h5 11 exd6 exd6 12 ♗e3 d5 and Black had equalised.

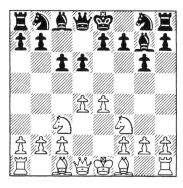

5 ♗g5!?

White has many options here:

a) The restraining 5 a4 has already been discussed in the last note above.

b) The move 5 h3 is highly important when it is the precursor of the system based on ♗e3 (see Game 10).

c) If 5 ♗e3 at once, rather than allow a transposition to Games 10 or 11, Black should take the chance to play 5...♗g4!, cutting across White's plans of an untroubled central build-up. Then 6 a4 (6 ♗e2 and 6 h3 are sound) 6...♗xf3 7 gxf3?! (no doubt White was afraid of 7 ♕xf3 ♕b6 hitting both b2 and d4, but then 8 ♗c4 looks like a good attacking move) 7...d5 8 a5 e6 with a position similar to that reached in our main game but without

Black having spent a move on ...♕b6, and White having played two rather superfluous moves with his a-pawn (Zapata-Chernin, St John 1988),

d) Another alternative is 5 ♗c4, when Black can play 5...b5, his standard plan in the next two games, with a gain of tempo. Play could go 6 ♗b3 (the sharp 6 ♘xb5, hoping for 6...cxd5?? 7 ♗d5, can be met by 6 ...d5, when 7 ♗b3 dxe4 8 ♘g5 cxb5 9 ♘xf7 ♕xd4 10 ♕xd4 ♗xd4 11 ♘xh8 e6! is better for Black) 6...a5 7 a4 b4 8 ♘e2 ♘f6 9 e5 ♘d5 10 ♘f4 ♘xf4 11 ♗xf4 d5 12 0-0 ♗g4 13 h3 ♗xf3 14 ♕xf3, as in De Firmian-Alburt, USA Championship 1984. Black has a solid and safe position, and the two white bishops aren't very imposing in view of the blocked centre. However, White has his customary space advantage.

e) Finally, 5 ♗e2 is well answered by 5...b5! With good reason, in Games 10 and 11 below, White prefers to develop this bishop to d3. Then ...b5-b4 is not much of a threat because of the simple retreat ♘e2, which keeps the knight nicely centralised. Here, however, with the bishop blocking the e2-square, the knight would be driven back to b1 or offside to a4. So White normally feels it is necessary to play 6 a3. This loss of a move allows Black to equalise and aim for more, e.g. 6...a6 7 ♗e3 ♘d7 8 0-0 ♗b7 (or 8...e5 9 ♕d2 ♗b7 10 ♖ad1 ♘gf6 11 ♗h6 0-0 12 ♗xg7 ♔xg7 13 h3 ♖e8 14 dxe5 dxe5 15 ♕e3 ♕c7 with equality in G.Garcia-Nogueiras, Granma 1987) 9 ♕d2 ♕c7 10 b4?! (10 ♖ad1 is more solid) 10...♘gf6 11 ♗h6 0-0 12 ♗xg7 ♔xg7 13 ♖fe1 ♖fd8 14 ♕e3 e5 15 ♖ed1 h6 16 h3 c5! and Black began the process of undermining White's weakened queenside in T.Olafsson-Conquest, Reykjavik 1998.

The move Polgar selects in the game leads to a highly interesting clash of plans in the middlegame.

5...♕b6!?

The idea of this move is to obstruct

White's most aggressive set-up, which consists of 6 ♕d2 and 7 0-0-0.

6 ♖b1

Instead, White could call Black's bluff with 6 ♕d2, when after 6...♕xb2 7 ♖b1 ♕a3, Shirov gives 8 ♗d3 h6 9 ♗e3 ♘f6 10 0-0 ♘bd7 11 h3 ♕a5 as unclear. More direct is 8 ♗c4, e.g. 8...♘d7 9 0-0 ♘b6 10 ♗b3 ♘f6 11 e5 dxe5 12 dxe5 ♘fd5 13 ♘e4 (thus far this is the game Kogan-Kantsler, Tel Aviv 1996; recapturing the pawn with 13 ♗xd5 etc. is the obvious alternative with unclear play) and now 13...♗f5 looks okay for Black.

The game move looks rather unnatural, but it doesn't indicate a lack of ambition. It becomes clear that Polgar intends to attack on the queenside, kingside and in the centre!

6...♗g4 7 ♗e3

The fact that the bishop could have gone to this square 'in one go' suggests that White's opening strategy may not be quite sound.

7...♗xf3 8 gxf3

Having declined the chance to sacrifice the b-pawn, White was hardly going to offer the d-pawn with 8 ♕xf3?

The doubled pawns give Polgar's kingside a slightly fragile look, but on the other hand she has a trump card in form of the light-squared bishop which now has no rival. Black decides to construct a cen-

tre pawn barrier on d5 and e6 to curb the bishop's activity. Meanwhile, White gains space on the kingside by advancing the h-pawn and is ready to pounce if a tactical opportunity presents itself.

8...♕c7

A necessary retreat, as Black wants to play ...e7-e6 without being embarrassed by a discovered attack on his queen after d5.

9 h4 e6! 10 h5 d5 11 ♕d2

Black's centre looks solid, but he has spent a lot of time setting it up. A more direct plan for White was 11 ♕e2, but Shirov shows that Black has nothing to fear: 11...♘f6 12 h6 ♗f8 13 ♗g5 ♗e7 and if 14 ♗xf6 ♗xf6 15 exd5 cxd5 16 ♘xd5 ♕a5+ 17 ♘c3 ♗xd4 18 ♕b5+ ♘c6! etc. is good for Black.

11...♘d7 12 b4

And here White can set her opponent problems with 12 exd5 exd5 13 ♗f4 ♕b6 14 ♕e3+. Now Shirov gives the long variation 14...♘e7 15 ♗d6 0-0!? 16 ♗xe7 ♖fe8 17 ♘e2 ♗f8 18 hxg6 hxg6 19 ♗c5 ♘xc5 20 dxc5 ♗xc5 21 ♕h6 ♗d4 22 ♔d1 ♗g7 23 ♕h4 ♖e5 when he concludes that Black's initiative against the white king gives him enough for the piece. Black is by no means forced into this, and could try the quiet 14...♔d8, when White has to think about defending his d-pawn.

12...♘gf6 13 h6 ♗f8 14 ♗f4 ♕d8

Black could force equality with 14...e5 15 dxe5 ♘xe5 16 ♗xe5 ♕xe5 17 f4 ♕e6 18 e5 ♘e4 (Shirov) but the game move keeps the tension.

15 ♗d3 ♗e7 16 ♘e2 0-0 17 c3 b5!

Black plans to undermine the white queenside and so begins by fixing the pawn on b4.

18 ♔f1 a5 19 a3 ♘b6 20 ♖e1 ♘e8

The outpost square on c4 attracts the attention of both black knights.

21 ♗e5!

Despite the fact that the kingside is virtually blocked, White succeeds in generating potent threats against the black king.

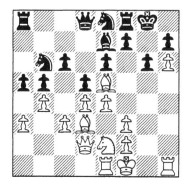

21...♘d6 22 ♗g7 ♘dc4 23 ♕c1 ♖e8 24 e5 axb4 25 axb4 ♖a2

Black has broken through on the queenside, but he has to be alert to danger on the other wing.

26 ♕f4

Now White plans ♕g4 and ♘f4 followed either by the sacrifice ♘xe6 when ...fxe6? ♕xe6 would be mate, or alternatively a double piece sacrifice on g6, followed by ♕xg6 and a quick mate. Black acts fast to exchange both the white bishop on d3 and the knight.

26...♖d2 27 ♗b1! ♘a4 28 ♔g2 ♘ab2 29 ♕g4! ♘a3!

The bishop on b1 will be eliminated just in time to thwart White's plan.

30 ♘f4 ♘xb1 31 ♖xb1 ♘d3 32 ♘xd3 ♖xd3

33 ♖a1?

White persists in trying to attack, but this just loses the queenside pawns. White had to defend c3 with 33 ♖hc1, when 33...f5! 34 exf6 ♗xf6 35 ♖a1! ♗xg7 36 hxg7 is unclear according to Shirov.

33...♖xc3 34 ♖a7 ♖c4! 35 ♖ha1 ♖xb4 36 ♕f4 c5 37 ♖xe7

This sacrifice is White's only chance to create a swindle.

37...♕xe7 38 ♗f6 ♕c7 39 ♖a6 ♖xd4 40 ♕g5 ♖a4 41 ♖d6 ♖aa8 42 ♖c6!?

No better is 42 ♗d8 f6. White was hoping against hope for 42...♕xc6?? 43 ♗e7, when 43...♖xe7 44 ♕f6! mates or 43...f5 44 ♕f6 etc. But Shirov is vigilant.

42...♕a7 43 ♗d8 f6!

Here 43...♖axd8? 44 ♕f6 is best avoided, e.g. 44...♔f8 45 ♖d6!!

44 ♗xf6 c4 45 ♕g4 ♕f7 46 ♕d4 ♖ec8 47 ♕b6 ♖xc6 48 ♕xc6 ♖b8 0-1

After 49 ♕d6 ♖c8 50 ♕a6 ♕d7 Black wins by pushing the c-pawn. An enthralling struggle.

Game 10
Van der Weide-Piket
Rotterdam 1998

---

1 e4 g6 2 d4 ♗g7 3 ♘c3 c6 4 ♘f3 d6 5 h3

White has adopted a Classical variation move order, but in fact he intends to play a system with ♗e3 similar to that discussed in the next main game. As a first step, he prevents Black from disturbing his build-up with 5...♗g4.

5...b5

As in the next game, Black's queenside expansion is enterprising but risky as it provides targets for the white pieces and pawns. There were two alternatives:

a) Black can strike at the centre immediately with 5...e5. However, he would be slightly worse after 6 dxe5 dxe5 7 ♕xd8+ ♔xd8 8 ♗e3 f6 9 ♗c4 etc. In particular, the bishop on c8 is deprived of good development squares.

b) More reasonable is 5...♘d7, planning ...e7-e5. Then after 6 ♗e3 e5 (6...♘gf6 7 e5 may be awkward) followed by 7...♘gf6 and 8...0-0 play would be similar to that in the Yudasin game with 5...♘d7 mentioned in the note to Black's fifth move in the next main game.

6 ♗d3 ♘d7

Not satisfactory is 6...e5 7 ♗e3 ♘d7?! (7...a6 or 7...♗b7 are necessary) 8 d5! b4 9 dxc6 bxc3 10 cxd7+ ♗xd7 11 bxc3 ♘f6 12 c4 ♗c6 13 ♘d2 (Yudasin) when White has a useful extra pawn.

7 0-0 ♗b7?!

Here 7...e5 8 d5 looks bad, but 7...a6 was more solid, when 8 a4 ♖b8 is the same idea as in the next main game.

8 ♗e3 a6

In view of the unexpected catastrophe awaiting him at move 12, all of Black's moves now appear wrong. Preferable was 8...e5 9 a4 b4, with a defensible position.

9 a4 e5?

Black goes confidently to his doom. Here he definitely had to try 9...b4, even though it weakens his queenside pawns.

10 axb5 cxb5

If 10...axb5 11 ♖xa8 ♗xa8 (11...♕xa8 12 d5! cxd5 13 ♘xb5 ♕b8 14 ♗a7 is a disaster for Black) 12 ♕a1 (12 d5!?) is good for White (Yudasin).

11 dxe5! dxe5

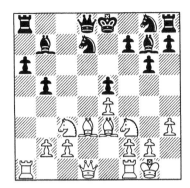

Perhaps Black thought he had a small advantage here, as after 12...♘gf6 next move the threat of ...b5-b4, winning the e4-pawn, is difficult for White to meet. However, Black isn't slightly better – he is completely lost! After White's reply he will never find time to play ...♘gf6.

12 ♗xb5!!

White blasts open the position. Despite the sacrifice of a piece he will always have the advantage in firepower where it matters, as Black's kingside pieces are unprepared for a battle in the centre. This is the type of breakthrough Black always fears when, in an opening like the Modern Defence, he has delayed the development of his pieces in search of immediate counterplay with his pawns on the queenside.

12...axb5 13 ♘xb5 ♗f8

Black has to staunch up the d6-square. If 13...♖xa1 14 ♕xa1 ♗c6 Yudasin gives the crushing variation 15 ♘d6+ ♔f8 16 ♘g5! ♘h6 17 ♘dxf7!, when Black is pulverised as 17...♘xf7 18 ♘e6+ wins his queen.

14 ♕d3

With the black king trapped in the centre, there is no need for White to rush. He clears d1 for his king's rook and intends to exchange the other rook on a8 followed by ♕c4!, when a subsequent ♘c7+ will drive out the black king.

14...≣a6 15 ≣fd1 ♕c8

The queen dodges the threat of 16 ≣xa6 ♗xa6 17 ♘xe5.

16 ≣xa6 ♗xa6 17 ♘d6+!

This forces the exchange of the only black piece actively resisting on the dark squares.

17...♗xd6 18 ♕xd6 ♗e2

This is a spirited attempt to eliminate one of the attackers. If instead 18...♘gf6 19 ♗g5 ♘xe4? 20 ♕e7 is mate.

19 ≣d5! ♘e7

If 19...f6 then 20 ♘xe5! ♘xe5 21 ≣xe5+! fxe5 22 ♕xe5+ ♔d7 23 ♕xh8 is winning. Perhaps the best chance for continued resistance was 19...♗xf3, but 20 ≣xe5+! ♘xe5 21 ♕xe5+ ♔d7 22 ♕xh8 ♗e2 23 ♕xh7 leaves White with four pawns for the piece and a continuing attack. Both of these variations are given by Petursson.

20 ♘xe5!

After this further sacrifice, Black's dark squares completely collapse.

20...♘xd5 21 ♘xd7! ≣g8

If 21...♕xd7 22 ♕e5+ ♘e7(?!) 23 ♕xh8+ picks up both rook and knight with check.

22 ♗g5! ♗a6

Or 22...♕xd7 23 ♕b8+ ♔d8 24 ♕xd8 mate.

23 exd5 ♕xd7 24 ♕e5+ 1-0

Black gave up as 24...♔f8 25 ♗h6+

wins the rook to start with. A brilliant attacking display by White.

Game 11
Gallagher-Irzhanov
Lucerne 1997

1 e4 g6 2 d4 ♗g7 3 ♘c3 c6 4 ♗e3 d6

In view of the difficulties Black encounters in this game, the reader is urged to investigate 4...d5!? here. Then after 5 ♕d2 dxe4 6 ♘xe4 ♘d7 7 0-0-0 ♘gf6 8 ♘c3?! (8 ♘xf6+ is better – Krasenkov) 8...0-0 9 f3 b5 10 ♔b1 ♘b6 11 h4 h5 12 ♗h6 ♗e6 13 ♗xg7 ♔xg7 14 ♘h3 b4 15 ♘e4 ♘a4! Black had excellent attacking chances based on ...♕a5 in Socko-Krasenkov, Poland 1996. Of course, White can also play less aggressively (perhaps recklessly is a better word) than this, but Black should hardly experience serious problems. Also possible is 5 f3, when 5...♘f6 6 e5 ♘fd7 7 f4 b5 8 ♗d3 ♘b6 9 b3 was murky but turned out well for White in Vujosevic-Sekulic, Yugoslavia 1995. Perhaps Black should take the bull by the horns with 5...dxe4 6 fxe4 e5!? which looks fine for him. (Incidentally, Irzhanov himself never had the chance to try 4...d5 as we cheated with the move order – the game actually began 3...d6 4 ♗e3 c6.)

Another alternative is 4...♕b6, as played in Adams-Shirov, Belgrade 1995. This audacious move, putting the queen on the same diagonal as White's bishop, aims to prevent White from achieving his most aggressive set-up with 5 ♕d2 and 6 0-0-0. After the game continuation 5 ≣b1 d6 6 ♘f3 ♘f6 7 ♗e2 ♕c7 8 0-0, Adams recommends 8...♗g4 when exchanging off the knight on f3 would be positionally well motivated. In case the reader doubts this, we should look at how much the knight contributed to Black's downfall in the game after the move actually played: 8...♘bd7?! 9 a4 0-0 10 ♘d2! e5 11 dxe5 dxe5 12 ♘c4 ♖d8 13 ♕d6! ♘e8 14 ♕xc7 ♘xc7 15 ♘d6 ♘e6 16 ♗c4 ♘b6 17 ♗xe6 ♖xd6 18 ♗b3! Here Black cannot easily untangle his pieces as 18...♗e6 19 ♗c5 ♖d2 20 ♗xe6 fxe6 21 ♖bc1! leaves him with weakened pawns. Nevertheless this is how he should play. In the game Shirov tried to keep his pawn structure intact and was defeated in classy positional style by Adams: 18...♘d7?! 19 ♖bd1 ♗f8 20 ♘b1! (an excellent move, planning to bring the knight to c4 via a3) 20...♖xd1 21 ♖xd1 ♔g7 22 ♘a3 ♗xa3 (this destroys the knight but severely weakens his dark squares) 23 bxa3 ♔f8 24 a5 ♔e7 25 f4! ♘f6? (25...b6! – Adams) 26 fxe5 ♘xe4 27 ♖d4 ♗f5 28 g4 c5 29 ♖c4 and Black resigned. A rather drastic defeat, but 4...♕b6 deserves attention. Nevertheless, we repeat that 4...d5 seems like the best option.

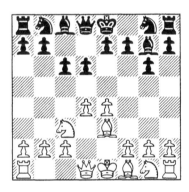

5 ♕d2

If 5 h3 Black can try 5...♕a5!? when after 6 f4 (by no means forced – 6 ♘f3 is also quite reasonable, when 6...e5 is probably best) 6...♘f6 7 ♗d3 e5 8 ♕f3? (8 ♘f3 ♘bd7 is unclear according to Korotylev), as in Sveshnikov-Korotylev, St Petersburg 1994, Black could have played 8...♘xe4!! as 9 fxe5 (9 ♕xe4 d5 10 ♕f3 exd4 wins for Black) 9...♘xc3 10 ♗d2 dxe5 11 ♗xc3 ♕c7 12 dxe5 0-0 is slightly better for Black – Sveshnikov.

During the course of the 1990s, White

developed a highly dangerous system against the Pirc/Modern set-up involving ♗e3. If it is a Pirc and Black has played ...♘f6 and ...0-0, White is ready to exchange dark-squared bishops with ♕d2 and ♗h6 and then launch a quick kingside attack with h2-h4 and h4-h5 (of course, White doesn't castle kingside). This direct attacking plan has proved surprisingly difficult to meet. In the Modern the knight remains on g8, which obstructs, or at least delays, the plan of ♕d2 and ♗h6. Meanwhile, Black is usually aiming for counterplay with a queenside pawn advance involving ...b7-b5. White normally responds by bunching his pieces in the centre, e.g. knights on c3 and f3, bishops on d3 and e3 and queen on d2, and then tries to undermine Black's pawn structure on the queenside. He is also waiting for ...♘f6, in the hope that the pawn advance e4-e5 will prove strong.

In passing, we should mention the independent line 5 h4!?, when 5...h5 6 ♘h3 ♘f6 (6...♗xh3 may be better, eliminating the knight before it reaches the impregnable g5-square) 7 f3 b5 8 ♘g5 was played in Onischuk-Irzhanov, Lucerne 1997. Here Onischuk gives 8...a6 9 e5 ♘d5 as unclear.

5...b5

Since Black has played ...c7-c6, this bid for counterplay is a natural plan. However, it proves double-edged as White can later play to undermine the black queenside pawns.

It was also possible to ignore the queenside and develop rapidly in the style of a Pirc defence with the aim of ...e7-e5, e.g. 5...♘d7 6 ♘f3 ♘gf7 7 h3 0-0 8 ♗d3 e5 9 0-0 ♖e8 10 ♖fe1 exd4 11 ♘xd4 ♘c5 12 ♗h6, as in Yudasin-Kakageldiev, Biel 1993, when Yudasin recommends 12...♗xh6! 13 ♕xh6 ♕b6 with unclear play. The queen on h6 is a terrible sight for Black, but meanwhile on the queenside he is threatening both 14...♕xb2 and

14...♘xd3, winning a piece.

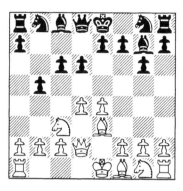

6 ♗d3

White has some important alternatives here:

a) 6 f3 may appear somewhat superfluous as the e-pawn is under no threat. However, the plan of castling queenside and then pushing the kingside pawns has been used in diverse forms by some of the best players in the world, so it deserves respect. Here after 6...♘d7 7 g4 ♘b6 8 h4, the vital block 8...h5! led to unclear play in Oll-S.Mohr, Debrecen 1989.

b) A second possibility is the attempt to land a blow in the centre with 6 0-0-0 ♘d7 7 e5!? when 7...♘b6 8 exd6 exd6 9 ♗g5 (Nunn and McNab suggest that 9 ♖e1 ♘e7 10 ♗h6 0-0 11 h4 is more dangerous) 9...f6 10 ♗f4 d5 11 ♗d3 ♔f7 12 h4 h5 13 f3 ♘e7 was unclear in Maros-Petran, Slovakia 1994.

6...♘d7 7 ♘f3

Another idea was 7 f4!? with a hybrid between the ♗e3 system and the Austrian Attack. One example is 7...♘b6 8 b3 ♘f6 9 ♘f3 a6 with a slight advantage for White in Granda-Kurajica, Groningen 1997.

7...a6 8 a4

White puts immediate pressure on the black queenside and is rewarded with control of the a-file.

8...♖b8

Black wants to keep his queenside

pawns compact, and thus avoids 8...b4 9 ♘e2 a5, when White can play c2-c3 to break them up. An important alternative was 8...♗b7, but this leaves the queenside vulnerable to a sudden breakthrough. For example, Yudasin gives the variation 9 0-0 e5 10 ♖fd1 ♕c7 11 axb5 axb5 12 ♖xa8+ ♗xa8 13 d5! breaking up the black queenside, with a clear advantage to White. Something even nastier happened to Black in the previous game.

9 axb5 axb5 10 0-0 b4

Black wants to play 10...e5 but 11 d5 is awkward for him, so first he chases back the white knight.

11 ♘e2 ♘gf6 12 ♗h6

The exchange of dark-squared bishops is an important theme in White's opening strategy. It weakens Black's kingside and removes most of his dynamic chances, leaving him to face a dour defensive task.

12...0-0 13 ♘g3 e5

It is important that Black achieves his space-gaining advance, but nonetheless the position remains worse for him. White now builds up an initiative on the kingside.

14 ♗xg7 ♔xg7 15 ♕g5! ♕c7 16 ♘f5+ ♔g8 17 ♖fe1 ♘e8

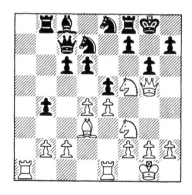

18 ♕h6?

This was tempting as 18...gxf5? would now leave Black facing a lethal attack after 19 ♘g5 ♘df6 20 exf5. A possible finish would be 20...♕e7 21 ♖e3 ♔h8 22 ♖h3, when h7 collapses with a quick mate. However, while it is true that some sacrifices, such as 12 ♗xb5 in the game above, are more determined than others not to be ignored, there is no rule in chess that says you have to accept every sacrifice! In this instance Black can simply decline the offer.

Much stronger for White was the quiet 18 ♗c4! (as recommended by Yudasin) which puts the bishop on an active diagonal where it exerts pressure on f7. Then 18...d5 19 exd5 ♘b6, trying to exploit the loose position of the bishop and knight, would fail for a number of reasons, e.g. 20 d6! when 20...♘xd6 21 ♘xd6 (or 21 ♘e7+) 21...♕xd6 22 dxe5 leaves White a pawn up for nothing. If instead Black plays quietly, the pin on f7 would be very awkward for him, as he is deprived of the plan of ...f7-f6 enabling his queen to defend the second rank on the kingside. With the bishop on c4 White's idea of ♕h6 combined with ♘g5 would therefore be much stronger. This was a very instructive moment as it shows the difference between a genuinely strong move and one which only makes a strong visual impression.

18...♘b6!

This takes away the c4-square from the white bishop (if White had played 18 ♗c4 last move he could now reply 19 ♗b3, keeping his bishop on the excellent diagonal). Black is therefore threatening 18...gxf5 when 19 ♘g5 f6 gives him a winning position.

19 ♘e3 f6 20 ♘c4 ♗e6

Black keeps up the fight for the c4-square.

21 ♘xb6 ♕xb6 22 ♖a6 ♕c7 23 ♖ea1

The possession of the a-file gives White an undoubted advantage, but on its own this should hardly be enough to win the game.

23...♘g7 24 dxe5 dxe5 25 ♖a7 ♖b7 26 ♕e3 b3!

This is a good defensive move, undermining the white bishop and getting rid of the potentially weak b-pawn.

27 cxb3 ♗xb3 28 ♖xb7 ♕xb7 29 ♕c5

If 29 ♖a7 ♕b4 30 ♕h6 ♖f7 is solid enough for Black.

29...♗f7 30 ♗c4 ♖a8

Definitely not 30...♕xb2? 31 ♗xf7+ ♔xf7 (31...♖xf7 32 ♖a8+) 32 ♕c4+! etc.

31 ♖d1 ♘e6 32 ♗xe6 ♗xe6 33 h3 ♗f7 34 ♖d2 ♔g7 35 ♔h2 ♖b8 36 ♕d6 ♕b5 37 ♕e7 ♖b7 38 ♕d8 c5??

Instead 38...♖b8 holds the draw.

39 ♖d6 1-0

Black resigned as f6 drops followed by e5. This was a sad end for Black, who after defending precisely for most of the game blundered just when the draw seemed in sight. However, a regular tournament player knows that a sudden collapse after a painstaking defence is by no means an unusual occurrence. Black was always having to find precise moves and side-step pitfalls, whereas White had the luxury of knowing that he could make an inaccurate move without jeopardising his safety (as happened at move 18). Gallagher knew that if he kept up the pressure there was a good chance Black would falter in the end.

Summary

After 4 ♘f3 d5 (Games 6-8) Black has good chances for equality, but he must play exactly. The quiet lines of the Pseudo-Classical after 4 ♘f3 d6 (in the notes to Game 9) don't seem particularly dangerous for Black (or White!), while 5 ♗g5 (Game 9) is interesting but probably inaccurate. More critical is the system with an early ♗e3 seen in Games 10 and 11. These games are hardly a great advertisement for the plan of queenside expansion with ...b7-b5, though with best play Black is okay but somewhat passive. Nevertheless, in particular after 4 ♗e3 (Game 11) 4...d5 is recommended.

1 e4 g6 2 d4 ♗g7 3 ♘c3 c6 *(D)*

4 ♘f3
> 4 ♗e3 – *Game 11*

4...d5
> 4...d6 *(D)*
>> 5 ♗g5 – *Game 9*
>> 5 h3 b5 6 ♗d3 ♘d7 7 0-0 – *Game 10*

5 h3 *(D)*
> 5 ♗f4 – *Game 8*

5...♘f6
> 5...♘h6 – *Game 7*

6 e5 ♘e4 – *Game 6*

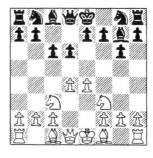

3...c6　　　　　*4...d6*　　　　　*5 h3*

CHAPTER THREE

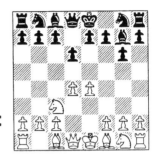

1 e4 g6 2 d4 ♗g7 3 ♘c3 d6: The Main Lines

---

1 e4 g6 2 d4 ♗g7 3 ♘c3 d6

In this chapter we examine lines beginning 1 e4 g6 2 d4 ♗g7 3 ♘c3 d6, where after 4 f4 or 4 ♗e3 or 4 ♘f3 (4 ♗c4 and 4 ♗g5 are to be found in Chapter 4) Black plays 4...a6. Note that 4...c6 would transpose to variations given in the previous two chapters, while 4...♘f6 leads to the Pirc Defence. Also, 4...♗g4 is briefly mentioned in the notes to Game 16.

All the games in the chapter have interrelated ideas and plans which makes the transpositional possibilities enormous. Black is not greatly concerned with the rapid development of his kingside pieces and aims for an immediate queenside expansion with ...a7-a6 and ....b7-b5, usually followed by ...♘d7 or ...♗b7. This strategy is seen at its best in Games 12 and 13, where White plays 4 ♗e3 a6 5 ♕d2 with the idea of a quick ♗h6 followed by an attack on Black's castled king. In the Pirc, where Black has already committed himself with ...♘f6, White has scored well using this system. However, by delaying ...♘f6 and concentrating on the queenside Black can take most of the sting out of White's attacking system, as Mikhail Gurevich proves in two fine games.

There are, however, two main sources of danger for Black in omitting an early ...♘f6. Firstly, White may achieve a breakthrough in the centre with e4-e5 and slay the black pieces while they are still on their starting squares. Anand tries this plan in Game 14 after the move order 3 ♘c3 d6 4 ♗e3 a6 5 ♘f3 etc., but Black's position should prove resilient enough. In fact, the plan of a central breakthrough is much more promising after the 'Austrian' move order 3 ♘c3 d6 4 f4, as White's e4-e5 advance will be bolstered by the pawns on d4 and f4. This is demonstrated in Game 16, where Black has some doubtful moments in the opening phase. However, it is clearly not any easy type of game for White to play either, as Black's heroic defence is rewarded with a battling victory.

The second danger facing Black is the attack on his b5-pawn beginning with a2-a4. This may or may not be combined with another idea such as an e4-e5 advance or ♕d2 and ♗h6. Ideally, Black would like to stand his ground with his pawns, but in most cases he is compelled to weaken them by advancing with ...b5-b4 or even playing the ugly ...b5xa4. White adopts the plan of a2-a4 in Game 15, where he responds to Black's provocative

Modern set-up in very classical style: he makes only two pawn moves in the opening (the two 'best' ones, e2-e4 and d2-d4, according to classical precepts), puts his knights on the well approved c3- and f3-squares, and then develops his bishop unpretentiously on e2. We may sneer at White's lack of sophistication, but in the game Black soon finds himself in serious trouble! Nevertheless, with accurate play Black can hold the balance.

> ### Game 12
> ### Skripchenko-M.Gurevich
> *Groningen 1997*

1 e4 g6 2 d4 ♗g7 3 ♘c3 d6 4 ♗e3

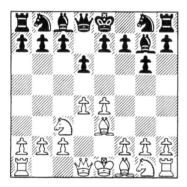

With 4 ♗e3 White declares his intention to play ♕d2 and ♗h6 followed by ♗xg7 to exchange off dark-squared bishops. Then, assuming Black has castled kingside, the next stage will be to launch a direct assault with h2-h4-h5 and h5xg6, breaking open the h-file. If all goes well, this will culminate in a quick mate, possibly heralded by ♕h6 with the queen supported by the rook on h1. White's king meanwhile will probably have castled on the queenside, so as to be secure and not get in the way of the attack of his own pieces. In tournament practice this simple plan has proved very dangerous for Black, who has often found himself the victim of

a crushing defeat. One counter method for Black is to avoid or delay castling kingside, but White can play ♕d2 and ♗h6 just the same, when after the exchange ...♗xh6 (probably forced as the bishop is undefended); ♕xh6 White's queen is forever threatening to infiltrate on g7. In that case, Black will probably start wishing he had castled, so that after the exchange ♗xg7 ♔xg7 at least his king would defending the dark squares!

However, Black has available a much more subtle response to White's direct plan. Thankfully, he has chosen a Modern Defence move order and his knight isn't yet on f6. So at the moment if White plays ♕d2 and ♗h6 Black simply takes the bishop and wins a piece (unfortunately things get more complicated than this!). Black's next move reveals his best strategy. **4...a6!**

Black leaves his knight back on g8 and instead prepares to expand on the queenside with ...b7-b5. There are two further advantages to this plan. Firstly, if White responds with 5 a4, then queenside castling becomes a less attractive option for him, which means that a gung ho attack with 0-0-0 and h2-h4-h5 becomes much less likely. And secondly, the white e-pawn could become a target after ...♗b7 or a later ...♘f6, threatening ...b5-b4.

Another 'Modern' alternative was 4...c6, which transposes to Chapter 2. On the whole, a queenside expansion with ...b7-b5 is more effective when it is supported by ...a7-a6 rather than with ...c7-c6. The latter, although solid, has several negative points.

Firstly, ...c7-c6 curtails the activity of Black's queenside pieces as it takes away the c6-square from the knight (though we should point out that d7 is often its best square) and leaves the queen's bishop blocked in after the plausible development ...♗b7. Also, ..c7-c6 exposes the centre to the undermining advance d4-d5!? and should Black ever choose to adopt the plan of ...c6-c5 to attack d4 he will probably have to spend a tempo safeguarding the b5-pawn with ...a7-a6, when he would be losing time compared with the immediate ...a7-a6 and ...c7-c5.

5 ♕d2

Black must eventually play ...♘f6, as it would be suicidal to leave his kingside permanently undeveloped. Therefore at some point White will get the chance to play ♗h6 and so prepares accordingly.

Of the alternatives, 5 ♘f3 is analysed in Game 14. There are also many transpositional possibilities here. We give two of the most important:

a) After 5 h4 h5 6 ♕d2 b5 7 f3 ♘d7 8 ♘h3 ♗b7 9 a4 c6 10 ♘g5 ♘gf6 11 ♗e2 0-0 12 0-0 e5 Black had equalised in Apicella-Hillarp-Persson, Zaragoza 1995. The critical test in this sequence has to be 9 0-0-0, which transposes to 7 0-0-0 mentioned at the end of the note to White's seventh move in Game 13. There 9...♖c8!? is suggested.

b) 5 f4 transposes to a variation of the Austrian Attack – see the notes at moves seven and eight in Game 16.

5...b5 6 a4

White decides to quell Black's queenside insurrection. This is a good time to strike as the pawns aren't yet supported by the pieces, and therefore cannot be maintained in a compact formation (obviously 6...c6? 7 axb5 cxb5 7 ♗xb5+ wins a pawn). So Black is compelled to break ranks with his b-pawn, when his queenside pawn structure becomes dislocated. But at least he has created some counterplay and discouraged White from ever castling queenside. This means that if, as occurs in the game, White reverts to the plan of a kingside attack, then it isn't just the black king which could find itself in danger.

The alternative 6 f3 in considered in

Game 13.

6...b4 7 ♘d1

Instead 7 ♘ce2 a5 8 ♘g3 was possible, as in Kaminiski-Ehlvest, Polanica Zdroj 1997, when 8...♘d7 was played. An interesting but risky-looking alternative would be 8...d5!?, e.g. 9 ♗d3 ♗b7 10 e5 c5!?

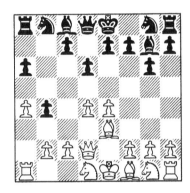

7...a5 8 c3 ♘f6 9 f3 bxc3 10 bxc3 0-0

An example of the dangers Black faces if he plays carelessly is Anand-Khalifman, Las Palmas 1993, which went 10...c6?! 11 ♗h6 0-0 12 h4 e5 13 h5 ♖e8 14 hxg6 fxg6 15 ♗xg7 ♔xg7 16 ♘f2 ♖a7?! (he should seek counterplay with 16...♘bd7! – Anand) 17 ♖b1! ♗e6 (still 17...♘bd7! was correct as the bishop becomes a target on this square) 18 dxe5 dxe5 19 ♕h6+ ♔g8 20 ♘gh3! ♕e7 21 ♘g5 ♗a2 22 ♖b2 ♕a3 23 ♖xa2! (giving up the exchange to gain time to smash Black's kingside) 23...♕xa2 24 ♘xh7! (White gets his attack in first) 24...♘xh7 25 ♕xg6+ ♔f8 26 ♖xh7 ♖xh7 27 ♕xh7 ♕g8 28 ♕h4! (of course he avoids the exchange of queens) 28...♘d7 29 ♘g4 ♕b3 30 ♕h6+ ♔e7 31 ♕xc6. White now has the material advantage of three pawns for the exchange plus continued attacking chances against Black's king which is denuded of pawn cover. Meanwhile, White's own king can slip away to g1 if necessary where it will be very secure. Anand eventually converted these advantages into a win.

11 ♗h6

Skripchenko has 'tidied up' the queen-side and now launches a kingside on-slaught. A less ambitious approach was 11 ♗d3 ♘bd7 12 ♘e2 c6 13 0-0, just developing the pieces. However, 13...e5 14 ♘f2 d5, as in Ljubojevic-Ehlvest, Linares 1991, gives Black plenty of play in the centre.

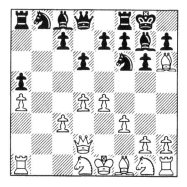

11...e5!

White has actually fallen behind in development, so it is natural for Black to try to open lines in the centre, especially since the white king could become vulnerable.

12 h4 ♖e8 13 d5

This keeps the centre blocked: Black mustn't be allowed to play ...d6-d5 himself.

13...c6 14 dxc6 ♘xc6 15 ♗xg7 ♚xg7 16 ♗b5 ♕c7 17 h5 ♗e6

Again Black tries to break out with ...d6-d5!

18 ♘e3

Instead 18 hxg6 fxg6 19 g4 ♖ed8 was unclear (Gurevich). The queen and king's rook have been unable to strike a decisive blow against Black's king, and so rather belatedly White brings the knights into the fray.

18...♖ed8 19 hxg6 fxg6 20 ♘e2 ♘e7!

Tactics come before strategy! Here 20...d5? looks very logical (indeed it has been Black's aim for some moves) but it fails to 21 exd5 ♗xd5 22 ♘xd5 ♖xd5 23

♕h6+ ♚h8 (23...♚g8 24 ♗c4) 24 ♕xg6 when White is winning (Gurevich). It will be seen that White's bishop, sitting unobtrusively on b5, plays a big part in Black's demise in this variation: there is a potential ♗c4 pin and also the latent threat of ♗xc6, driving the black queen away from the defence of h7 after the recapture ...♕xc6 and so making ♕h6+ very strong. It is the fortune or misfortune of this bishop which will decide who comes out on top in the resulting struggle.

21 c4

White stops ...d6-d5 once and for all, which is a very important achievement, though in the process the dark squares, especially d4, are weakened. The bishop is also not too happy, as it finds its retreat cut off.

21...h5!

An excellent move which plans to seize the initiative on the king's wing.

22 ♖d1

Perhaps White should have played 22 ♘d5, so that after 22...♘exd5 23 cxd5 the bishop is freed from its prison on b5.

22...♕c5

The queen stations herself on the weakest diagonal in White's position.

23 ♘g3 ♚f7!?

A cunning move, which sets a positional trap.

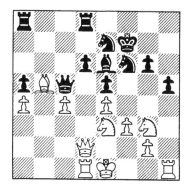

24 ♖f1?

The sight of the black king on f7 provokes an intemperate reaction from White, who prepares f3-f4 without more ado. However, this allows Black to gain a dark-squared bind on the kingside. It really was time for White to free the poor bishop on b5 with 24 ♘d5!, when Gurevich gives 24...♘exd5 25 cxd5 ♗d7 26 ♖c1 ♕a7 27 ♕f2 as unclear.

24...h4! 25 ♘e2 g5 26 ♖c1 ♕a7 27 ♘c3?

This was the last chance to force Black to capture on d5 with 27 ♘d5! Now the bishop will remain entombed on b5 while the battle is lost.

27...♘h5!

The knight heads for f4 to strengthen the dark-square stranglehold.

28 ♘ed5 ♘f4 29 ♘xf4 exf4!

This clears a wonderful outpost on e5 for the other knight.

30 ♘d5 ♘g6

Of course, Black isn't interested in 30...♘xd5? 31 cxd5, when he frees White's bishop and clears the c-file for White's rook. A long manoeuvring phase now begins.

31 ♔e2 ♖ac8 32 ♖fd1 ♘e5 33 ♖c3 ♖h8 34 ♖h1 ♖c5 35 ♕d4 ♔g6 36 ♖g1 ♖hc8 37 ♖gc1 ♕f7 38 ♘b6 ♖d8 39 ♘d5 ♖h8 40 ♖h1 h3?!

At last Black judges it is the right moment to attempt a breakthrough. This looks strong, but as will be seen in the next note, it is another instance in which we can say that tactical accuracy is more important than positional considerations. Black should have prepared this move with 40...♕f8. Pragmatically speaking, it is surprising that Gurevich decided to force things on the last move of the time control.

41 gxh3 ♕f8!

Black wakes up to the danger just in time, for if 41...♖xh3? 42 ♖xh3 ♗xh3 43 ♘xf4+! wins for White. Now White could

avoid the worst with 42 h4 according to analysis by Gurevich, the main idea being that 42...♖xh4?! 43 ♖xh4 gxh4 44 ♘xf4+! ♕xf4 45 ♕xd6 ♕h2+ 46 ♔f1! would be unclear.

42 ♖cc1? ♖xh3 43 ♖xh3 ♗xh3

Black's attack will soon become irresistible, as the wretched situation of the white bishop on b5 means that he is playing with an extra piece.

44 ♖g1 ♗e6 45 ♕d2 ♗xd5 46 cxd5 ♔f6!

This releases the queen for a decisive breakthrough on either h8 or, in support of the rook, on c8, without allowing ♕xf4 in reply. White cannot defend against both of these threats.

47 ♖c1 ♕h8! 48 ♖xc5 ♕h2+ 49 ♔d1 ♕xd2+ 50 ♔xd2 ♘xf3+ 0-1

White resigned as after 51 ♔e2 ♘d4+ 52 ♔d3 dxc5 Black wins by advancing his passed pawns as quickly as possible.

This game was a very useful lesson in manoeuvring by Mikhail Gurevich, who is also the hero of our next game.

Game 13
Xie Jun-M.Gurevich
Haarlem 1997

---

1 e4 g6 2 d4 ♗g7 3 ♘c3 d6 4 ♗e3 a6 5 ♕d2 b5 6 f3

White prepares a pawn storm on the kingside. This is a common plan in similar positions and requires vigilance from Black, since one blunder can be fatal when the king is threatened by an all-out attack.

However, Xie Jun's move is somewhat double-edged, as the knight on g1 is deprived of its best square on f3. Another drawback is that a slight weakness is created on the dark squares. At the moment this weakness is barely perceptible, but should White continue with ♗h6 at some point in order to exchange bishops and pursue the attack on Black's king, it could become significant.

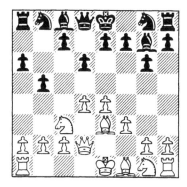

6...♘d7

The only good move! Instead, 6...♗b7 would commit the bishop too early while 6...♘f6 allows 7 ♗h6. On d7 the knight supports ideas of ...c7-c5 or ...e7-e5, which are always nice option to have when the opponent is planning a wing attack.

7 h4

An interesting alternative was the wing development of the knight with 7 ♘h3 which is only possible now, as having put his knight on d7, Black cannot reply ♗xh3 breaking up White's pawns. The knight can be regrouped to the f2-square, where it doesn't obstruct the bishop on f1. However, the knight can no longer support the d4-pawn and in Rashkovsky-Khalifman, Kazan 1995, Black exploited this with 7...c5! There followed 8 a4 b4 9 ♘d1 ♘gf6 10 ♘hf2 0-0 11 ♗e2?! (accord-

ing to Khalifman it was better to close the centre with 11 d5, when 11...a5! 12 ♗b5 ♘b6 13 c4 bxc3 14 ♘xc3 e6 is unclear) 11...cxd4 12 ♗xd4 a5 13 0-0 ♗b7.

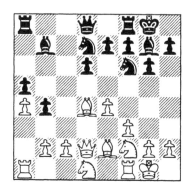

Here Black has his ideal position in this variation. He has no weaknesses and his pieces are smoothly developed, while there is an obvious plan of attack along the c-file. Meanwhile, White's pieces are somewhat cluttered. Khalifman went on to win in good style after 14 ♗b5 ♕c7 15 c3 ♘c5! 16 ♗xc5 dxc5 17 ♘e3 ♖fd8 18 ♕e2 ♘e8!, attacking c3 and planning 19...♘d6.

A second possibility was 7 0-0-0, when after 7...♗b7 8 h4 h5 (Black could also try 8...h6!? when 9 ♘h3 ♖c8 or 9...c5 look more enterprising than 9...e6, which was played in Gufeld-Kindermann, Dortmund 1983) 9 ♘h3 ♘gf6 (perhaps not best – see below) 10 ♔b1 ♖c8 11 ♕e1! (the threat is 12 e5, and if 11...e6 12 ♗g5 looks awkward) 11...e5 12 d5 c6 13 dxc6 ♖xc6 14 ♘g5 White had the edge in Anand-Davies, Moscow 1987, as the bishop on g7 is shut out of the game. However, this didn't stop Nigel Davies from making an enterprising sacrifice after 14...♕c7 15 ♕d2 ♖xc3 (or else 16 ♘d5 is difficult to meet) 16 ♕xc3 ♕xc3 17 bxc3 d5, and although Anand must be a bit better here he later faltered and lost. It will be seen that 9...♘gf6?! exposed the knight to attack by e5 and so forced Black to block in his own bishop on g7. Therefore, 9...♖c8!? looks better, preparing ...c7-c5 without further ado.

7...h6!?

Black fights for the g5-square. Instead 7...h5 8 ♘h3! (compared to the Khalifman game of the last note, the knight is heading for a much more attractive square than f2) 8...♗b7 9 ♘g5 (the knight is virtually immovable from this excellent outpost, as ...f7-f6, ruining his pawn structure, is hardly ever likely to be a practical proposition for Black) 9...♘gf6 (nevertheless, Black is solidly placed) 10 a4 c6 11 ♗e2 e5 12 dxe5 dxe5 13 0-0 and White had an edge in Armas-Nogueiras, Matanzas 1994.

8 g4

If 8 h5 g5!

8...h5!

With the white pawn back on g2 we saw that the manoeuvre ♘h3 and ♘g5 was strong (see the note to Black's seventh move). But here, with the pawn on g4, 9 ♘h3 can be answered by 9...hxg4 10 fxg4 ♖xh4. Alternatively, 9 gxh5 ♖xh5 10 ♘ge2 e5 11 ♘g3 ♖xh4 12 ♗g5 ♗h6! (Gurevich) gives Black a clear advantage. Therefore, Xie Jun is obliged to block the kingside in order to secure the safety of her pawns. Of course, this cannot have pleased her as she wanted to open lines to further her attack.

9 g5 e6

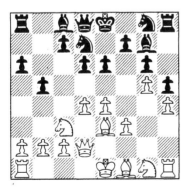

Black clears e7 and at last attends to the development of his king's knight. The flexibility of the Modern Defence is a real plus point over the Pirc when facing the ♗e3 system, since keeping the knight back on g8 cuts out many of White's attacking options.

10 ♘ge2 ♘e7 11 ♘g3

After 11 f4 d5 12 ♗g2 ♘b6 gives Black counterplay.

11...d5

Black doesn't leave his opponent in peace to prepare a build-up such as ♗h3, ♖f1, f3-f4 and f4-f5.

12 ♘ce2 ♗b7 13 c3 ♕c8

This natural move prepares ...c7-c5 to continue the process of undermining White's centre. However, Gurevich later suggested the more dynamic approach 13...c5!, when the forcing variation 14 dxc5 ♕c7 15 b4 ♘e5 16 ♗g2 ♘c4 17 ♕c1 a5 gives Black a strong initiative for his pawn.

14 ♗h3 c5

Black has now solved all his opening problems and begins to attack White's pawn chain on the queenside.

15 0-0 ♕c6 16 b3 0-0 17 e5 a5 18 ♘f4 b4 19 cxb4 axb4 20 ♘fxh5?!

Since Black's methodical play is gradually dismantling her position on the queenside and in the centre, Xie Jun makes a radical attempt to gain counterplay by offering a piece. This looks like a dangerous sacrifice, but Black defends with just the right mixture of caution and greed.

20...gxh5 21 ♘xh5

White now intends 22 ♘f6+ with ideas of h4-h5 combined with h5-h6 or ♕c2 etc. The knight would be immovable except at the cost of opening lines and exposing the black king to a withering attack. Therefore it is essential that Black destroys his opponent's grip on the centre before the knight reaches f6.

21...cxd4 22 ♗xd4 ♗xe5! 23 ♗xe5 ♘xe5 24 ♕f4

Things still look dangerous for Black, as White threatens both the knight and 25 ♕f6! with unstoppable mate on g7. However, his next move meets both threats and kills off the attack.

24...♕c3!

A great defensive move. If now 25 ♕f6 ♘eg6! or 25 ♖ac1 ♘d3! both win for Black.

25 ♘f6+ ♔g7 26 ♘h5+ ♔g8 27 ♘f6+ ♔h8 28 g6

The last throw of the dice, but Black can force a decisive simplification.

28...♘g8 29 ♘xg8 ♘xg6! 30 ♕h6+

Of course, if 30 ♕f6+ simply 30...♔xg8.

30...♔xg8 31 h5 ♕d4+ 32 ♔g2 ♕f4 0-1

Game 14
Anand-Svidler
Linares 1998

---

1 e4 g6 2 d4 ♗g7 3 ♘c3 d6 4 ♗e3 a6 5 ♘f3 b5 6 ♗d3

White adopts the same system of development which proved so effective against 3...c6 4 ♗e3 d6 in Games 10 and 11 of Chapter 2. Basically, he masses his minor pieces in the centre, fortifying his pawn centre, and keeps all his options open. Thus he may decide to attack on the queenside with a2-a4, or on the kingside with ♕d2 preparing ♗h6 (he would probably preface the latter idea with h2-h3, to rule out ...♗g4 in reply). Anand chooses a third idea: attack in the centre.

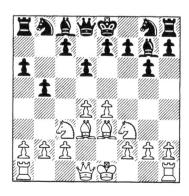

6...♘d7!

As usual this is a key move in Black's set-up. It would be less good to play 6...♘c6?!, which blocks the c7-pawn and so deprives Black of the possibility of a quick ...c7-c5.

7 e5

White continues in 'classical' style: Black's lack of development is to be punished by a rapid breakthrough in the centre. However, the white pieces aren't well placed to follow up this action.

7...♗b7!

The bishop seizes the diagonal which White has so kindly opened for it. This is a much better idea than 7...dxe5?! 8 ♗e4 ♖b8, when 9 dxe5 threatens to win the exchange with 10 ♗a7.

8 e6

Instead 8 exd6 cxd6 is slightly better for Black: the c7- and e4-pawns are worlds apart in value, and White should only permit their exchange if he has a strong tactical blow prepared. Therefore White prefers to make a positional pawn sacrifice to disrupt Black's development and keep the initiative.

8...fxe6 9 ♘g5 ♘f8 10 0-0 ♘f6 11 ♖e1

♕d7 12 ♗d2

White plans 13 ♕e2 to intensify the pressure on e6. If he succeeds in recapturing the pawn then he should have a slight edge in view of his more solid pawn structure.

12...h6

Black has to force back the knight if he wishes to safeguard e6 and also be able to develop his kingside at some point.

13 ♘f3 ♖b8

Instead 13...0-0-0?? would be suicidal as 14 a4 would give White a big attack. The black king does better to stay in the centre or go to the kingside where, despite the evident weaknesses in the pawn structure, at least he would be surrounded by defenders.

14 a4 b4 15 ♘e4

Anand considers that 15 ♘e2!? is interesting here. After 15...♗xf3 16 gxf3 White's kingside is wrecked, but on the other hand he can follow up with ♘f4 to attack both e6 and g6, to say nothing of the hanging pawn on a6. The game move leads to the forced exchange of White's bishop on d3 which has been hindering the development of Black's kingside by its persistent attack on g6.

15...♘xe4 16 ♗xe4 ♗xe4 17 ♖xe4 ♕c6!

18 ♖e3 ♕c4

Black's queen manoeuvre staunches up the queenside and prevents, or rather prof-

itably delays, White's breakthrough there.

19 c3 b3

Of course, he cannot allow the opening of the c-file after either 19...bxc3? 20 ♖xc3 or 19...a5? 20 cxb4 axb4 21 ♖c1, when in either case White will capture on c7 after the black queen moves, with a huge advantage. After the game move, the b3-pawn will eventually be lost to a combination of the moves ♖a3 and, after moving the bishop from d2, ♘d2. However, while White is thus engaged in regaining his pawn his opponent Black can develop his kingside and achieve good counterplay.

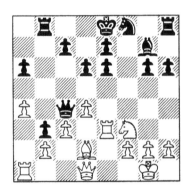

20 ♖e1 g5 21 ♗e3 ♕d5 22 ♕d3?

Better was 22 ♘d2 followed by ♖a3 and ♖xb3 with equality (Anand). White's plan to oust the black queen from d5 with c3-c4 weakens his own centre.

22...a5 23 ♖a3 ♔f7 24 ♘d2 ♘g6 25 ♕e2 ♘h4! 26 f3 ♘g6

The knight provokes a weakness in White's camp and promptly retreats again. This weakness will become more pronounced after White's next move, which leaves his d4-pawn less solidly defended. Although this is an excellent manoeuvre by Svidler, it seems to make him overconfident.

27 c4 ♕f5 28 ♘e4 ♔g8 29 ♕d1 ♖b4?

Black misses his chance. Instead Anand recommends 29...g4! when he says that 30 ♖xb3 (or 30 ♘g3 ♕c2!) 30...♖xb3 31

₩xb3 gxf3 is slightly better for Black.

30 ♖xb3 ♖xc4?!

The consistent move, but 30...♖xb3 31 ₩xb3 ♔h7 was better, with unclear play (Anand).

31 ♖b5 ₩f7 32 ♖xa5 ♔h7 33 ♖b5 d5?

The third and fatal mistake, after which the rook finds itself cut off from safety and eventually lost. The cautious 33...♖c6 looks better.

34 ♘c5 ₩f5

This is Black's idea, which plans a big attack with ...♘h4 in combination with ...♖c2. Unfortunately for him it is tactically flawed.

35 b3! ♖c3

If 35...♖c2 36 g4 wins the rook. A forcing variation now begins.

36 ₩d2! ♖c2 37 g4! ♘h4 38 gxf5 ♘xf3+ 39 ♔h1 ♘xd2 40 ♖e2 ♘c4

The only chance was 40...♖xc5 41 ♖xc5 ♘e4 42 ♖xc7 exf5, planning ...f5-f4 (Anand), but Black would still be in deep trouble.

41 ♖xc2 ♘xe3 42 ♖e2 1-0

Black resigned as 42...♘xf5 43 ♘xe6 is entirely hopeless.

Game 15
Rublevsky-Ibragimov
Elista 1998

1 e4 g6 2 d4 ♗g7 3 ♘c3 d6 4 ♘f3 a6

Sometimes 4...♗g4 is played, but this seems better when combined with ...♘f6 in the Pirc. Here an attempt to put immediate pressure on d4 is not very promising, e.g. 5 ♗e3 ♘c6 6 ♗b5! a6 7 ♗xc6+ bxc6 8 h3 ♗xf3 9 ₩xf3 ₩b8 (9...₩d7 10 e5! is a good pawn offer known from the game Tal-Hort, Moscow 1975) 10 e5! (attacking c6) 10...₩b7 11 0-0 ♘h6 12 ♖ad1 0-0 13 ♗c1 and Black had no active play in Kindermann-Hickl, Munich 1987.

5 ♗e2

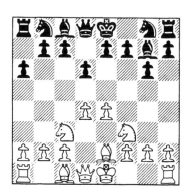

White decides on the 'standard' Classical set-up rather than 5 ♗e3, which would transpose to the previous game after 5...b5. In committing his bishop to e2 he is foregoing any attempt at an outright refutation of Black's set-up by a rapid breakthrough in the centre with e4-e5, as if that were his aim then d3 would be a more appropriate square for the bishop. Of course, White hasn't rejected forever the possibility of an advantageous e4-e5, as the game continuation will show: it simply isn't a priority for him at the moment. However, it does mean that White's only remaining plan over the next few moves, other than generally efficient development, is to undermine the black queenside pawns as soon ...b7-b5 is played.

Instead 5 a4 would stop Black playing ...b7-b5 in the first place, but this can hardly be the refutation of 4...a6. Black

could play 5...&f6 or speculate with
5...&g4 which tries to exploit the insertion
of a2-a4 and ...a7-a6 as there is no &b5
response available to White. Play could
continue 6 &e2 (or 6 &c4 – with the
threat of 7 &xf7+! – 6...e6 etc.) 6...&c6 7
&e3 e5 8 dxe5 dxe5 9 ₩xd8+ &xd8 10
&d5 &d7 with a very slight edge for
White in the endgame.

5...&d7 6 0-0 b5 7 a4! b4 8 &d5 a5

Notwithstanding our comment above
about the somewhat placid nature of
White's opening moves, if Black tries to
equalise too quickly then the white pieces
will show their fangs. Black would like to
play 8...&b7, when 9 &xb4 &xe4 would
exchange off his vulnerable b4-pawn for
White's proud e4-pawn. However, although strategically speaking this would
be a great achievement for Black, his neglect of development makes this idea tactically unsound. White could punish him
with 10 &g5! &b7 11 &c4 e6 (a variation
on a well-known theme is 11...&h6? 12
&xf7+! &xf7 13 &e6 etc.) 12 &xe6! fxe6
13 &xe6 ₩c8 14 &xg7+ &f7 15 &h5 gxh5
16 ₩xh5+ &f8 17 &d5, and White, whose
ideas include &a3 followed by &f3+, has a
very strong attack. This variation is given
by Rublevsky in *Informator 72*.

9 c3 e6

Nothing as drastic as the variation of
the last note above happens after 9...bxc3
10 bxc3, but in relinquishing the tension
between the pawn structures on the
queenside Black would leave himself
rather passive. On a less abstract note,
White would perhaps be able to exploit
the open b-file.

10 &e3 &b7 11 ₩c2

Of course, if he has no strong tactical
follow-up White should avoid the unequal
exchange 11 cxb4? &xe4.

11...&gf6 12 e5!

Finally White makes a bid to increase
his space advantage in the centre.

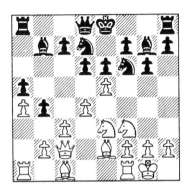

12...&e4?

This is a serious error, after which
Black will have to spoil his pawn structure
in order to defend the knight. Correct was
12...dxe5, when 13 &xe5 (if 13 dxe5 &d5
14 &c4 0-0 15 &g5 ₩c8 16 &fe1 is good
for White according to Yudasin, so perhaps Black should try 14...h6!? in this sequence) 13...0-0 14 &3c4 leaves White
with just a slight edge according to
Rublevsky.

13 &d3 f5

After 13...d5 14 c4, the tactical threat of
15 cxd5 exd5 16 &xd5 &xd5 17 &xe4
would be difficult to meet.

14 exf6 &dxf6 15 cxb4!

White saddles Black with a weak pawn
on b4 before he has the chance to play
...b4xc3.

15...axb4 16 &d2!?

Instead 16 &b5+ is interesting, but after
16...&f7 White wouldn't have enough
firepower directed at e4 to dislodge the
black knight from this centre square.

16...&xd2 17 &xd2

Rublevsky points out that the
zwischenzug 17 &b5+?? ends in embar-
rassment for White after 17...c6! 18 &xc6+
&f7! 19 &xd2 (19 &xb7 &xf1 20 &xa8
&xe3) 19...&c8 pinning the bishop.

17...0-0

Black's inaccuracy at move twelve has
led almost by force to the loss of the b-

pawn. He realises that his one chance of safety is to activate his pieces and pawn centre.

18 ♗xb4 ♘h5 19 ♗e4 ♗xe4 20 ♕xe4 ♘f4 21 ♘c2 c5!? 22 dxc5 d5 23 ♕e3 e5

If 23...♗xb2 24 ♖ad1, when 24...♖xa4 fails to 25 ♕b3 (Rublevsky). Instead Black tries to create complications with his passed pawns, but White's accurate play dashes all his hopes.

24 g3 ♘e6 25 ♖ad1 d4 26 ♕b3 ♕e8 27 ♖fe1 ♔h8 28 ♘xd4!

White exploits the potential pin on the black queen to smash the black centre.

28...♘g5

Instead 28...♘xd4 29 ♖xd4 exd4 30 ♖xe8 ♖fxe8 31 ♗d2 d3? (but otherwise Black has no counterplay and White begins to advance his pawns) 32 ♕xd3 ♖ad8 33 ♕b5! wins for White.

29 f4 ♕xa4 30 fxg5 exd4 31 ♕xa4 ♖xa4 32 ♗a3

The dust has settled and the white passed pawns should win the day. Black's bid to free his kingside makes it much easier for White.

32...h6 33 ♖e6 ♔h7 34 c6 ♖c8 35 gxh6 ♗xh6 36 ♖e7+ ♔g8 37 c7 1-0

> ### Game 16
> ### Lanka-Beim
> *Linz 1997*

1 e4 g6 2 d4 ♗g7 3 ♘c3 d6 4 f4 a6

We should remind the reader that besides 4...♘f6 (transposing to a Pirc) and 4...c6 (mentioned very briefly in Chapter 1) Black can also play 4...♘c6, which however we do not choose to discuss here as after 5 ♗e3 ♘f6 it transposes to a Pirc set-up.

5 ♘f3 b5 6 ♗d3

White can play also 6 ♗e3, or ♗e3 at some other point in this sequence, for which see the next note and the second paragraph of the note to Black's eighth

move below.

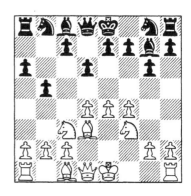

6...♗b7 7 e5!

This is the critical test of the validity of Black's 4...a6 idea against the Austrian. White sets up a solid wedge of pawns in the centre. Instead 7 ♗e3 b4 8 ♘e2 ♘f6 9 e5 ♘d5 10 ♗d2! c5 (10...a5!? – Beliavsky) 11 c4 bxc3 12 bxc3 cxd4 13 cxd4 gave White a slight advantage in Svidler-Beliavsky, Dortmund 1998 (by transposition).

7...♘d7 8 0-0 e6

The natural counterattacking move is 8...c5, but this is well answered by 9 ♗e4! when Bareev-Pekarek, Dortmund 1990, continued 9...♗xe4 10 ♘xe4 cxd4 11 exd6 (also quite strong is 11 e6 fxe6 12 ♘eg5 ♘f8 13 ♘xd4) 11...♕b6 12 f5! gxf5 13 ♘g3 e6 and here according to Bareev White could gain a strong attack against Black's king with 14 ♕e1 (threatening 14 ♘xf5) 14...0-0-0 15 a4 b4 16 a5 ♕xd6 17 ♖a4 etc.

Here we should mention the game B.Lalic-Polzhin, Dresden 1998, which began 3 ♘c3 d6 4 f4 a6 5 ♘f3 ♘d7 6 ♗e3 b5 7 ♗d3 c5 8 e5 ♗b7 as the position reached is identical to 8...c5, except that White has played ♗e3 rather than 0-0. This difference is vital, since after 9 ♗e4 ♗xe4 10 ♘xe4 ♘h6! 11 dxc5 ♘g4 (exploiting the bishop on e3 to gain time) 12 ♕e2 dxe5 13 0-0-0 ♕c7 14 fxe5 Black could have equalised with 14...♘dxe5! according to Bogdan Lalic. As a rule, ideas involving 7 ♗e3, or an earlier ♗e3, seem on the whole less effective against the 4...a6 Austrian as the bishop often blocks White's own attack down the e-file. Of course, if the game had begun 3 ♘c3 d6 4 ♗e3 a6 5 f4 then White would have no choice but to have his bishop on this square.

Returning to our main game, Beim avoids the complexities above with a solid move which keeps his pawn structure more compact and rules out any e5-e6 pawn sacrifice.

9 a4

White could still play aggressively in the centre with 9 d5!?, when Beim gives the variation 9...exd5 (9...b4? 10 dxe6 bxc3 11 exf7+! ♔xf7 12 ♘g5+ ♔e7 13 exd6+ cxd6 14 ♕e2+ is winning for White) 10 exd6 cxd6 11 f5! ♘e7 and White's initiative gives him more than adequate compensation for the pawn, though Black looks fairly solid.

9...bxa4

Positionally speaking, this is a very ugly move which gives up any hope of keeping the queenside pawns intact. However, after 9...b4 10 ♘e4 White's build-up in the centre looks very threatening, so Black is sensible to try to distract his opponent by introducing play on the queenside.

10 ♘g5

White, however, refuses to be distracted from his planned attack. Nevertheless, the simple 10 ♖xa4 deserved attention, planning to gang up on the weak a6-pawn with 11 ♕e2.

10...♘h6?

Black reserves e7 for his queen, but this seems a serious mistake as White can now profit from the absence of the knight from the centre by playing 11 d5! Then 11...exd5 12 e6 ♘c5 13 exf7+ ♘xf7 14 ♘xf7 ♔xf7 15 f5 gives White a highly dangerous attack (Yudasin). Therefore Black should have played 10...♘e7!

11 ♘ce4? 0-0 12 c3 ♗c6 13 ♕f3 ♗b5

Black seeks counterplay by forcing White to weaken the d4-square or allow the exchange of bishops.

14 c4 ♗c6 15 ♕h3 ♖e8 16 ♘c3 ♘f8 17 d5

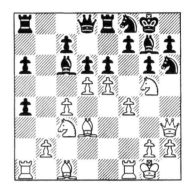

Having deployed his pieces to aggressive squares, White clears the lines of attack with some violent pawn stabs.

17...♗d7 18 f5 ♘xf5?

Black goes wrong. Instead Beim gives 18...exf5! 19 e6 fxe6 20 dxe6 ♘xe6 21 ♘xe6 ♗xe6 22 ♗xh6 f4! (the point) 23 g4! fxg3 24 ♕xg3 ♗xh6 25 ♗xg6 ♖e7!! 26 ♗f7+ ♔h8 27 ♗xe6 ♖xe6 and Black has a clear advantage. Of course, it would have been extremely difficult for Black to have calculated this accurately during the game, especially when facing such a daunting attack. Therefore we can conclude that although White's attack was unsound, it offered him good practical chances as there was little chance that Black would find the one refuting variation.

Evidence of this is that a former World Championship candidate, who has annotated this game independently from Beim, stopped his analysis of the above variation at 20...♘xe6 by gracing this move with two question marks as it appears to lose a piece to 21 ♘xe6 ♗xe6 22 ♗xh6: he simply didn't see that Black can win back the piece advantageously with 22...f4! As a consequence, he was very appreciative of White's moves 17 d5 and 18 f5, giving them both an exclamation mark; and Black's serious blunder 18...②xf5, which turns a very good position into a bad one, is also given an exclamation mark, as it seems the best fighting chance! It makes you wonder how many other games have been completely misassessed just because one vital move has been missed at the end of an obscure variation.

19 g4 ♗xe5!

This is forced, as 19...②h6 20 dxe6 fxe6 21 ②ce4 gives White a massive attack.

20 gxf5 exf5

Beim's sacrifice has secured his kingside. However, the extra piece gives White a definite advantage, especially as the black pawns are reduced to a purely defensive function.

21 ②f3 ♗g7

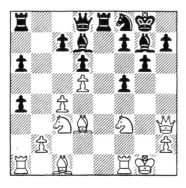

22 ♗c2?

After an exciting tactical phase, White finds that he can attack no more as the black kingside is solidly defended by a wall of pawns. He must therefore turn his attention to the more mundane task of exploiting Black's weaknesses on the a-file. Evidently this is psychologically difficult, as he seems to have little enthusiasm for the task and makes a succession of errors which eventually lead to defeat. Here, for example, he allows Black to gain counter-play by attacking the c4-pawn. The simple 22 ②xa4 was called for.

22...♖b8 23 ♗xa4 ♖b4 24 ♗xd7?!

White activates Black's knight for him. Beim suggests 24 ♗d1!? ♖xc4 25 ♔h1 with obscure play.

24...②xd7 25 ♖xa6 ♖xc4 26 ♖c6??

This is a terrible blunder in time pressure which loses the exchange. Instead 26 ♔h1 was unclear.

26...♖g4+ 27 ♔h1 ②b8! 28 ②g5

The black rook and three pawns should prove too much for White's knights in the long run, especially as the white king is open to attack. However, Lanka's attempt to land an immediate blow only leads to further material losses, after which White could resign.

28...h5! 29 ②b5 ②xc6 30 dxc6 ♖xg5 31 ♗xg5 ♕xg5 32 ②xc7 ♖c8 33 ♕b3 ♕d8

Black avoids the last trap 33...♖xc7? 34 ♕b8+ and wins easily enough, but 33...♕d2 34 ♕b7 ♗e5! (Beim) 35 ♕xc8+ ♔h7 with unstoppable mate on h2 would be a prettier finish.

34 ②d5 ♖xc6 35 ♕b7 ♖c2 0-1

Perhaps Black is taking some risks in playing the Modern, but fighting wins like this are rare in openings such as the Petroff Defence!

Summary
After 3 ♘c3 d6 4 ♗e3 a6, White's plan of 5 ♕d2 aiming for ♗h6 is not so effective when Black has delayed ...♘f6 (Games 12 and 13). Black should also have adequate chances after 5 ♘f3 (Game 14), as White's attempt to play in the centre with e4-e5 isn't particularly well supported by his pieces. The quiet line 4 ♘f3 a6 5 ♗e2 (Game 15) contains some poison and requires careful play from Black. Finally, 4 f4 (Game 16) is White's most dangerous line when combined with the e4-e5 advance. Black seems to be under some pressure here.

1 e4 g6 2 d4 ♗g7 3 ♘c3 d6 *(D)*

4 ♗e3
    4 f4 – *Game 16*
    4 ♘f3 a6 5 ♗e2 – *Game 15*
4...a6 *(D)* **5 ♕d2**
    5 ♘f3 – *Game 14*
5...b5 *(D)* **6 a4**
    6 f3 – *Game 13*
6...b4 7 ♘d1 – *Game 12*

3...d6

4...a6

5...b5

CHAPTER FOUR

1 e4 g6 2 d4 ♗g7 3 ♘c3 d6: Other Lines

1 e4 g6 2 d4 ♗g7

To complete our study of the Modern Defence without c2-c4 we shall look at four ideas for White which didn't fit comfortably into the earlier chapters. These are 3 ♘c3 c6 (or 3...d6) 4 ♗c4 (Game 17); 3 ♘c3 d6 4 g3 (Game 18); 3 ♘c3 d6 4 ♗g5 (Game 19); and 3 c3 (Game 20). In the notes to Game 19 we also look at early h2-h4 ideas.

In Game 17, the highly interesting 3 ♘c3 c6 4 ♗c4 d6 5 ♕f3 leads to some complex strategical play which is laced with tactical ideas. Black seems fine, but he must tread very carefully in the early middlegame. A much quieter approach is 3 ♘c3 d6 4 g3, as in Game 18, but this can also be dangerous for Black if he fails to act resolutely and falls into a positional bind. Black can try an aggressive response, but this isn't without risks. We examine 3 ♘c3 d6 4 ♗g5 in Game 19, but this shouldn't cause Black too many problems. In Game 20 we look at 3 c3, where White foregoes active play in the opening in order to set up a very solid fortress. This is an ambitious stance by White and by no means a bad one, but in rejecting the option of a ♗e3 development he is leaving his d4-pawn slightly vulnerable to a coun-

terattack. This can cause him serious problems if he plays in a risky style, as the game demonstrates.

Game 17
Izmukhambetov-Bologan
Sevastopol 1997

1 e4 g6 2 d4 ♗g7 3 ♘c3 c6

Or 3...d6 4 ♗c4 c6 transposing.

4 ♗c4

One of the useful things about this move is that it deters Black from playing 4...d5, as then 5 exd5 b5 (forced) 6 ♗b3 b4 7 ♘ce2 cxd5 8 ♗d2! a5 9 a3 bxa3 10 ♖xa3 leaves Black under pressure because of the vulnerable pawn on a5. This has been proved many times, e.g. in I.Almasi-Teplitsky, Budapest 1993. It therefore cuts down on the amount of theory White has to learn and may also have the bonus of depriving Black of his favoured pawn structure in the Modern.

4...d6 5 ♕f3

This primitive-looking move conjures up memories of the schoolyard. Nevertheless, it has been tested at the highest level, and at the time of writing is one of the most critical lines after 3...c6.

Alternatives here are hardly as dangerous for Black. If 5 ♘f3 we transpose to 4 ♘f3 d6 5 ♗c4 which is mentioned in the note to White's fifth move in Game 9 of Chapter 2.

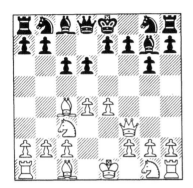

5...e6

The seemingly impossible 5...♘f6 has also been tried. Then a forcing variation runs 6 e5 dxe5 7 dxe5 ♘d5 8 ♘xd5 cxd5 9 ♗xd5 0-0 10 ♗xb7 ♕a5+ 11 c3 ♗xb7 12 ♕xb7 ♘a6. Here in Thipsay-Koshy, India 1994, White found a neat way to kill off Black's counterplay: 13 ♕f3! ♖ad8 14 ♘e2 ♘c5 15 0-0 ♘b3 16 axb3! ♕xa1 17 ♘d4 ♕a6 (17...♗xe5 allows a fork on c6) 18 ♗f4 and the combination of White's compact queenside pawns and impregnable knight on d4 were worth more than the rook.

6 ♘ge2

White could also speculate with 6 ♗f4!? when 6...♗xd4? would be highly risky as after 7 0-0-0 Black is forced to play the ghastly looking 7...♗c5.

The most enterprising response for Black is an expansion on the queenside with 6...b5 7 ♗b3 a5. In Stefansson-Shirov, Clichy 1995, this led to wild play after 8 a4 b4 9 ♘ce2 d5 10 h4 (10 e5 ♘d7 is unclear) 10...dxe4 11 ♕xe4 ♘f6 12 ♕f3 ♗b7 13 0-0-0 ♘bd7 14 ♕h3 c5

see following diagram

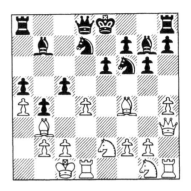

Here 15 dxc5 ♘e4! 16 ♗xe6 fxe6 17 c6 ♕f6! 18 cxd7+ ♔f7 19 ♕b3 ♘c5 would be very strong for Black. The game actually continued 15 ♘f3 ♗a6 16 ♗xe6! (if 16 d5 ♘xd5 17 ♗xd5 exd5 18 ♖xd5 ♗c4, planning ...♗e6, is better for Black) 16...0-0 (Black is curiously helpless after 16...fxe6 17 ♗d6!) 17 ♗xd7 ♗xe2 18 ♗c6 ♗xd1 19 ♖xd1 and now Shirov says he should probably have played 19...b3!? with at least an equal game for Black in the melee. This analysis is based on Shirov's comments in his book *Fire on Board* – a very apt title in view of what we have just seen!

If the reader regards this line as frighteningly complex or too theoretical (or maybe both?) then he or she will be pleased to know that Black can also play in solid style with 6...♘d7, when 7 0-0-0 (not of course 7 ♗xd6?? ♘b6 winning a piece; a common theme in this line) 7...♕e7 8 ♕e2 e5 9 dxe5 dxe5 10 ♗e3 ♘gf6 was equal in Fishbein-Webster, Oakham 1990.

6...b5

It is natural to adopt the plan of a queenside expansion as Black gains time by attacking the bishop. Playing for ...e6-e5 is less promising, e.g. 6...♘d7 7 0-0 (7 ♗f4 ♕e7 8 ♗b3 e5 9 dxe5 dxe5 10 ♗g5!? ♘gf6 11 0-0-0 h6 12 ♗e3 was about equal in Konguvel-Mohr, Linares 1996) 7...♘gf6 8 ♗b3 0-0 9 ♗g5 ♕a5 10 ♗h4 e5 gave

White a slight edge in Milov-Segal, Israel 1993.

7 ♗b3 a5 8 a3

This is better than 8 a4 b4 9 ♘d1 ♗a6, when White must worry about the threat of 10...♗xe2 winning his d-pawn.

8...♗a6 9 d5

The critical move which prevents Black from setting up his favoured pawn structure with ...d6-d5. Also of interest is 9 0-0!?, when 9...♘d7 10 ♗f4 ♕e7 11 ♖ad1 e5 12 ♗g5 ♘gf6 13 d5?! c5 was good for Black in Nunn-Shirov, Germany 1996. Later 11 e5 d5 12 ♕e3 was suggested as an improvement for White and this was tested in the game Nunn-Chandler, Birmingham 1998, when 12...h6 13 ♕d2 ♕d8 14 ♖fe1 ♘e7 15 ♘g3 c5 16 ♘ce2 cxd4?! 17 ♘xd4 turned out very well for White. After the game Nunn suggested the plan of 16...c4, when following 17 ♗a2 and a subsequent c2-c3 to bring the bishop back into the game via b1, Black can block the queenside with ...a5-a4. Then it isn't clear that White's attack over the limited area on the kingside is enough to win the game. Nevertheless, it is understandable that Black avoided such a passive approach.

9...cxd5 10 exd5 e5

Black now has a nice pawn structure on the kingside and aims to prove that the bishop on b3 is shut out of the game. But in his rather undeveloped state will he survive the immediate attack from White's active pieces?

11 ♘e4 h6

The answer to the question above was 'no' in the game J.Polgar-Shirov, Amsterdam 1995, which went 11...♕c7? 12 c4! bxc4 (or else 13 c5 follows) 13 ♗a4+ (the fact that this bishop has come to life shows that Black's opening plan has suffered a fiasco) 13...♘d7 14 ♘2c3 ♔e7? (he had to try 14...h6) 15 ♘xd6! ♕xd6 16 ♘e4 ♕xd5 17 ♗g5+ ♘df6 18 ♖d1 ♕b7 19

♖d7+ ♕xd7 20 ♗xd7 h6 (20...♗b7 was the only chance) 21 ♕d1! 1-0. After 21...hxg5 22 ♕d6+ ♔d8 23 ♗b5+ Black is ripped to shreds.

Black has to play more cautiously. Therefore, Bologan gains control of the g5-square and aims for ...f7-f5 without allowing ♘g5 and ♘e6 in reply. White cannot ultimately prevent this but can try to make it work in his favour by exploiting the weaknesses created in Black's kingside structure.

12 g4 ♘f6 13 ♘2g3 ♘xe4 14 ♘xe4 0-0 15 ♕h3 f5

Finally Black has achieved this key advance, but forceful play will be necessary to prove that it is tactically watertight.

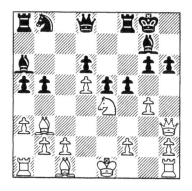

16 gxf5 ♗c8!

The bishop returns to the fray. If instead 16...♖xf5 17 ♗xh6 is strong for White.

17 ♘g3

Whereas now 17 ♗xh6? ♗xf5 wins a piece.

17...♖xf5!

Black is forced to offer the exchange. It is clear that 17...♗xf5 18 ♘xf5 ♖xf5 19 ♗xh6 ♖h5 20 ♕e6+ is good for White, while in *Informator 70* Bologan demonstrated why 17...gxf5 is also insufficient: 18 ♗xh6! f4 19 ♕h5 fxg3 20 ♗xg7 ♔xg7 (or 20...gxf2+ 21 ♔d2 ♔xg7 22 ♖hg1+ fxg1♕ 23 ♖xg1+ ♔f6 24 ♖g6+ ♔e7 25 ♖g7+ ♔f6

26 ♕g6 mate) 21 ♖g1 ♗f5 22 ♖xg3+ ♔f6 23 ♕g5+ ♔f7 24 ♕xf5+ and White wins.

18 ♘xf5?

The acceptance of the sacrifice gives Black excellent counter-chances. Therefore, in Anand-Shirov, Dos Hermanas 1996, White preferred to decline the offer with 18 ♕g2! Then play continued 18...a4 (Black rules out c2-c3 followed by ♗c2, but this leads to the partial blocking of the queenside and so allows White's king to find a safe haven there) 19 ♗a2 ♖f4!? (still trying to sacrifice this exchange, this time to free the other bishop) 20 c3 ♖h4 (Anand recommends 20...♕h4 21 h3 ♘d7 22 ♗e3 with unclear play) 21 h3 ♗f5? (this leaves the white bishop on a2 with no rival; better was 21...♘d7 22 ♘e4 ♘f6 – Stohl) 22 ♘xf5 gxf5 23 ♕g6! ♕f8 24 ♗e3. White then castled queenside when the fragility of Black's light squares and open g-file gave him good attacking chances against the black king.

18...♗xf5 19 ♕g3

If 19 ♕g2 ♘d7, planning 20...♘c5 or if White prevents this with 20 ♗e3 then 20...e4 and 21...♘e5 gives Black active play.

19...♘d7 20 ♗e3 ♖c8?

This is one preparatory move too many. Instead Black should play 20...e4! to activate his bishop. Then 21 c3 can be met with 21...♘e5, planning to jump into d3 or f3. If instead 21 ♕xd6, Bologan gives the variation 21...♗xb2 22 ♖b1 ♗c3+ 23 ♗d2 ♗xd2+ 24 ♔xd2 ♕g5+ 25 ♔e1 e3!, when Black has a huge attack.

21 c3 ♘f6 22 a4?

Now it is White's turn to blunder. This is a disastrous idea that undermines his bishop on b3 and so leads to the destruction of his queenside pawn structure. Instead White should play 22 0-0, when Bologan gives 22...♘h5 23 ♕g2 ♕h4 24 f3 ♘f4 (24...♗h3 25 ♕xg6) 25 ♗xf4 exf4 26 ♖fe1 ♗e5 27 ♗c2 as winning for White.

However, Black doesn't have to rush into a kingside attack. Instead 22...♕d7, keeping open options of ...♔h7, ...♘h5 or...♗h3 at some point, gives Black dynamic play. White's king is somewhat unsafe, the bishop on b3 is passive and the d5-pawn weak. Certainly it would be difficult for White to exploit his material advantage.

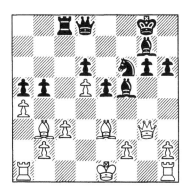

22...♖b8!

As Black has only just developed his rook to c8 it is possible that White 'forgot' that he could change his mind and move it to b8!

The immediate threat is 23...bxa4, when 24 ♗xa4 ♘xd5 destroys White's centre.

23 axb5 ♖xb5 24 ♖a3 ♕b8

Now White can no longer prevent a breakthrough on the b-file.

25 ♗a2 ♖xb2 26 0-0 ♘e4 27 ♕f3 ♘xc3!
28 ♗a7

A desperate move, but if 28 ♖xc3 e4! picks up the rook.

28...♕xa7 29 ♕xc3 e4 30 ♕xa5 ♕xa5
31 ♖xa5 ♗d4 32 ♖a3 ♗c5 33 ♖a8+ ♔g7
0-1

White lost on time but his position is in any case completely hopeless. There is no possible defence against the threat of 34...♗h3, or perhaps even stronger, 34...e3 when after 35 fxe3 ♗xe3+ 36 ♔h1 ♗e4+ mates.

Game 18
Geller-Hickl
Dortmund 1989

1 e4 g6 2 d4 ♝g7 3 ♞c3 d6 4 g3

A sneaky move order is 4 ♞ge2, hoping to entice us into the Pirc after 4...♞f6 5 g3. We proudly decline with 4...♞c6, but then White can avoid g2-g3 in favour of the more direct 5 d5, when 5...♞e5 6 f4 ♞d7 7 ♝e3 ♞gf6 8 ♞d4 0-0 9 ♝e2 ♞b6 10 0-0 ♝d7 11 a4 a5 12 ♝f3 c6 13 ♛e2 gave White the better chances in Muller-Seul, Germany 1992. Perhaps 5...♞b8, planning ...c7-c6, is a better approach.

After 4...♞c6 White could also try 5 ♝e3 but unless he continues g2-g3 at some point his knight will be misplaced on e2, where it blocks in the bishop on f1 and has less scope than on f3. Therefore 5...e5 should equalise for Black.

4...♞c6!

Here 4...♞f6 would transpose to the Pirc. Black seeks an independent path by putting immediate pressure on d4.

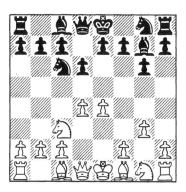

5 ♝e3

Instead 5 ♞ge2 ♝g4! looks awkward for White. However, 5 d5 is a serious alternative, e.g. 5...♞e5 (Riskier is 5...♞d4 as the knight may find itself cut off in enemy territory. However, there seems no good way for White to arrange c3 to capture it,

as 6 ♞b1? c6 7 a4? cxd5 8 exd5 gives the knight an escape route on f5. Instead the more normal 6 ♝g2 – not 6 ♞ge2?? ♞f3 mate – 6...c5 7 ♞ce2 f5 gave Black active play in Tempone-Conquest, Buenos Aires 1994.) 6 f4 ♞d7 7 ♝g2 c6 8 ♞f3 cxd5 9 ♞xd5 ♞b6 10 0-0 ♞xd5 11 ♛xd5 ♛b6+ 12 ♚h1 ♞f6 13 ♛d3 0-0 14 ♝e3 ♛c7 15 ♝d4 ♝d7 16 c4 ♝c6 and Black was comfortable in Spasov-Speelman, Biel 1993, as the white knight is a long way from d5! White prepared the plan of e4-e5, but he was a little careless and allowed his pawns to fragment after 17 ♜ae1 ♜ad8 18 ♝c3 b6 19 ♛c2?! ♝b7 20 b3?! (20 e5!?) 20...b5! 21 e5 dxe5 22 fxe5 ♞d5! 23 ♝d2 (23 cxd5 b4 regains the piece with some advantage) 23...bxc4 24 ♛xc4 ♛xc4 25 bxc4 ♞b6 26 ♝b4 ♜fe8 and Black had the better endgame.

5...e5

5...♞f6 6 h3 e5 7 dxe5 ♞xe5 transposes to our main game, where we would prefer to have the knight on e7 rather than f6 – see the note to Black's seventh move.

6 dxe5 ♞xe5 7 h3

White guards the g4-square, as 7 f4 allows 7...♝g4! when after 8 ♝e2 (or 8 ♛d2 ♞f3+) 8...♝xe2 (8...♞c4 9 ♝d4!) 9 ♞gxe2 ♞d7 the exchange of bishops has left the pawn on g3 looking rather silly. However, perhaps 7 ♝g2 is possible, as 7...♞c4?! (7...♞e7) 8 ♝d4! ♞xb2? (8...♞f6 intends to answer 9 b3 with 9...c5!? but 9 ♛e2! may be awkward in view of 9...♞xb2? 10 ♛b5+ winning a piece) 9 ♝xg7 ♞xd1 10 ♜xd1 followed by 11 ♝xh8 is clearly good for White. In the game White spends a tempo on a pawn move rather than developing a piece, despite the fact that the situation in the centre isn't completely stable. This suggests that Black should be able to break out and equalise. However, he has to act before his opponent completes his development, as in that case White will have a good position in view of his control of the d5-square.

7...♘f6?

Much better was 7...♘e7! as Black keeps the option of attacking White's centre with ...f7-f5. Then 8 f4 ♘5c6 9 ♗g2 (Ledger-McNab, Bayswater 1990) 9...f5!?, planning 10...fxe4 and 11...♘f5, looks fine for Black. Even the immediate 7...f5 is possible, e.g. 8 exf5 (8 ♗g2 ♘e7, recapturing on f5 with the knight if necessary) 8...♗xf5 9 ♗g2 c6 and Black is ready to play moves such as ...♘f6, ...0-0 and ...d6-d5.

8 f4! ♘ed7

The chance for activity has gone. If 8...♘c6 9 ♗g2 0-0 10 ♘ge2 leaves Black with no way to put serious pressure on White's centre.

9 ♗g2 0-0 10 ♘ge2 ♖e8 11 0-0 ♘b6

The combinative 11...♘xe4? 12 ♘xe4 f5 fails to 13 ♘g5!, threatening a check on d5 (Cabrilo).

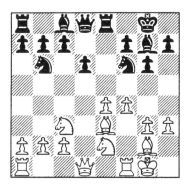

12 ♗d4!

White removes his bishop from any tactical tricks on the e-file and ties down the knight on f6, which can now only move on pain of allowing an exchange of dark-squared bishops, which would weaken the kingside.

12...♗e6 13 b3!

White prevents 13...♗c4!, when the bishop finds a much more active diagonal.

13...c5!?

Hickl knows that the only chance of securing a safe position is by generating some counterplay. Therefore he tries to force through the central pawn advance ...d6-d5.

14 ♗f2 ♕e7?

If 14...d5 15 e5 ♘fd7 16 ♘xd5 ♘xd5 17 ♗xd5 ♗xh3 or 15 exd5 ♘fxd5 16 ♘xd5 ♗xd5 both bring Black's pieces to life. However, White has a third option in 15 f5!, when 15...gxf5 16 exf5 ♗xf5 17 ♗xc5 ♕c8 18 ♗d4 looks very good for him. After the game move, Black is ready to play 15...d5, but Geller's accurate reply crushes this hope.

15 g4!

Evidently Black should have prevented this with 14...h5! last move.

15...♗d7

Instead 15...d5? 16 e5 ♘fd7?! 17 ♘xd5 would be a disaster for Black.

16 ♕d2 ♗c6 17 ♘g3 ♖ad8

All the black pieces are centralised or controlling centre squares, but there is no constructive plan available apart from the ...d6-d5 breakout. With his next few moves Geller wins the battle for this square, which leaves Black almost totally passive.

18 ♖ae1 ♕c7 19 g5!

Again the g-pawn is just in time to stop ...d6-d5.

19...♘fd7 20 ♘d5 ♗xd5 21 exd5

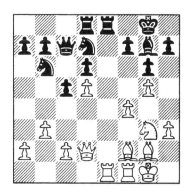

White's pressure has yielded a space advantage in the centre and on the kingside. He now plans a direct attack on the black king. In this he is greatly helped by the fact that Black's knights have no good squares in the centre.

21...♘c8 22 c4 a6 23 h4 b5 24 ♗h3

This bishop will win the game for White as the constricted black knights can do little to oppose its control of the light squares.

24...♘cb6 25 ♕c2 bxc4 26 bxc4 ♘f8 27 h5 ♖b8 28 hxg6 hxg6 29 f5! ♖xe1 30 ♖xe1 ♗e5 31 ♘e4 ♘bd7 32 ♕e2 ♖b2

At last Black achieves some significant looking counterplay, but things on the kingside have growing alarming for him..

33 ♕g4 ♕a5 34 fxg6 fxg6 35 ♕h4!

White finds the winning idea of 36 ♗e6+ ♘xe6 (36...♔g7 37 ♕h6 mate) 37 dxe6, when the passed pawn is unstoppable. So Black makes a desperate sacrifice, but it can only delay the killing bishop check.

35...♖xf2 36 ♔xf2 ♕xa2+ 37 ♖e2 ♗d4+ 38 ♔f1 ♕xc4 39 ♗e6+ ♘xe6 40 dxe6 ♕c1+

Of course, 40...♕xe6 41 ♘f6+ wins the queen. Black can only give some spite checks before resigning.

41 ♖e1 ♕c4+ 42 ♔g2 ♕a2+ 43 ♔h1 ♘f8 44 e7 1-0

Game 19
Spangenberg-Azmaiparashvili
Moscow 1994

---

1 e4 g6 2 d4

Over the next three moves we will consider lines where White plays an early h2-h4. We begin with 2 h4, after which 2...h5 should equalise for Black, but a logical alternative is 2...d5, responding to the wing move with a counterattack in the centre. Then 3 exd5 ♕xd5 4 h5 ♗g7 5 ♘c3 ♕a5 6 ♗c4 ♘c6 reached a strange

kind of Scandinavian position in Casagrande-Beim, Linz 1997. Nunn's verdict of 'murky' seems most appropriate here!

2...♗g7 3 ♘c3

If 3 h4 then besides 3...h5, Black can choose 3...d5!? 4 e5 h5 5 ♘e2 c5 6 c3 ♘c6 7 a3 ♘h6 8 b4 cxd4 9 cxd4 ♘f5 10 ♘bc3 e6 with a strange French-Gurgenidze hybrid in Granda-Kakageldiev, Yerevan 1996, which looks very solid.

3...d6 4 ♗g5

After 4 h4 c6 (or 4...h5) 5 h5 ♕b6 6 ♘ge2 e5 7 h6 ♗f6 8 d5 ♘e7 9 dxc6 ♕xc6 10 ♗e3 (winning the queen costs too much after 10 ♘d4 exd4 11 ♗b5 dxc3 etc.) 10...0-0 11 ♕d2 ♗h8 (Black retreats the bishop, as if it is exchanged, e.g. after ♗g5, then Black would be in grave danger of being mated on g7) 12 0-0-0 ♖d8 13 ♔b1 ♕e8 14 f3 ♗e6 was unclear in Spasov-Azmaiparashvili, Groningen 1989. As a final word concerning h2-h4 ideas, we should mention that after 4 ♗e2 c6 5 h4?!, 5...♕b6 6 ♘f3 ♗g4 looks awkward for White.

Here we turn our attention to White's bishop move in the game. It is an aggressive move, but it seems slightly illogical for the bishop to be aiming at a 'brick wall' on e7 whereas on e3 it could be defending the sensitive d4-pawn and still be able to join in an attack on the kingside after ♕d2 etc.

4...a6

Black prepares an immediate expansion on the queenside, which is the same plan as he adopted in Chapter 3 after 4 ♗e3 and 4 ♘f3. In fact, similar positions to those in Chapter 3 could easily arise, for example if Black played ...h7-h6 and White retreated his bishop to e3, or if White played ♕d2 and ♗h6, in which case it wouldn't matter whether the bishop came from g5 or e3. These possibilities could also happen in combination with ♘f3, leading to other games in Chapter 3.

Another possibility for Black was 4...♘c6, immediately attacking the d4-pawn which White's bishop has so pointedly snubbed. Then 5 ♗b5 (5 d5 ♘e5 is unclear) 5...a6 6 ♗xc6+ bxc6 7 ♘ge2 ♖b8 8 b3 gave White a very slight advantage in Winants-Speelman, Brussels 1988.

Black could also try 4...c6, when 5 ♕d2 b5 6 f4 (6 ♘f3 ♘d7 7 ♗d3 was more solid) 6...♘d7 7 ♘f3 ♘b6 8 a4 b4 9 ♘d1 a5 10 c3 bxc3 11 bxc3 ♘f6 12 ♘f2 0-0 13 ♗d3 was Dreev-Seirawan, Wijk aan Zee 1995. Black is well entrenched and there is no serious danger facing him but White has a small space advantage and an impregnable centre. This outcome of the opening struggle is typical of Black's plan of ...c7-c6 and ...b7-b5 not just against 4 ♗g5 but also in Chapter 2 against 4 ♘f3 and 4 ♗e3. We therefore concentrate on 4...a6 here, which seems to give greater chances of counterplay.

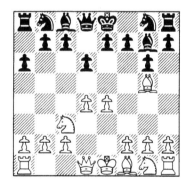

5 ♕d2

After 5 ♗c4 b5 6 ♗d5 (it's not clear that White should want to provoke a move that helps to stabilise Black's centre) 6...c6 7 ♗b3 ♘d7 8 ♘f3 ♕c7 9 a4 b4 10 ♘e2 ♘gf6 Black had equalised in Smirin-Kantsler, Rishon le Zion 1997. Alternatively White could try the 'Austrian' 5 f4, when 5...b5 6 ♘f3 ♗b7 7 ♗d3 ♘d7 8 ♘e2 c5 9 c3 cxd4 10 cxd4 ♘gf6 11 ♘g3 gave

balanced chances in Krays-Kantsler, Israel 1996. (Judging from these two examples Kantsler always solves his opening problems by playing his knight to f6 on move 10!)

5...b5 6 0-0-0?!

Since White has preferred 4 ♗g5 to 4 ♗e3, not only is the d4-pawn more vulnerable in itself but it is also easier for Black to arrange to attack it with ...c7-c5. After all, with the bishop on e3, ...c7-c5 could often be met by d4xc5, planning either to win a pawn or perhaps to follow up with ♗d4, challenging the bishop on g7. It is therefore rather reckless of White to put his king on the queenside when Black can so easily achieve ...c7-c5, breaking open the long diagonal for his bishop. Probably White does best with the standard plan of 6 a4 attacking Black's queenside pawns, when 6...b4 7 ♘d5 a5 8 c3 gave him some advantage in Filipenko-Schekachev, Smolensk 1992.

6...♗b7 7 f3 ♘d7 8 h4?

This is redolent of the cavalier style in which White used to play against the Modern in its early days, when it was thought that direct methods of attack could refute all this 'nonsense' with ...g7-g6 and ...♗g7. We shouldn't be too contemptuous of this opinion, as Anand and others have occasionally bashed the Modern through castling queenside and launching a pawn storm on the kingside! Nevertheless, in this instance we can surely be critical of White's play. The bishop on g5, rather than being the spearhead of an attack, is a useless piece. Even if White succeeds in finding time for h4-h5 followed by h5xg6 and an exchange of rooks on the h-file, he wouldn't have a decisive attack in sight. His other bishop on f1 is denied its favourite attacking square by the 'Modern' pawn on c4. So in 'undoing' the potential 'work' of this bishop with the pawn moves ...a7-a6 and ...b7-b5 it could be claimed that Black has achieved the equivalent of developing a piece of his own.

Although formally undeveloped, the knight on g8 is doing a great job in defending the weakest point in Black's position, the h6-square. As long as White is prevented from playing ♗h6 he cannot infiltrate on the dark squares and cause problems for the black king.

Instead of the pseudo-attacking 8 h4, White should have prepared to defend his queenside with either 8 ♔b1 or 8 ♘ge2.

8...c5!

This heralds Black's attack which becomes overwhelming in just a few moves.

9 ♘ge2 ♕a5 10 ♔b1 b4 11 ♘d5 ♗xd5 12 exd5 ♘b6 13 ♘c1 c4!

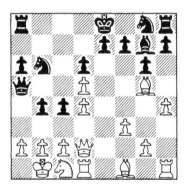

This is a wonderful all-purpose move. It closes the centre and so prevents any counterplay White might have achieved with d4xc5 and (after the recapture ...d6xc5) d5-d6. It also rules out 14 ♘b3 and denies the white pieces the d3-square. And lastly, it threatens ...c4-c3 in some lines to break up White's queenside defences.

14 ♕e1

Here we see the 'undeveloped' knight on g8 is doing another useful job in defending e7 against mate!

14...♕b5!

This defends c4 and so threatens

15...♘xd5. White cannot let this happen unopposed, but the 'remedy' proves fatal for his king's health.

15 b3 h6!

This is a shameful moment for the proud bishop on g5, which is kicked backwards by the pawn to make way for the grand entrance of the knight on g8.

16 ♗f4 ♘f6! 17 ♗xd6 ♘fxd5!

Now Black simply intends to castle kingside with a huge attack. White's next move makes things easier for him.

18 a4 ♘xa4! 19 bxa4 ♕xa4 20 ♗xc4

If 20 ♘e2 b3 is decisive, so White has to give up his queen.

20...♘c3+ 21 ♕xc3 bxc3 22 ♗b3 ♕a5 23 ♖he1 ♗f6 24 ♘a2 0-0 25 ♗b4 ♕b5 26 ♗xe7 ♗xe7 27 ♖xe7 ♕a5 28 ♖e5 ♕a3 29 ♘xc3 ♖ab8 30 ♖d3 a5 31 ♖b5 ♖fe8 0-1

Game 20
Magomedov-Ftacnik
Yerevan 1996

---

1 e4 g6 2 d4 ♗g7 3 c3

This is White's most solid response to Black's fianchetto, blocking out the bishop on the long diagonal. An obvious drawback is that the queen's knight is deprived of its best square on c3, and instead has to be deployed in far less promising fashion to d2. Since virtually all of White's attacking variations begin with the move ♘c3, it would be easy to conclude that he is not showing much ambition in this game. However, this isn't necessarily the case. Although he is not aiming to cause Black any immediate problems in the opening, White is keeping a small positional plus and maintaining the tension. He hopes that Black will overpress in search of counterplay or, if he responds to White's set up in a quiet style, make one or two slight errors in his piece disposition. Then White will have gained winning chances without taking any risks or needing to demonstrate a huge amount of sharp opening theory.

Here we should admit to having taken enormous liberties with the move order in this game, which actually began 1 e4 d6 2 d4 ♘f6 3 ♗d3 g6 4 h3 ♗g7 5 ♘f3 0-0 6 0-0 ♘c6 7 ♖e1 ♘d7. It is no surprise that the non-critical nature of the play allows the same position to be reached in manifold ways. Therefore, we have chosen a 'route' which allows us to view as many 'side paths' as possible.

3...d6

4 ♘f3

White has a couple of important alternatives here:

a) After 4 f4 ♘f6 5 ♗d3 (or 5 e5 dxe5 6 fxe5 ♘d5 7 ♘f3 0-0 8 ♗c4 c5! – planning to answer 9 dxc5 with 9...♗e6 10 ♘g5 ♘c6 – 9 0-0 cxd4 10 cxd4 ♘c6 11 ♘c3 ♗e6 gave Black a comfortable game in Plachetka-Hoi, Ostrava 1992) 5...0-0 6 ♘f3 Black can hit out at White's centre with the pawn sacrifice 6...c5 7 dxc5 ♘bd7! This has been a pet line of David Norwood, who has shown that Black gets enough pressure on e4 to win back the pawn with equal chances. For example, 8 cxd6 (if 8 b4 a5!) 8...exd6 9 0-0 ♘c5 10 ♕c2 (10 e5 dxe5 11 ♘xe5 ♘g4! 12 ♗c4 ♘xe5 13 fxe5 ♕xd1 14 ♖xd1 ♗e6 15 ♘a3 ♗xe5 led to a draw in Lodhi-Norwood,

Dhaka 1993) 10...♖e8 11 ♘bd2 ♗d7 12 ♘d4 ♖c8 13 ♔h1 ♕e7 14 f5 ♘fxe4 15 ♗xe4 ♘xe4 16 fxg6 hxg6 17 ♘xe4 ♕xe4 18 ♕b3 ♗e6 19 ♘xe6 ♖xe6 and Black was at least equal in Hodgson-Norwood, Plymouth 1989.

b) 4 ♗g5 ♘f6 5 ♘d2 0-0 6 ♘gf3 c5! (this seems a more attractive plan than preparing ...e7-e5 as in that case the bishop on g5 would be exerting extra pressure on f6) 7 dxc5 dxc5 8 ♗c4 (a more active square for the bishop than e2, when after 8...♘c6 9 0-0 ♕c7 10 ♕c2 ♖d8 11 ♖fe1 h6 12 ♗h4 ♘h5 13 ♘c4 ♗e6 14 ♘e3 ♘f4 15 ♗f1 ♘e5 the World Champion was striving for the initiative in Yusupov-Kasparov, Riga 1995) 8...♘c6 9 ♕e2 ♕c7 10 0-0 h6 11 ♗h4 ♘h5 12 ♕e3 b6 (instead 12...g5 {or 12...♘a5} 13 ♗g3 – not 13 ♕xc5? b6 – 13...♘xg3 14 hxg3 b6 would equalise) 13 ♖fe1 g5 and now rather than acquiesce in 14 ♗g3 ♗xg3 15 hxg3, White preferred to speculate with 14 ♗xg5 hxg5 15 ♕xg5 in Speelman-Howell, Calcutta 1996, whereupon Black should have played 15...♘f4 16 e5 ♘e6 or 16...b5 with unclear play.

4...♘f6 5 ♗d3

The super-solid 5 ♘bd2 (or 5 ♕c2 0-0 6 ♗e2 ♘c6 7 0-0 e5 also looks equal) 5...0-0 6 ♗e2 isn't really much of an attempt to gain the advantage. After 6...♘c6 7 0-0 e5 8 dxe5 ♘xe5 9 ♘xe5 dxe5 Black was fine in Kovacevic-Ftacnik, Vinkovci 1995.

5...0-0 6 0-0 ♘c6

As is usual in this system, Black has the choice between preparing ...e7-e5 or playing ...c7-c5. Here 6...c5 should be okay for Black but it tends to leave White with an irritating, if tiny, edge, e.g. 7 h3 cxd4 8 cxd4 ♘c6 9 ♘c3 e5 10 dxe5 dxe5 11 ♗c4!? (more usual is 11 ♗e3, but White wants to deter 11...♗e6) 11...b6?! (11...♗e6, despite allowing doubled pawns was perhaps still best) 12 b3! h6 13 ♗a3 ♖e8 14 ♘b5 and White suddenly had a big advantage in McDonald-McShane, London 1997.

7 ♖e1 e5

Also 7...♗g4 is possible, when 8 ♘bd2 e5 9 h3 ♗d7 10 dxe5 ♘xe5 11 ♘xe5 dxe5 12 ♘c4 ♖e8 was equal in Salov-Topalov, Dos Hermanas 1997, but playing the bishop to g4 and then back to d7 seems a little indulgent.

8 h3 ♘d7

Black clears the way to advance ...f7-f5. Solid alternatives include 8...♗d7 and 8...h6 to rule out 9 ♗g5.

9 ♗f1

A more aggressive bishop move is 9 ♗b5, but 9...♘e7 10 ♘bd2 a6 11 ♗f1 b6 12 a4 a5 13 ♗b5 (back again!) 13...♗b7 was safe for Black in Godena-Ftacnik, Pula 1997. White can also choose to obstruct Black's plan with 9 ♗g5 f6 10 ♗h4, which gave him some advantage in Kindermann-Hickl, Bad Homburg 1997, after 10...♕e7 11 ♘a3 ♘d8 12 ♘c4 ♘f7 (a notable knight manoeuvre) 13 b4 c6.

9...h6 10 dxe5 dxe5 11 ♘bd2 f5

This is the thematic bid for activity in such positions, but on the other hand White's system of development has been specially designed to prove that it is wrong! A hard struggle now develops with White trying to undermine the black centre by attacking from the queenside.

12 b4 ♕f6 13 b5 ♘e7 14 ♗a3

It was hard to decide whether White should prefer 14 exf5, when after 14...gxf5 15 ♗a3 ♖e8 16 ♘c4 it is easier for him to attack the black centre, but at the same time the centre is no longer pegged back by the pawn on e4 and so has more dynamic potential.

14...f4 15 ♘c4 ♖e8 16 ♖e2! a6!

Since the struggle in the centre is delicately balanced, both sides hope to decide it in their favour by bringing their rooks into the game. Thus while White begins a manoeuvre to increase the pressure along the d-file, Black forces open the a-file.

17 bxa6 ♕xa6 18 ♖d2 ♕c6 19 ♕b3 ♔h7

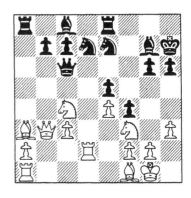

20 ♘cxe5?

Despite his passive opening we cannot accuse White of lacking fighting spirit! This sacrifice looks highly dangerous, but it contains a flaw. Instead White should have continued his build up in methodical style via 20 ♖ad1 with unclear play.

20...♘xe5 21 ♘xe5 ♗xe5 22 ♗b5

This appears very strong as the black queen and rook on e8 are skewered. However, White had overlooked Black's 23rd move, after which it is a case of the trapper trapped.

22...♕f6?!

In fact, according to Ftacnik the sharp 22...♕xc3!, planning to answer 23 ♕f7+ with 23...♗g7 24 ♗b2 ♗e6! (driving the queen away from f7 so that 25...♕xd2 doesn't allow mate on g7) was even better.

23 ♗xe8 ♗e6! 24 ♗xe7 ♕xe7 25 ♕xb7?

The bishop should sell itself as dearly as possible with 25 ♗xg6+! – Ftacnik.

25...♖xe8 26 ♖ad1 f3!

Now Black gains a decisive attack before White can exploit the open d-file.

27 ♕b5 ♕g5 28 g3 ♖e7 29 a4 h5 30 ♖d3 ♗xh3 31 ♖e1 ♗g2 32 ♕c5 ♖g7 33 ♖d5 ♕g4 34 ♖xe5 ♕h3 35 ♖xh5+ gxh5 36 ♕f5+ ♕xf5 37 exf5 ♖f7 38 a5 ♖xf5 39 ♖a1 ♖f8 40 ♔h2 ♖a8 41 a6 ♖a7 42 ♖a5 ♔g6 43 ♖a1 ♔f5 44 ♖a4 ♔e5 45 ♖a5+ ♔e4 46 ♖c5 ♖xa6 47 ♖xc7 ♖a1 0-1

Summary

In Game 17, White's choice of 3 ♘c3 c6 (or 3...d6) 4 ♗c4 d6 is a good way to avoid the ...d7-d5 ideas of Chapters 1 and 2. It leads to a hard struggle with chances for both sides.

In Game 18, 3 ♘c3 d6 4 g3 ♘c6 should be okay for Black if he plays energetically, while White's quiet system with 3 c3 in Game 20 allows Black a dull equality if he wishes it, but if he desires to create winning chances then he has to take some risks. Finally, in Game 19 3 ♘c3 d6 4 ♗g5 is interesting, but requires an accurate follow-up from White.

1 e4 g6 2 d4 ♗g7

3 ♘c3
> 3 c3 *(D)* – *Game 20*

3...d6 *(D)* **4 ♗c4**
> 4 g3 – *Game 18*
>
> 4 ♗g5 – *Game 19*

4....c6 5 ♕f3 *(D)* – *Game 17*

3 c3

3...d6

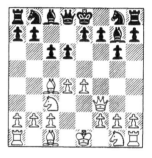

5 ♕f3

CHAPTER FIVE

Averbakh Variation with 4...♘c6 5 d5 ♘d4

1 d4 g6 2 c4 ♝g7 3 e4 d6 4 ♘c3 ♘c6 5 d5 ♘d4

In the rest of this book we shall focus on lines after 1 d4 g6. The most critical of these is 2 c4 ♝g7 3 e4 d6 4 ♘c3 (Chapters 5-8), when Black has a choice between transposing to a King's Indian Defence with 4...♘f6 and taking play along Modern Defence lines.

One very popular line here is 5 ♝e3 (Chapter 6), but first we consider 5 d5, the most direct way to try and take advantage of Black's system. Although Black almost always replies 5...♘d4, of course 5...♘e5 is also playable and indeed in my database it has scored slightly over fifty percent: but that's probably because it's generally employed by stronger players trying to bamboozle weaker ones! Perhaps this line will really catch on one day but here we restrict ourselves to one rather vile example of the suffering Black may have to endure against a sensible strong opponent.

Before passing on to the main line we should mention 6 ♝e3 c5 7 dxc6 ♘xc6 (Game 21) which is perfectly sensible for White, reaching a Maroczy Bind pawn structure. Of course White can't play as in the Sicilian with the knight on d4 – not only would this leave him a tempo adrift

of normal variations but it's also necessary to lose a further tempo with h2-h3 to stop ...♘g4. But there is an alternative plan of ♖c1 followed by f2-f3 and ♘g1-e2-f4, when nobody has found any particularly wonderful way of exploiting White's somewhat ponderous development.

Instead the main line continues 6 ♝e3 c5 7 ♘ge2 ♕b6 (7...♘xe2 8 ♝xe2 is awfully comfortable for White – see the notes to Game 22) when we reach an important parting of ways:

a) 8 ♘xd4 cxd4 9 ♘a4

This used to be the most popular line. Whilst there's much to be said for an attempt at direct exploitation if not refutation of Black's play, this is extremely committal. White can generate extremely quick play on the queenside but in return he gives Black a potentially annoying pawn on d4 and good development.

9..♕a5+

The splendid queen sacrifice 9...dxe3?! was first played by Ray Keene against Agdestein. Unfortunately, it doesn't really work, as you can see from Game 22.

10 b4

Unfortunately, if White is sufficiently wimpy (or the players have nefariously agreed beforehand) then a draw is to be had here. Neither side can now deviate from the forced sequence 10...♕xb4+ 11 ♗d2 ♕a3 12 ♗c1 ♕b4+. So if Black has to win at all costs then he *can't* play this line.

If instead of 10 b4, White plays 10 ♗d2 then there is a choice between 10...♕c7 and 10...♕d8 (not 10...♕a6 11 c5). My feeling is that if it's playable then the queen should go to the more active c7 rather than d8. This encourages c4-c5 but, as the excellent game Parker-Martin (Game 23) shows, Black has serious resources. My battle against Korchnoi was less frantic but I also got the advantage rather quickly.

b) 8 ♘a4 ♕a5+ 9 ♗d2

Here Black must choose between retreating to c7 or d8, which are fairly similar after 10 ♗c3! (see Game 24), and the current main line.

9...♕a6

The point of this rather ugly move is to prevent 10 ♗c3 in view of 10...♗d7, when Black gets a fine game (though he must be a tiny bit careful, see Johannes-van Hoolandt in the notes to Game 25). Obviously the queen would much prefer to be on c7 or d8, but since the lines after 10 ♗c3 are somewhat depressing, 9...♕a6 has become the main line. Normally White exchanges

10 ♘xd4 ♗xd4

and, having done it's work, the knight

returns to c3, reaching the next diagram.

11 ♘c3

The first thing I should say is that this is an extremely sharp position. Either player can quickly get into a real mess after just a couple of inaccuracies. It's therefore ideal for the sort of player prepared to venture the Modern. But it does place great demands particularly on Black, who may have to continue by 'non-standard means' in order to justify his previous play.

Black has a perfectly good Benoni pawn structure and with some space disadvantage is very happy to have already exchanged a pair of minor pieces. As to development, he has amassed a very reasonable 'quantity' of this though the quality is rather more in doubt. The path divides here between the 'obvious' 11...♗d7 (Game 25) and the absolutely most critical move 11...♕b6 (Game 26).

c) 8 ♕d2

Despite appearing less fearsome than the attempts at direct refutation, this eminently sensible move looks like a very good bet for White, since with accurate play he should be able to reach a pretty favourable version of a 'normal' position.

Unfortunately for Black, the natural continuation 8...♗g4 runs into 9 f3! after which 9...♗xf3 10 ♘a4! turns out to be winning for White (see the notes to Game

27). Norwood recommends the rare 8...f5. This is a very nice idea – Black needs to destabilise the position in some way and ...f7-f5 is the very simplest, but as the notes to Game 27 show, White could have obtained rather a nice advantage.

So the most 'rational' continuation is **8...♞f6**

Now 9 ♞xd4?! isn't absolutely clear but should surely be avoided by White – see Game 28. The critical line is 9 f3 after which the most accurate continuation is 9...♞d7 10 ♖d1 0-0 11 b3! (see Game 29). Now Black is finally forced to exchange on e2, after which Hernandez obtained a rather dangerous initiative which he quickly converted with some apparently brutally efficient play into a won position. This game seems to have scared off Black players from repeating the line, but there are certainly improvements for him and whilst it is risky, it does look very reasonably playable to me pending further evidence.

Game 21
Muir-Webster
British Championship 1993

---

1 d4 d6 2 e4 g6 3 c4 ♝g7 4 ♞c3 ♞c6 5 d5 ♞d4 6 ♝e3 c5 7 dxc6!?

In *Informator 35*, Suba went as far as to give this an '!' when annotating his game against Jonathan Mestel – see the note below.

7...♞xc6 8 ♛d2

8 ♖c1 ♞f6 9 f3 0-0 10 ♞ge2, trying to take advantage of the knight on g1 rather than apologise for it, looks more logical:

a) 10...a6 was played in Suba-Mestel, Las Palmas Interzonal 1982, which continued 11 ♞f4 ♝d7 12 ♝e2 (Suba suggests that 12 ♛d2 is even better) 12...e5?! (this is surely too radical) 13 ♞fd5 ♞xd5 14 ♞xd5 ♞d4 15 0-0 ♝e6 16 ♝d3 ♚h8 17 ♛d2 (this is rather like a Sicilian Sveshnikov or even

more so the Kalashnikov with a ridiculously early ...e7-e5) 17...b5 18 f4 f5 19 ♝xd4! exd4 20 cxb5 ♝xd5 (20...axb5 21 ♞c7) 21 exd5 axb5 22 a3 ♖b8 23 ♖fe1 ♛d7 24 ♖e6 ♖f6 25 ♛e2 ♖xe6 26 dxe6 ♛b7 27 ♖e1? (27 e7 ♖e8 28 ♛e6 to be followed by ♖e1, ♛f7 and ♝xb5 is very strong) and Jonathan had to navigate several more dicey moment before eventually salvaging a draw.

b) 10...♛a5 11 ♛d2 ♝d7 12 ♞f4 ♖fc8 13 ♝e2 ♞e5 14 b3 ♝c6 15 0-0 ♛d8, as in Plauth-Buchal, San Bernardino open 1992, was an admission that Black can't immediately profit from his temporary 'initiative'. But although outrated by almost 200 points Black obtained the advantage before a nauseating blunder cost him the game.

8...♞f6 9 h3 0-0 10 ♞f3 ♝e6 11 ♖c1 a6 12 ♝e2 ♛a5 13 0-0 ♖fc8

Clearly in this type of position the knight isn't well placed on f3, where it blocks the f-pawn and has no influence on the queenside. So Black ought to be doing rather better than in similar positions in the Sicilian. Muir now played the normal Sicilian move:

14 ♞d5 ♛xd2 15 ♞xd2 ♞d7 16 b3

16...♝xd5!? 17 exd5!?

17 cxd5 looks safer and now:

a) 17...♞d4 18 ♝g4! f5 19 ♝xd4 ♝xd4 (19...fxg4 20 ♝xg7 ♚xg7 21 hxg4 is simply bad, but would be playable if White had interpolated 19 exf5 gxf5 since then the d5-pawn would be loose) 20 exf5.

b) 17...♞b4 18 ♗g4! again causes trouble. Now 18...f5 19 exf5 h5 20 ♗f3 gxf5 is a mess but one in which White is very happy to have the two bishops.

17...♞d4 18 ♖fe1 b5 19 ♗xd4?!

This rather backfires. After 19 ♗f1 White remains very comfortable.

19...♗xd4 20 cxb5 ♖xc1 21 ♖xc1 axb5 22 ♞f3

Not 22 ♗xb5? ♖xa2 when if 23 ♞f3 ♗xf2+.

22...♗b2! 23 ♖c2 ♖xa2 24 ♗xb5

White can't exploit the pin since if:

a) 24 ♔h2? ♗e5+ 25 ♞xe5 ♖xc2 26 ♞xd7 ♖xe2 wins.

b) 24 ♗f1 is the only other way to prevent the rook escaping with check but Black can simply hit the knight when it moves to e1 en route to d3.

24...♞f6 25 ♗c4 ♖a1+ 26 ♔h2 ♗a3

Since the b-pawn is going nowhere, Black's more compact position – one pawn island against three – gives him good chances. However, White has a clear target on e7 and with the minor pieces flying around had several opportunities (during what I presume must have been a time scramble) to stabilise the position before emerging at the time control with a lost game.

27 ♞d4 ♗c5 28 ♞c6 ♞e4!

If 28...♔f8 29 ♖e2 not only hits the e-pawn again but also cuts out Black's play.

29 ♞xe7+ ♔f8 30 ♞c6 h5

If 30...♗xf2 31 g4 gives the king space.

31 g4

31 g3 (Fritz) is possible and if 31...♗xf2 32 ♗d3 ♞c5 33 ♖xf2 ♞xd3 34 ♖f6.

31...hxg4 32 hxg4 ♞xf2 33 ♗e2 ♖b1 34 ♔g2 ♞e4 35 b4! ♗xb4!?

see following diagram

36 ♖c4?

36 ♗d3! (Fritz) comes extremely close to winning a piece and in any case should force a draw. Of course it's nothing to do with the opening but the analysis is fun:

a) 36...♞f6? 37 ♖f2.

b) 36...♞g5 37 ♖a2! wins a piece albeit for some compensation, i.e. 37...♖b3 38 ♗c2 ♖c3 39 ♞xb4 ♖c4 40 ♞c6 ♖xg4+ and Black has very reasonable drawing chances but certainly no more.

c) 36...f5 37 gxf5 gxf5 when:

c1) 38 ♖f2 forces a dead draw after 38...♞xf2 39 ♗xb1 ♗c5 40 ♗xf5.

c2) 38 ♖a2!? ♖b3 39 ♗c2! ♖g3+ 40 ♔h2 ♗d2! 41 ♗xe4 ♗f4 42 ♖a8+ ♔g7 43 ♖a7+ (protecting the rook with tempo) 43...♔f6 and White can do no better than 22 ♗h1, after which Black has immediate perpetual on the g-file, as 44 ♗g2!? ♖c3+ 45 ♔g1 ♗e3+ 46 ♔f1 ♗xa7 47 ♞xa7 is of course absolutely fine for Black.

36...♞c3 37 ♞xb4?

37 ♗d3 ♖b2+ 38 ♔f3 ♞a2 looks tougher.

37...♞xe2 38 ♖c8+ ♔g7 39 ♞c6 ♞f4+

Now Black has untangled and has an easily winning position.

40 ♔f3 ♞xd5 41 ♖d8 ♖b3+ 42 ♔e4 ♞f6+ 43 ♔f4 ♖b1 44 g5 ♖f1+ 45 ♔e3 ♞h7 46 ♖xd6 ♞xg5 47 ♞d4 ♖e1+ 48 ♔d3 ♞e6 49 ♞f3 ♞f4+ 50 ♔d2 ♖e2+ 51 ♔d1 ♖e3 0-1

Game 22
Miles-Rohde
London (Lloyds Bank) 1984

1 d4 g6 2 e4 ♗g7 3 c4 d6 4 ♘c3 ♘c6 5 d5 ♘d4 6 ♗e3 c5 7 ♘ge2 ♕b6

I really don't like the submissive 7...Ìxe2. White gets a perfectly ordinary position with a tempo or so extra in view of the knight's journey via d4. True Black has freed himself by exchanging off a pair of minor pieces – always nice when one has a space disadvantage – but vigorous play makes the black position look pretty dubious, e.g. 8 ♗xe2 ♘f6 9 f4 0-0 10 0-0 e6 11 dxe6 ♗xe6 (if 11...fxe6 12 e5! leaves Black with an inferior pawn structure after 12...dxe5 13 ♗xc5) 12 f5 ♗c8 13 ♕d2 with a very pleasant game for White in Vaisser-Turner, European Club Cup, Athens 1997.

8 ♘xd4 cxd4 9 ♘a4 dxe3?!

As mentioned in the introduction to this chapter, although this is a splendid idea I simply don't believe it. Not only does Black end up with just two pieces and some initiative for the queen with no extra pawns; but most importantly he is left with sick doubled b-pawns which provide an excellent target for the queen once White has consolidated.

10 ♘xb6 exf2+ 11 ♔xf2 axb6 12 ♕d2!

Keeping control of d4. The stem game Agdestein-Keene, Gausdal 1983, went 12 ♕c2 ♗d4+ 13 ♔e1 ♘f6 14 ♗e2 0-0 15 ♖d1 ♗e5 16 a4 h5 17 b3 ♗d7 18 ♕d3 e6 19 dxe6 ♗xe6 20 ♗f3 ♘d7 21 ♔f2 b5! 22 axb5 (or 22 cxb5 ♘c5 23 ♕e3 ♗xb3 annihilating most of White's queenside) 22...♖a2+ 23 ♖d2 ♘c5 24 ♕e3 ♖xd2+ 25 ♕xd2 ♘xb3 26 ♕c2 ♗d4+ 27 ♔g3 ♗e5+ 28 ♔f2 ♗d4+ and Agdestein settled for a draw with 29 ♔g3.

12...♘f6 13 ♗d3 ♘g4+ 14 ♔e2 0-0 15 h3 ♘e5

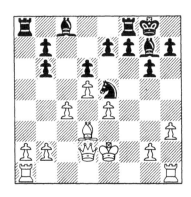

16 b3!

Offering to return the exchange, after which the dynamism would go out of Black's position and he would be left with a material disadvantage for nothing. Rohde manage to get some more mileage out of his bishops before accepting the bait, but not nearly enough.

16...f5 17 a4 ♘xd3 18 ♕xd3 fxe4 19 ♕e3!

Keeping the e-file blocked to avoid any excitement after 19 ♕xe4 ♗f5 20 ♕e3 e6!, when White's king could easily get into serious trouble.

19...♗xa1

Surrender. Once this proud prelate has gone, the white king is quite safe and Miles easily converts the victory.

20 ♖xa1 b5 21 cxb5 ♖f5 22 ♕d4 ♗d7 23 ♖c1 ♗xb5+!?

Desperation.

24 axb5 ♖a2+ 25 ♔e3 ♖ff2 26 ♖c8+ ♔f7 27 ♕h8 ♖fe2+ 28 ♔f4 g5+ 29 ♔xg5 ♖xg2+ 30 ♔h5 1-0

Game 23
Parker-A.Martin
British Championship, Hove 1997

1 d4 g6 2 c4 ♗g7 3 e4 d6 4 ♘c3 ♘c6 5 d5 ♘d4 6 ♗e3 c5 7 ♘ge2 ♕b6 8 ♘xd4 cxd4 9 ♘a4 ♕a5+ 10 ♗d2

As mentioned in the introduction to

this chapter, White can force a draw here with 10 b4 ♕xb4+ 11 ♗d2 ♕a3 12 ♗c1 ♕b4+.

10...♕c7

Black would presumably prefer to keep the queen developed rather than retreat it to d8 if possible, as 10...♕d8 11 c5! dxc5 12 ♘xc5 ♘f6 13 ♕a4+ ♘d7 14 ♗b5 favoured White in Khasin-Mikac, Pula 1989.

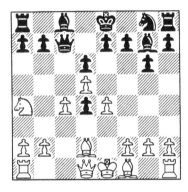

11 c5!?

The sharpest, trying to demolish Black's structure immediately.

In Beersheva 1987 Victor Korchnoi played the calmer 11 ♗d3 against me (JS). After 11...♘f6 12 b4 ♘g4 13 ♖c1 0-0 14 0-0 ♘e5 15 ♘b2 I tried 15...a5!?, breaking up the queenside since White can't simply maintain his phalanx with 16 a3 in view of 16...axb4 17 axb4? ♖a2, when 18 ♖b1 loses to 18...♖xb2!, so the best White can do is to jettison a pawn with 18 f4. Instead 16 bxa5 looks critical. I simply can't remember what I intended but presume it was 16...b6 (16...♖xa5 17 ♗xa5 ♕xa5 looks extremely dubious, particularly against a man as materialistic as Victor Lvovich) when 17 axb6? ♕xb6 is extremely pleasant for Black but White can either force events with 17 f4!? or perhaps try something quiet like 17 ♖e1 bxa5 18 ♗f1, though e.g. 18...a4 looks very reasonable for Black. In the game Victor tried 16 ♗b1?!, but after 16...axb4 17 ♗xb4 b6 18

a3 ♘d7 19 f4 ♘c5 Black has an excellent structure and stands at least equal.

11...♘f6!

Putting development above all else. 11...dxc5 led to very serious trouble in Seirawan-Keene, Holland 1982, after 12 ♗b5+ ♗d7 13 ♗xd7+ ♕xd7 14 ♘xc5 ♕b5 15 b4 ♘f6 16 a4 ♕b6 17 0-0 ♖d8 8 ♕e2 0-0 19 ♖fc1 a6 20 a5 ♕a7 21 ♗f4 when Black's position is absolutely vile.

12 f3?!

Rather weakening. There are two important alternatives here:

a) 12 ♗b5+ is positionally desirable but loses time – probably too much time. For example, 12...♗d7 13 ♗xd7+ (13 c6 bxc6 14 dxc6 ♗e6 15 ♕c2 0-0 16 0-0 d5 was played in Danailov-Garkov, Bulgaria 1984 – White has a huge c-pawn but the rest of the position is very nice for Black. Still unless White has a big improvement in the line below then, having initiated with 12 ♗b5+, this is the logical way to continue.) 13...♘xd7 14 cxd6 ♕xd6 15 ♕b3 ♕a6 16 ♖c1 0-0 17 ♘c5 ♘xc5 18 ♖xc5 ♖ac8! If he could consolidate then White would have an excellent game but Black is too far ahead in development and went on to win in Agnos-Webster, London 1990.

b) The less ambitious 12 ♗d3 seems better. After 12...0-0 13 ♖c1 e6 reaches the position in the main game, but with White having played the developing move ♗d3 rather than f2-f3. Still Black was doing very well after 14 dxe6 ♗xe6 15 cxd6 ♕xd6 16 ♘c5 ♖fc8 17 b4 ♗xa2 18 ♘xb7 ♕b6 19 ♘c5 a5 20 bxa5 ♖xa5 21 ♘d7 ♖xc1 22 ♘xf6+ ♗xf6 23 ♕xc1 ♖c5 24 ♕a3 ♗b1 25 0-0 ♗xd3 26 ♕xd3 ♖b5 in the game E.Agdestein (Grandmaster Simen's brother)-Villamayor, Moscow Olympiad 1994, though White just held on.

12...0-0

Playing consistently for the initiative. It's also possible to take the pawn with

12...dxc5 13 ♖c1 b6 14 b4 and here not the submissive 14...0-0 15 bxc5 bxc5 16 ♘xc5 ♕b6 17 ♕a4 e6 18 dxe6 ♗xe6 19 ♘xe6 ♕xe6 20 ♗c4 ♕e5 21 0-0, which left White with much the better structure in Mohr-Marangunic, Croatian Team Championship, Makarska 1994, though it was later drawn, but rather 14...♘d7! trying to suck White into further adventures. The important thing here is to force White to make sufficient concessions in establishing his positional advantage on the queenside that Black's initiative more than compensates, and the plan worked very well in Muellen-Lorscheid, Germany 1983, which concluded 15 ♗b5 0-0 16 ♗c6 ♖b8 17 bxc5 ♘xc5 18 ♘xc5 bxc5 19 ♖xc5 ♗a6 20 ♕c1 ♕d6 21 ♔f2 d3 22 ♖a5 ♗b2 23 ♕e1 ♗d4+ 24 ♔f1 ♗c4 25 ♕c1 ♖b2 26 ♕xc4 ♖b1+ 0-1.

13 ♖c1

Natural, but if he wants to play ♗b4 then it probably ought to be this move rather than next.

13...e6! 14 ♗b4 exd5 15 cxd6 ♕d8 16 e5 ♖e8

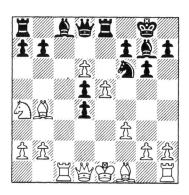

White has a glorious centre but lacks development so badly that he is in serious trouble. The submissive 17 ♗e2 ♖xe5 18 0-0 is unpleasant and if 17 ♕xd4? ♘g4! creates mayhem – of course White can't defend the e-pawn with 18 f4 in view of 18...♘xe5! So Parker tried:

17 f4!? ♘e4?

Obvious, but as Martin told me, 17...♘h5! is even stronger since now if 18 ♕xd4 (18 g3 ♘xf4 19 gxf4 ♕h4+ with a violent attack, e.g. 20 ♔d2 ♕f2+! 21 ♗e2 ♕xf4+ 22 ♔c2 d3+ wins easily) 18...♘xf4! and if 19 ♕xf4 ♗xe5 demolishes White.

18 ♕xd4

18 g3 afforded some sort of defence since after 18...♘xd6 19 ♗xd6 ♕xd6 20 ♕xd4 Black can't crash through immediately with 20...♗xe5? 21 fxe5 ♖xe5+ 22 ♗e2 ♖e4 23 ♕d1 ♗g4 24 ♘c3, but simply 20...f6 21 ♗g2 fxe5 22 ♕xd5+ ♕xd5 23 ♗xd5+ ♔h8 gives Black a big advantage.

18...♕h4+ 19 g3 ♘xg3 20 hxg3 ♕xh1

Although the d-pawn could become dangerous, Black's material advantage together with the somewhat exposed white king and the possibility of returning a piece with ...♗xe5 to blast open the e-file should prevail.

21 ♔f2

If 21 ♘c3 ♗h3! (not 21...h5 22 ♕xd5 ♕g1 23 ♘e2) 22 ♕f2, when after the obvious 22...♗xe5!? 23 fxe5 ♖xe5+ 24 ♔d2 ♖f5 25 ♕d4 ♗xf1 is easy enough, but after 24 ♘e2 ♗xf1 25 ♕xf1 (25 ♔d2 ♕h6+) 25...♖xe2+ 26 ♔xe2 ♕e4+ 27 ♔f2 ♕xb4 28 d7 the d-pawn still needs to be rounded up.

21...h5 22 ♖c3?

Unpinning the bishop but helping Black by vacating the bank rank since there will be no threat of ♖h1 with the queen on h2 and bishops on g2 and h3.

If 22 ♘c3 h4 23 ♕xd5 hxg3+ 24 ♔xg3 (24 ♔e1 ♕h4) 24...♕g1+ 25 ♔f3 (25 ♕g2 ♕e3+) 25...♗g4+ 26 ♔e4 ♕f2 wins, but 22 ♕e3 looks like a better chance, e.g. 22...♕h2+ 23 ♗g2 ♗h3 24 ♕f3 ♗xe5 (if 24...♖c8 either 25 ♘c5 or perhaps 25 ♘c3) 25 fxe5 ♖xe5 26 ♖h1 ♕xg2+ 27 ♕xg2 ♗xg2 28 ♔xg2 ♖d8 Black must be better but the d-pawn remains a serious pest.

22...h4 23 ♗g2 ♕h2 24 gxh4?!

If 24 ♔f1 simply 24...hxg3 should be decisive – not 24...♗h3 when 25 ♕g1 forces the queens off.

24...♕xh4+ 25 ♔e3

Defending the queen to prevent ...♗xe5. Now White is blown away but 25 ♔g1 ♗xe5 was also hopeless.

25...♖xe5+! 26 fxe5 ♗h6+ 27 ♔d3 ♗f5+ 28 ♗e4 ♗xe4+ 29 ♔e2 ♗f3+ 30 ♔d3 ♗e2+ 0-1

Game 24
Gelfand-Azmaiparashvili
Dortmund 1990

---

1 d4 g6 2 e4 ♗g7 3 c4 d6 4 ♘c3 ♘c6 5 d5 ♘d4 6 ♗e3 c5 7 ♘ge2 ♕b6 8 ♘a4 ♕a5+ 9 ♗d2 ♕d8?!

I suspect that 9...♕c7 is better, but after 10 ♗c3 e5 11 dxe6 ♘xe6 we still reach the same pawn structure as in the main game, e.g. 12 ♗xg7 ♘xg7 13 g3!? (13 ♕d2, in similar fashion to Gelfand-Azmaiparashvili, was very possible) 13...♘f6 14 ♗g2 0-0 15 0-0 ♗d7 16 ♘ac3 ♗c6 17 ♕d2 ♖fe8 18 f3 ♖ad8 and Black had a very playable position in Tisdall-Davies, Oslo 1988. For 9...♕a6 see the next main game.

10 ♗c3!

Much the simplest approach though 10 ♘xd4 is also very playable, hoping to reach the previous game with the queen

already committed to d8 – which is a good reason why Black should prefer 9...♕c7 rather than 9...♕d8. Moreover, in the game continuation Black would be slightly happier with the queen on c7 since then he could defend the d6-pawn in one move with ...♖d8. Petursson-Hoi, Nordic Zonal 1992, continued 10...♗xd4 11 ♗c3 ♗xc3+ 12 ♘xc3 ♘f6 13 ♗e2 0-0 14 0-0 a6 15 f4 ♕c7 16 ♕d2 ♗d7 17 ♕e3 b5 18 e5 and despite the exchange of two pairs of minor pieces – helpful to the side with a space disadvantage – White was obviously somewhat better, though the game was drawn in 34 moves.

10...e5

10...♗g4?! is the prelude to an extremely speculative sacrifice. At a less exalted level, and particularly when playing at a fast time limit, it is perfectly plausible for Black to aim for this variation – just so long as he realises that he's bluffing! For example, 11 f3 ♗xf3 (forced since if 11...♗d7? Black loses a clear pawn: 12 ♘xd4 cxd4 13 ♗xd4 ♗xd4 [13...♗xa4 14 ♕xa4+ is check] 14 ♕xd4) 12 gxf3 ♘xf3+ 13 ♔f2 ♘e5, when Black has two pawns for the piece and some short-term prospects against the white king but I really don't believe it if White plays well. P.H.Nielsen-Danielsen, Esbjerg 1997, continued 14 ♗h3! h5 15 ♘g1! g5?! 16 ♘f3 with a clear advantage.

11 dxe6 ♘xe6 12 ♗xg7 ♘xg7 13 ♕d2!

Preparing to attack d6.

13...♘f6 14 f3 ♗e6 15 ♘f4 ♕e7 16 0-0-0 ♖d8 17 ♘c3 0-0 18 g4!

Now aiming to force control of the d5-square. While this position is far from lost, Black is very passive and over the following moves Gelfand gradually asserts more and more control.

18...♘d7 19 h4 ♘b6 20 b3 f6 21 ♘fd5! ♘xd5 22 exd5

Ridding his opponent of the weak d-pawn but in return setting up a juicy target for his pieces on e6.

22...♗c8 23 h5! gxh5

If 23...g5 24 h6 ♘e8 25 ♗d3 would be most unpleasant.

24 ♖e1 ♕f7 25 ♗d3 ♔h8 26 ♕h6 f5 27 gxh5 ♕f6 28 ♕xf6 ♖xf6 29 h6! ♘e8 30 ♖e7 ♖g6 31 ♘e2 ♘f6 32 ♘f4 ♖g3 33 ♖h3 ♖gg8 34 ♘e6

Fixing on the weak f5-pawn.

34...♖d7 35 ♖g7!

Winning the exchange. There are some technical difficulties in the ending in view of Black's extra pawn and compact position – but White is very much favourite to win in the end.

35...♖gxg7 36 hxg7+ ♖xg7 37 ♘xg7 ♔xg7 38 ♖g3+ ♔f7 39 ♔d2 ♗d7 40 ♖g1 ♘g8 41 ♖h1 ♔g7 42 ♖b1 ♘e7 43 b4

Opening up a second front on the queenside.

43...cxb4 44 ♖xb4 b6 45 a4 ♘c8 46 a5 ♔f6 47 f4

Denying the black king either dark square and incidentally fixing the f5-pawn on a light square where it blocks its bishop and is firmly in the white bishop's sights.

47...♔e7 48 ♖b1 bxa5 49 ♖h1 ♔f6 50 ♖xh7 ♘e7 51 ♔e3 ♗e8 52 ♖h8 ♗d7 53 ♖d8 ♗c8 54 ♖xd6+

The end. Azmaiparashvili carried on for several more hopeless moves.

54...♔f7 55 ♗c2 ♘g6 56 ♖c6 ♗d7 57 ♖c7 ♔e8 58 ♖xd7! 1-0

Of course this wasn't all forced from the opening, but the whole business is very depressing for Black; hence his attempts at more active play in the following games.

> ## Game 25
> ### Levitt-Efimov
> *Amantea 1991*

1 d4 d6 2 e4 g6 3 c4 ♗g7 4 ♘c3 ♘c6 5 d5 ♘d4 6 ♗e3 c5 7 ♘ge2 ♕b6 8 ♘a4 ♕a5+ 9 ♗d2 ♕a6 10 ♘xd4

Of course 10 ♗c3 is bad (that's the whole point of 9...♕a6) after 10...♗d7! 11 b3 ♗xa4 12 bxa4:

a) 12...♕xc4? is a bad mistake, e.g. 13 ♖c1 ♘xe2 14 ♗xg7 ♕xc1 (or 14...♕b4+ 15 ♔xe2 and White wins) 15 ♗xe2!

♕xd1+ 16 ♔xd1 f6 17 g4! ♘h6 (or 17...♔f7 18 ♗xh8 ♘h6 19 g5! and White wins) 18 ♗xh6 ♔f7 and White won in a dozen more moves in A.Johannes-P.Van Hoolandt, Belgian League 1996/97.

b) Simply 12...♘f6! is very strong since 13 ♘xd4? fails to 13...♘xe4!, so White has to acquiesce in 13 ♘g3 0-0 when Black has a splendid game.

10...♗xd4 11 ♘c3

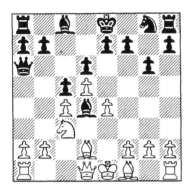

11...♗d7

11...♗g7 is no worse than this move but after 12 ♗d3 (12 ♘b5 ♕b6 is Game 26) Black must take the precaution of playing 12...♗d7! Instead 12...♘f6? walks into 13 ♘b5!, i.e. 13...♕b6?? (the very ugly 13...♔d8 was absolutely forced) 14 ♕a4 ♗d7 (or 14...0-0 15 ♗a5 ♕a6 16 ♘c7 b5 17 cxb5 winning) 15 ♗a5 ♕a6 16 ♘c7+ and Black resigned in Degraeve-Baudot, European Club Championship 1996. Ljubojevic's 11...♕b6!? is the subject of the next main game.

11...♗d7 is the 'normal' move, and if Black is going to play it then I suppose he should really do so at once. There's a potentially rather large psychological advantage in trying it on with 11...♕b6 and after 12 ♗d3 reverting to 12...♗d7, but from a technical point of view it seems better to delay committing the queen.

12 ♗d3 ♘f6

Although it must be playable, the re-

treat 12...♗g7 is rather tame. Black should instead try to make something of the bishop's position on d4, where it is rather exposed but also quite aggravating for White. After 12...♗g7 the game Lautier-Spraggett, 6th matchgame, Correze 1989, continued 13 0-0 ♘f6 14 ♕e2 0-0 15 f4 ♘e8 16 e5, when White had a space advantage but Black's position was still fairly robust.

13 0-0 0-0 14 ♘e2

The most forcing but the calm 14 h3! may be better.

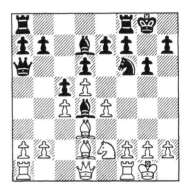

14...b5?!

Launching into a very messy tactical sequence but I suspect that other lines were better:

a) If 14...♗xb2 15 ♖b1 gives very good compensation since the bishop gets tracked down after 15...♗d4 (15...♗e5 is also possible first if Black judges that is on balance after 16 f4 ♗d4+ 17 ♘xd4 cxd4 the inclusion of 16 f4 is unfavourable to White – but I don't really believe this) 16 ♘xd4 cxd4 17 ♗h6 ♖fe8 18 c5 is very unclear. Black can try to keep his structure with 18...♕a3 or take the money with 18...♕xa2 19 cxd6 exd6 20 h3 ♘xe4 21 ♗xe4 ♖xe4 22 ♖xb7, when Black has several pawns but the dark squares round his king are pretty sick.

b) 14...♗g4 is safer and now:

b1) Levitt gives 15 ♗h6! ♖fe8 16 h3

forcing 16...♗xe2 17 ♕xe2, when White has successfully untangled and defended his b-pawn. Even so 17...♘d7 is very messy, e.g. 18 ♔h1 (if 18 ♖fc1 ♘e5 19 ♗b1 ♕b6 20 ♖c2 ♘xc4! 21 ♕xc4 ♗xb2; or 18 ♖ac1 ♕xa2 but conceivably 18 b3!?) 18...♘e5 19 f4 ♘xd3 20 ♕xd3 ♗xb2!? 21 ♖ab1 and either 21...♗g7 or maybe 21...♗h8, when White has a lot of play for the pawn but Black also reasonable defensive chances. Black could also have moved his rook to b8 rather than e8, when 20...b5 is an option instead of grabbing the pawn with 20...♗xb2. Although I would generally prefer to play actively rather than grabbing material, I suspect that in this case it is worse, e.g. 21 f5 bxc4 22 ♕f3 ♗f6 23 g4 c3 24 bxc3 ♕c4 25 g5 ♗e5 26 fxg6 fxg6 27 ♖ae1 and it looks like Black will be mated.

b2) I also wondered about the wild exchange sacrifice 16 ♔h1 ♗xb2 (16...♗xe2 17 ♕xe2 gives White an extra tempo compared to the previous line) 17 f3!? ♗xa1 18 ♕xa1 ♗d7 19 g4. I don't really believe it but there are entertaining lines like 19...♕a3 20 ♘f4 ♖eb8 21 g5 ♘e8 22 e5 b5 23 e6 fxe6 24 dxe6 ♗xe6 25 ♕e1 ♗f7 26 ♕xe7 ♘g7 27 ♕f6 ♘e8 with a forced draw by repetition.

15 ♘xd4!

15 cxb5 ♗xb5 16 ♗xb5 ♕xb5 17 ♘xd4 cxd4 18 ♗h6 ♖fb8 would be excellent for Black.

15...bxc4 16 ♘c6 ♗xc6

Forced since if 16...cxd3? 17 ♘xe7+ ♔g7 18 ♗c3 the pin will be decisive.

17 ♗c2 ♗d7 18 h3?!

Levitt criticises this preferring not 18 ♗c3? ♘g4! (en route via e5 to d3) but the very direct 18 f4! His assessment depends upon just how playable Black's improvement is after the next diagram.

18...♘e8 19 f4 ♘c7 20 f5

If 20 a4, to keep the knight away from d4, 20...e6! gives counterplay.

20...♘b5 21 f6!?

After 21 ♗h6 ♘d4! White would probably eschew the exchange, aiming to transpose back into the game after 22 f6, though then the manic 22...♖fb8, intending 23 fxe7 ♖xb2, is very unclear.

21...exf6 22 ♖xf6 ♘d4 23 ♗h6 ♕b6 24 ♖b1

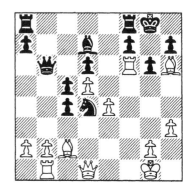

24...♖fe8?

A mistake because now White manages to consolidate his grip on the f6-square, after which the black king must soon perish. Instead Levitt recommends 24...♕d8 25 ♖xd6 'unclear'. Black could then continue 25...♖e8 and if 26 ♗a4 (26 ♖xd7 ♕xd7 27 ♗a4 ♕e7 28 ♗xe8 ♖xe8 is quite good for Black) 26...♕h4 27 ♗xd7 ♕xh6 28 ♗xe8 ♖xe8 he has quite serious compensation for the exchange – particularly if White is running short of time.

In fact, 25 ♕f1 is also possible, e.g. 25...♘xc2 26 ♖xd6 ♘d4 (again maybe 26...♕h4!? 27 ♗xf8 ♖xf8 28 ♖xd7 ♕xe4) 27 ♗xf8 (27 ♖xd7? ♕xd7 28 ♕f6 ♘e6! 29 dxe6 fxe6 30 ♗xf8 ♖xf8 is good for Black) 27...♔xf8. In any case, Black had to try this because now the game more or less plays itself.

25 ♕d2 ♖e7 26 ♕f2 ♕d8

Not 26...♗e8? 27 ♖xg6+! hxg6 (or 27...fxg6 28 ♕f8 mate) 28 ♕f6 and mates.

27 ♖f1 ♕e8 28 ♗b1 ♖b8 29 ♔h1 ♖xe4

29...♖b6? loses at once to 30 ♖xg6+!

Perhaps 29...♗b5 30 ♖xd6 f5 31 exf5 was worth a try, though after 31...c3, 32 fxg6! is absolutely terminal.

30 ♗xe4 ♕xe4 31 ♖f4! ♕xd5 32 ♖xd4! 1-0

The thematic finale. Black resigned in view of 32...cxd4 (or 32...♕xd4 33 ♕xf7+) 33 ♕f6! ♕e5 34 ♕xf7+ ♔h8 35 ♕f8+!

Although White won this game well, it shouldn't be too discouraging for Black players since Black passed up several unclear and very possibly playable lines along the way.

Game 26
Andruet-Todorcevic
Montpellier 1989

---

1 d4 g6 2 c4 ♗g7 3 ♘c3 d6 4 e4 ♘c6 5 d5 ♘d4 6 ♗e3 c5 7 ♘ge2 ♕b6 8 ♘a4 ♕a5+ 9 ♗d2 ♕a6 10 ♘xd4 ♗xd4 11 ♘c3 ♕b6!?

This wonderful move was, I believe, introduced by Ljubomir Ljubojevic (see the notes to Black's 12th move below).

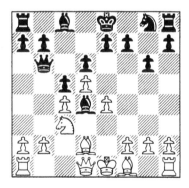

12 ♘b5

The most critical move, but I suspect that the best move is the simple 12 ♗d3. Now taking on b2 is very bad and 12...♗g7 will at best transpose to Lautier-Spraggett in the notes to the previous game, so I wondered whether Black could continue the provocation with 12...♘f6!?

My rough analysis isn't very cheery for Black, but even so it seems worth showing as an example of the very sharp play which can develop in this and similar lines. After 13 ♘b5 ♘g4 (trying to force White to capture) play might continue:

a) 14 ♕a4? 0-0! (not 14...♗d7 15 ♗a5 ♕a6 16 ♘c7+ ♔f8 17 ♕a3 ♗xb2 18 ♕xb2 ♕xa5+ 19 ♔e2 and White wins) 15 ♗a5 ♕a6 is very bad for White:

a1) 16 ♘c7 ♗d7! totally refutes White's play because of 17 ♕a3 ♗xb2.

a2) 16 ♘xd4 cxd4 17 ♕a3 ♘e5 leaves White all over the place. If 18 ♗f1 ♘xc4 simply wins a pawn.

b) 14 ♘xd4 cxd4 15 b3 0-0! prepares 16 0-0 (16 ♗c1 looks absurd though 16...♕b4+ 17 ♔e2 isn't absolutely clear) 16...♘e3! 17 fxe3 dxe3 18 ♔h1 (18 c5? ♕xc5 simply loses a pawn) 18...exd2 19 ♕xd2 when Black has a reasonable game.

c) But the best is the very simple 14 0-0! preparing to capture on d4 next move and then play ♗c1 when there is no check on b4. This seems to yield a clear advantage. For example:

c1) 14...♗xb2? 15 ♖b1 ♗g7 16 ♕a4 0-0 17 ♗a5 ♕a6 18 ♘c7 and White wins.

c2) 14...0-0 15 ♘xd4 cxd4 16 ♗c1 f5 17 exf5 with a clear advantage.

c3) 14...♗g7 15 ♕a4 0-0 16 ♗a5 ♕a6 17 ♘c7 ♗d7 18 ♕a3 ♗xb2 19 ♕xb2 ♕xa5 20 ♘xa8 again with a clear advantage.

c4) 14...♘e5 is more sensible, but after 15 ♘xd4 (15...♘xd3 16 ♘b5 ♘e5 17 b3 also gives White a large clear advantage) 15...cxd4 16 ♗c1 Black has plenty of time to prepare something against White's plan of b2-b3, ♗b2 moving the light-squared bishop and removing the d-pawn, but even so White is very much in the driving seat.

The conclusion is that while 11...♕b6 is a splendid idea, it's a little 'less accurate' than 11...♗d7 not only because the line which Black is daring White to play may not be too wonderful, but much more importantly because White can profitably duck the challenge.

12...♗g7!

12...♗xb2? was played in the stem game of this variation. After 13 ♖b1 ♗g7 14 ♕a4 ♔f8 (forced – 14...♗d7 loses to 15 ♗a5 ♕a6 16 ♘c7+ ♔f8 17 ♕a3) 15 ♗a5 ♕a6 16 ♕a3! b6 17 ♘c7 ♕xa5+ 18 ♕xa5 bxa5 White has:

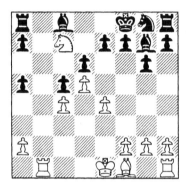

a) 19 ♔d2! now gives a big edge since the bishop can't get to b4 blocking the b-file. This refinement has been enough to put 12...♗xb2? out of commission.

b) But in the superb game Polugayevsky-Ljubojevic, Reykjavik 1987, Black's boldness was rewarded, as Polugayevsky couldn't resist the temptation and captured on a8 immediately with 19 ♘xa8? ♗c3+ 20 ♔d1 ♘f6 21 ♗d3 (if 21 ♖b8 ♔g7 22 f3 ♘d7! repulses the invader – but not 22...♘xe4? 23 ♔c2! ♘f2 24 ♗xc3 ♘xh1 25 ♔d2 when the knight is trapped on h1) and now 21...♗b4! (not 21...♔g7 22 a3) blocked the b-file with equality.

13 ♕a4 ♗d7 14 ♗a5 ♕a6

The position is on a knife edge. Black has now been forced to position his men ready to be family forked, but as a result of the pin and various hanging white pieces it turns out that the best that White can achieve – and indeed the only thing that he can do – is to take the exchange in return for serious compensation:

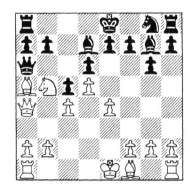

15 ♘c7+ ♔f8 16 ♕a3 ♗xb2! 17 ♕xb2 ♕xa5+ 18 ♔e2 ♖c8 19 ♕xh8

19 ♘e6+ ♗xe6 20 ♕xh8 ♗d7 is also possible, reaching the same position as in the game except that the black rook is on c8 rather than c7. There may be some exotic reason why this is important but I can't see it and suspect that it's irrelevant.

19...♖xc7 20 ♕b2 b5 21 ♔e3

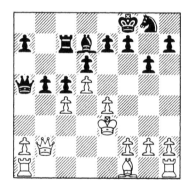

My strong impression is that Black *can't* win by direct attack here. But he already has a pawn for the exchange and after sensible moves should continue to hold very reasonable compensation even if White manages to get his king into safety.

21...♖b7

Possibly an improvement on the earlier game Lautier-Chabanon, Rouen 1987. There Black played 21...f5!?, which exposes the white king further but also opens lines up towards his own monarch. After 22 f3 fxe4 23 fxe4 ♞f6 24 h3 ♖b7 25 ♗d3! Chabanon played for mate with 25...bxc4?, but after 26 ♕xb7 ♕c3 27 ♕b1 Lautier had defended himself. The game continued 27...♗b5 (27...♕d4+ 28 ♔e2 doesn't help, e.g. 28...cxd3+ 28...♗b5 29 ♗c2! and White wins – 29 ♕xd3 ♕b2+ 30 ♔f3 ♗b5 31 ♕e3 etc.) 28 ♔f3 ♕xd3+ 29 ♕xd3 cxd3 30 ♖hb1 ♗c4 31 ♖b8+ ♔f7 32 ♔e3 and White went on to win.

Instead Black should just play the ending with 25...♖b6 26 ♕d2 ♕xd2+! (not 26...♕a3 27 ♖ac1 bxc4 28 ♖c3 ♕b2 29 ♕xb2 ♖xb2 30 ♖c2) 27 ♔xd2 bxc4 28 ♗c2 e6, when he seems to have enough play in the centre even though White can force the exchange of rooks.

22 cxb5?

22 ♗d3 was much better, as in Lautier-Chabanon above:

a) 22...bxc4 still doesn't work due to 23 ♕xb7 ♕c3 24 ♕b1 ♕d4+ 25 ♔e2 cxd3+ 26 ♕xd3 ♕b2+ 27 ♔f3 etc.

b) But 22...♞f6 is quite playable, e.g. 23 f3 ♖b6 24 ♕d2 ♕a3 25 ♖ac1 bxc4 26 ♖c3 ♕a6 27 ♗xc4 ♗b5 28 ♗xb5 ♖xb5 29 ♖b3 ♖xb3+ 30 axb3 ♕b6 31 ♖b1 when White is a little better but would have to play very well to make something of it.

22...♗xb5 23 ♗xb5 ♖xb5 24 ♕d2 ♖b4 25 f3 ♞f6

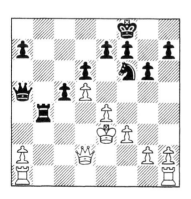

26 ♖hd1

To protect the queen, for if 26 ♖hb1? ♞g4+! 27 fxg4 ♖xe4+!

26...♕a3+ 27 ♕d3 ♕b2 28 ♖ab1 ♕xg2

With a clear advantage since Black already has more than enough material for the exchange and with the disappearance of this pawn the white king will never find more than temporary peace against the marauding queen and knight.

29 ♖xb4 cxb4 30 ♖d2 ♕h3

30...♕g1+ looks better.

31 ♔d4! ♞d7 32 f4 ♕h4 33 ♕e3 ♕f6+ 34 ♔c4 ♕a1 35 ♕d4 ♕f1+ 36 ♔xb4 f6

White has done very well over the last few moves but even so Black has plenty of play and when White pushes his luck it is he who goes over.

37 e5?

Trying to destabilise Black but the result is the opposite.

37...dxe5 38 fxe5 ♞xe5 39 ♕c3 ♕b1+ 40 ♔a3?!

40 ♔a4 would deny the queen an excellent square.

40...♕b5! 41 ♖d4 ♞f7! 42 ♕c6 ♞d6

Completing an excellent regrouping. Not only does the knight menace the enemy king from d6 but it protects its own monarch and most importantly directly prevents d6.

43 ♖b4 ♕d3+ 44 ♖b3 ♕d2 45 ♖b2 ♕f4 46 ♖c2 a5 47 ♕c5 ♔f7 48 ♔b3

If 48 ♕xa5 ♞c4+ 49 ♖xc4 ♕xc4, when although the a-pawn could be annoying Black has wonderful winning chances.

48...a4+ 49 ♔a3 ♕e4 50 ♖c3 f5 51 h3 g5 52 ♔b2?

Allowing an immediate win.

52...♕e5! 53 ♔b1 ♞e4 54 ♖e3 f4 0-1

> *Game 27*
> **Ivkov-Hübner**
> *West Germany 1975*

1 d4 g6 2 c4 ♗g7 3 ♞c3 d6 4 e4 ♞c6 5

d5 ♘d4 6 ♘ge2 c5 7 ♗e3 ♕b6 8 ♕d2 f5!?

Immediately attacking White's centre. This is a very good idea if it can be made to work, but apart from the stem game here, I could find only one other theoretically uninteresting example in the notes since people have presumably been put off the line by the improvement for White mentioned by Ivkov in *Informator 20*. It's a shame but my feeling is that this line is in serious need of inspiration if it is to be resuscitated.

Black would like to play 8...♗g4?, of course, since if he can exchange off two pairs of minor pieces or even better just bishop for knight and maintain the cavalry on d4 then he will be doing splendidly. But unfortunately after 9 f3! the abject 9...♗d7 seems to be forced since after the consequent 9...♗xf3? the tactics heavily, indeed apparently decisively, favour White, i.e. 10 ♘a4! ♕a6 (if 10...♕b4 simply 11 ♘xd4 ♕xd2+ 12 ♗xd2 ♗xe4 13 ♘b5 or 13 ♘f3 wins a piece for only two pawns) 11 ♘xd4 cxd4 12 ♗xd4 ♗xd4 13 ♕xd4 and now:

a) 13...♘f6 14 c5 ♕a5+ 15 ♘c3 dxc5 16 ♕e5! and Black was in dire trouble in Timman-Suttles, Hastings 1973.

b) Since that continuation is so foul for Black, I had a go at making 13...♕xa4 work. Unfortunately, however, the very best that Black can rationally hope for after this is perpetual check; and I believe that accurate play denies him even this, e.g. 14 ♕xh8 ♕b4+ 15 ♔f2 ♗xe4 16 ♕xg8+ ♔d7 and now:

b1) 17 ♕xa8 ♕xb2+ 18 ♔e3 (18 ♗e2 ♕d4+ 19 ♔g3 ♕e5+ looks drawn too) 18...♕c3+ 19 ♔xe4 f5+ 20 ♔f4 ♕e5+ 21 ♔f3 ♕e4+ 22 ♔f2 ♕d4+ 23 ♔e2 ♕xc4+ must surely be perpetual.

b2) 17 ♕xf7 ♕xb2+ 18 ♗e2 ♕d4+ 19 ♔g3 ♕e3+ 20 ♗f3 ♕g5+ 21 ♗g4+ ♗f5 22 h3 ♕e3+ 23 ♗f3 ♕e5+ is also I believe a

draw.

b3) But 17 ♕g7! looks winning, e.g. 17...♕b6+ 18 ♔e1 (18 ♔e2 f6 19 b3 ♕d4 20 ♖d1 ♕e5 21 ♖d3 also looks good enough) and now:

b31) If 18...f6 19 ♗e2! ♗xg2 20 ♗g4+ f5 21 ♗xf5+! gxf5 22 ♕xg2.

b32) 18...♕e3+ 19 ♔d1 f6 20 ♕f7 and:

b321) 20...♗f5 21 ♗e2 ♖f8!? 22 ♕xf8 ♗c2+ 23 ♔xc2 ♕xe2+ 24 ♔b3 ♕d3+ 25 ♔b4 ♕d2+ 26 ♔a4! wins.

b323) 20...♕d4+ 21 ♔e1 ♗f5 22 ♗e2 ♕e3 23 ♖f1 ♖f8 24 ♕xf8 ♗d3 25 ♖f2 ♗xe2 26 ♕xe7+! (26 ♖xe2 ♕g1+ 27 ♔d2 ♕d4 is perpetual) 26...♕xe7 27 ♖xe2 with excellent winning chances.

9 0-0-0!

This looks best. The alternatives are:

a) 9 ♘a4 ♕b4 10 ♕xb4 ♘c2+ 11 ♔d2 ♘xb4 is fine for Black.

b) 9 f3?! was played in a game Holstein-Bogdanov, Copenhagen open 1991, but after 9...fxe4 10 fxe4 ♗g4 Black already has a fine game and in fact went on to win in 36 moves.

9...♘xe2+ 10 ♗xe2

10...♘f6

Allowing an unfortunate exchange of bishops. My feeling is that Black should be looking for an improvement here but the problem is that if he tries to prevent ♗h6 with ...h7-h6 or ...h7-h5 perhaps then the g6-pawn is weakened and this will certainly be a problem, at least until Black gets castled. If 10...fxe4 11 ♘xe4 and:

a) 11...♗f5 12 ♘c3 ♘f6 (if 12...♕a5 maybe 13 g4 ♗d7 14 g5!?, playing against the g8-knight but perhaps 12...h5!?) 13 ♗h6 transposes to Ivkov-Hübner.

b) 11...♘f6 12 ♘c3 (better than 12 ♘xf6+ ♗xf6 13 ♗g5 ♕b4 14 ♕xb4 ♗xg5+ 15 ♕d2 ♗xd2+ 16 ♔xd2 with equality) 12...♗f5 (12...h6 13 ♗d3) 13 ♗h6 again transposes.

11 exf5 ♗xf5 12 ♗h6!

By exchanging bishops, White reduces the dynamism of Black's position and also removes some of the clutter on the e-file as he prepares to target the e7-pawn.

12...♗xh6 13 ♕xh6 0-0-0 14 ♖he1 ♖hf8 15 ♗f3?

A mistake because Black now gets serious counterplay against the c4-pawn. Ivkov indicated 15 ♗f1 with a clear advantage – this looks like rather a big assessment but certainly the e6-square and e7-pawn are weak so it is at least slightly better for White.

15...♕a6 16 ♕h4

Certainly not 16 ♖xe7? ♘g8.

16...♖f7 17 ♖e3 ♖g8!

Ivkov already assesses this as somewhat better for Black.

18 ♖de1 g5 19 ♕g3 ♖gg7

19...h5 also looks quite nice.

20 ♗e2 ♔d8 21 a3 ♕a5 22 h3

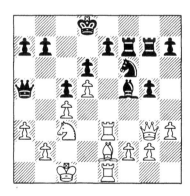

22...a6

As Ivkov pointed out, this was the moment to strike with 22...b5! and now:

a) The point is that if 23 cxb5?! ♘xd5! 24 ♘xd5? ♕xe1+ 25 ♗d1 ♕a5 26 ♖xe7 ♖xe7 27 ♕xd6+ ♔e8 White has at most a draw and probably not even that.

b) But if White continues 23 ♗g4 ♗xg4 24 hxg4 and if 24...b4 (24...bxc4!? is also quite possible) not 25 axb4? ♕xb4 when the c4-pawn drops off, but simply 25 ♘b1 when although the black position has improved White still has a perfectly reasonable game.

23 ♗g4 ♗xg4 24 hxg4 ♘d7 25 f3 ♖f4

25...b5!? was still possible though not, of course, as effective as in the previous note.

26 ♖e4 ♘e5 27 ♔c2 ♖gf7?

A mistake, presumably in time trouble.

28 ♖xe5!

This thematic sacrifice gives White not only a strong initiative but also much the better structure for only a very small material investment. In time trouble, the black position is now critical, though it looks as though there were still defences before it slipped to lost.

28...dxe5 29 ♖xe5 h6 30 ♖e6 ♖7f6 31 ♕e1 ♖xc4?

An attempt to create counterplay which ought to have lost. 31...♕c7 32 d6 is terminal, but there doesn't seem to be a knockout after 31...♖xe6 when:

a) 32 ♕xe6 ♖f6! defends and if 33 ♕g8+ ♔d7 34 ♘e4 ♖b6!

b) 32 dxe6 is very menacing but neither:

b1) 32...♖xc4 33 ♕e5 ♔c8 34 ♕h8+ ♕d8 35 ♕xh6 ♖d4 36 ♕xg5 ♕d6.

b2) Nor even 32...♕c7 33 ♘d5 ♖xc4+ 34 ♔b3 ♕d6 35 ♕a5+ b6 36 ♕xa6 ♖a4!! 37 ♔xa4 ♕c6+ 38 ♕b5 ♕a8+ 39 ♔b3 ♕xd5+ 40 ♕c4 ♕d1+ 41 ♔a2 ♔c7 (to attack the e6-pawn) 42 b4! is totally clear.

32 ♖xe7 ♖xc3+ 33 bxc3 ♕a4+ 34 ♔d2 ♖b6 35 ♕e5 ♕f4+

The only chance since if 35...♖b2+ 36 ♔e1 ♖b1+ 37 ♔f2 ♖b2+ 38 ♔g1 the king escapes, after which White immediately delivers mate.

36 ♕xf4 gxf4

This ending should be winning though Hübner did just manage to salvage the draw.

37 ♖h7 c4 38 ♔c2 ♖b3 39 ♖xh6

39 a4! should win.

39...♖xa3 40 ♖h7?

40 ♖f6 was still good enough.

40...b5 41 ♖f7 ♖a2+ 42 ♔b1 ♖xg2 43 ♖xf4 ♔e7! 44 ♖e4+ ♔d6 45 ♖e6+ ♔xd5 46 ♖xa6 ♔e5 47 ♖a2 ♖g1+ 48 ♔b2 ♔f4 49 ♖a5 ♔xf3 50 ♖xb5 ♖xg4 51 ♔a3 ♔e4

And they agreed the draw.

Game 28
Farago-Keene
Esbjerg 1981

---

1 d4 g6 2 c4 ♗g7 3 ♘c3 d6 4 e4 ♘c6 5 d5 ♘d4 6 ♗e3 c5 7 ♘ge2 ♕b6 8 ♕d2 ♘f6 9 ♘xd4?!

This is what Black is hoping for, and although the mess which results is far from totally clear, White would be unlikely to play 9 ♘xd4 'voluntarily', especially given that 9 f3 gives him a good game (see Game 29). However, it does occur from time to time and if Black is going to set this 'trap' then he should know something about the possible consequences.

9...cxd4 10 ♗xd4

10 ♕xd4 is perfectly playable. After 10...♕xb2 White has:

a) 11 ♘b5? ♘xe4! 12 ♕xb2 ♗xb2 13 ♖b1 ♗c3+ 14 ♘xc3 (14 ♔d1 ♗a5) 14...♘xc3 yields Black a pawn for rather minimal compensation.

b) 11 ♖b1 ♕a3 12 ♕d2 ♕a5 13 f3 0-0 14 ♘b5 ♕xd2+ 15 ♔xd2 b6 gave Black a very comfortable position in Donner-Ree, Wijk aan Zee 1972.

10...♘xe4! 11 ♗xb6 ♘xd2

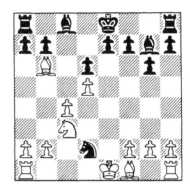

12 ♘b5!?

A brave move initiating immense complications, which, however, seem to be clearly in Black's favour. The alternatives are:

a) 12 ♗e3? allows 12...♘xf1 13 ♖xf1 ♗xc3+ 14 bxc3 b6 when the organic weakness of the c-pawns leaves White with an absolutely vile position.

b) 12 ♔xd2 axb6 is reasonably playable though. This position would be pleasant for White if he could exchange off the light-squared bishops and ideally keep on the other pair of minor pieces since he would have a nice plan of fixing the doubled pawn on b6 and then gradually aiming to attack it. But of course Black should not allow this. Instead he can use the dynamism inherent in the two bishops to annoy White. And he should be able at least to equalise by ...e7-e6 at the right moment with ...♗xc3+ if necessary before taking on d5.

12...axb6!?

Accepting the challenge. Instead 12...♔d7 is safe and gives a very reasonable position, e.g. 13 ♘c7 (13 ♔xd2 axb6 14 ♔c2 ♔d8 is about equal; and 13 ♘xa7/♗xa7 ♗xb2 14 ♖d1 ♘xf1 should also be very playable for Black) 13...♗xb2 14 ♖d1 ♗c3 15 ♘xa8 (if 15 ♖xd2 ♖b8 16 ♗xa7 ♔xc7 17 ♗xb8+ ♔xb8 18 ♔d1

♗xd2 19 ♔xd2 ♗d7 White's weakened queenside give Black the advantage) 15...♘c4+ 16 ♔e2 ♘xb6 17 ♘xb6+ axb6 must be fine for Black.

13 ♘c7+ ♔d8 14 ♘xa8 ♗xb2 15 ♖d1 ♘e4

As long as the knight can't escape via b6 and take the bishop, Black will have massive compensation for the exchange. Although the lines are very complex, it would be most surprising if any were good for White – there are simply too many possibilities at Black's disposal.

16 ♗d3

16 f3 ♗c3+ 17 ♔e2 ♗a5 is simple and strong. 16 ♘xb6 is much more interesting but ultimately seems excellent for Black, e.g. 16...♗c3+ 17 ♔e2 ♗a5 18 ♘a4 ♗d7 19 ♖d4 and now 19...f5 looks best: 20 f3 ♘f6 21 c5 dxc5 22 ♘xc5 ♗b6 23 ♖c4 ♗b5 24 ♘xb7+ ♔d7 25 ♔d2 ♗xc4 26 ♗xc4 ♖b8 (26...♔c7 27 ♖e1! ♔xb7 28 ♖xe7+ ♔b8 gives White reasonable play for the piece) 27 ♗a6 ♖a8 28 ♗b5+ ♔c7 29 a4 ♘xd5 30 ♖c1+ ♔xb7 31 ♗c6+ ♔a7 32 ♗xa8 ♔xa8 and Black should win.

16...♘c5 17 ♘xb6

This looks like the place to look for an improvement but if e.g.

a) 17 0-0 ♗g4 18 f3 ♘xd3 19 ♖xd3 ♗f5 20 ♖dd1 ♗a3 21 ♔h1 ♗c5 22 g4 ♗c2 23 ♖d2 ♗a4 24 ♖b1 b5! 25 cxb5 ♔d7 winning the knight.

b) 17 ♔e2 ♘a4 18 ♔e3 ♗a3.

c) 17 ♗c2 ♗c3+ 18 ♔e2 ♗a5 19 ♖b1 ♗f5! (the important thing is to evacuate the bishop so that if the knight emerges on b6 it has nothing to take) 20 ♗xf5 gxf5 21 ♖b5 ♘a4 22 ♖hb1 White will at best get a fairly balanced rook ending.

17...♗g4 18 f3 ♗xf3! 19 gxf3 ♗c3+ 20 ♔e2 ♔c7

Trapping the beast.

21 h4

21 ♖b1 ♗a5 doesn't help White.

21...♔xb6

Whereas White has no real targets for his rooks or chances of setting up a passed pawn, Black already has a pawn for the exchange and much the better pawn structure. So although White can still fight, his opponent has excellent winning chances.

22 h5 ♖a8 23 ♗b1

If 23 hxg6 ♖xa2+ 24 ♔f1 hxg6 25 ♖h7 ♘xd3 26 ♖xd3 ♗f6 27 ♖xf7 ♔c5 with a big advantage.

23...♗f6 24 hxg6 hxg6 25 ♖h7 ♘a4 26 ♖c1 ♖f8 27 ♗e4!?

Offering a pawn to get active.

27...♘c3+ 28 ♔d3 ♘xa2 29 ♖b1+ ♔c7 30 c5 dxc5 31 d6+ ♔xd6 32 ♖xb7 ♔e5 33 ♖h2

33 ♔c4 was better.

33...c4+!?

Returning a pawn to get co-ordinated.

34 ♔xc4 ♖c8+

35 ♔d3?

The obvious move but as by Keene showed in *Informator 32*, 35 ♔b3! is a much tougher defence since after 35...♘c1+ (35...♘c3 36 ♖c2 ♔f4 37 ♗d5!) 36 ♔b2 ♔f4+ 37 ♔b1 the knight is trapped. If then 37...♖c3 38 ♖c2 ♖xc2 39 ♔xc2 ♘e2 40 ♔d3 ♘d4 41 ♖b4 ♘xf3 42 ♗xg6+ ♔g5 43 ♗e4 White must be able to draw.

35...♘c1+ 36 ♔d2 ♗g5+ 37 ♔e1 f5

Now Black can co-ordinate his forces and it's all over.

38 ♗b1 ♖c3 39 ♖g2 ♔f6 40 ♖b6+ e6 41 ♖c2

41 ♖xe6+ ♔xe6 42 ♖xg5 ♔f6 43 ♖g3 ♘b3 should be a technical win.

41...♖e3+! 42 ♔f2

If 42 ♔f1 ♖xf3+ 43 ♔g2 ♖b3!

42...♘d3+ 43 ♔g3 ♗f4+ 44 ♔g2 ♘e1+ 45 ♔f2 ♘xc2 46 ♗xc2 ♖c3

The rest was pretty simple.

47 ♖b2 ♗e5 48 ♖a2 ♗d4+ 49 ♔g2 ♔e5 50 ♗d1 ♔f4 51 ♖c2 ♖d3 52 ♗e2 ♖e3 53 ♖a2 e5 54 ♖d2 g5 55 ♖a2 ♖c3 56 ♗d1 ♖c1 57 ♗e2 ♖g1+ 58 ♔h2 g4 59 fxg4 fxg4 60 ♗c4 g3+ 61 ♔h3 ♖h1+ 62 ♔g2 ♖h2+ 63 ♔f1 ♖xa2 64 ♗xa2 ♔f3 0-1

Game 29
R.Hernandez-Calderin
Colon 1991

1 d4 g6 2 c4 ♗g7 3 ♘c3 d6 4 e4 ♘c6 5 d5 ♘d4 6 ♗e3 c5 7 ♘ge2 ♕b6 8 ♕d2 ♘f6 9 f3 ♘d7 10 ♖d1

Alternatively:

a) 10 ♘a4 isn't unplayable due to 10...♕a6 11 ♘xd4 ♕xa4 12 ♘b5 0-0 13 ♗h6 ♗xh6 14 ♕xh6 a6 (14...♕b4+ 15 ♕d2 ♕xd2+ 16 ♔xd2 is fine for Black too) 15 ♘c3 ♕b4 16 ♕d2 f5 17 exf5 ♖xf5 18 ♗e2 ♘e5 19 b3 b5 20 cxb5 g5 and Black was doing well in Donner-Timman, Wijk aan Zee 1974, though Donner later caught

Timman in some tactics and won.

b) 10 0-0-0 forces 10...♘xe2+ 11 ♗xe2, but gives Black much more counterplay than if the white king takes refuge on the kingside.

10...0-0 11 b3!

A novelty at the time, this is much more testing than 11 ♘xd4 cxd4 12 ♗xd4 ♗xd4 13 ♕xd4 ♕xb2 when Black is comfortable.

11...♘xe2 12 ♗xe2

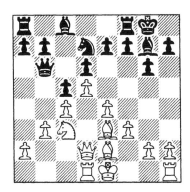

12...♕a5

This must be correct, improving the queen's position with tempo. Here or on the next move, Black may clarify the kingside with ...f7-f5 but the resultant structure with potentially weak pawns on both f5 and e7 is rather unpleasant for him, so I would much prefer instead to initiate play on the queenside as quickly as possible.

After 12...f5 13 exf5 gxf5 Black is threatening 14...f4! so White has:

a) In Sadler-Webster, Dublin Zonal 1993, Matthew reacted with 14 g3 ♕b4 15 ♖c1 ♘e5 16 0-0 a6 17 ♗h6 ♖f7 18 ♗xg7 ♖xg7 19 ♖fe1 b5 20 f4 ♘g4 21 ♗d3 ♗d7 22 ♖e2 ♖f8 23 ♖ce1 ♖ff7 24 ♘b1 ♕xd2 25 ♘xd2 ♔f8 26 ♘f3 ♔e8 27 ♘g5 with a good ending though Black held on to draw in 55 moves.

b) 14 ♗h6 at once has been suggested and if 14...♖f7 15 0-0 ♘e5 16 ♗xg7 ♖xg7 17 f4 ♘g6 18 ♗h5! Black has no real play to counteract White's structural advantage.

13 ♖c1 a6

Instead 13...f5 14 exf5 gxf5 15 ♗h6 ♖f7 16 ♗xg7 ♖xg7 17 0-0 was also rather grim in a Dutch correspondence game Van den Langenberg-Van Putten, 1995-97. White crashed through after 17....a6 18 f4 ♘f8 19 ♗d3 ♗d7 20 ♕c2 ♖f7 21 ♖ce1 ♘g6 22 ♖e3 ♖af8 23 ♖g3 ♖g7 24 ♘d1 e5 25 dxe6 ♗xe6 26 ♘e3 ♘e7 27 ♖xg7+ ♔xg7 28 g4 ♘c6 29 ♗xf5 ♘d4 30 ♕b2 ♔f7 31 ♗xh7 ♖h8 32 f5 ♖xh7 33 fxe6+ ♔xe6 34 ♕g2 1-0.

Given that he doesn't want to play ...f7-f5, 13...a6 is obvious. But since White now quickly develops a dangerous attack, I wondered if Black could spend a move playing 13...♖e8!? so as to meet 14 ♗h6 with 14...♗h8 (not 14...♗d4? 15 ♘b5!) when I think it must be to Black's advantage to retain the bishops, e.g. 15 h4 a6 16 h5 b5 17 hxg6 fxg6 (or even 17...hxg6!?) with a splendidly messy position which needs to be tested.

14 ♗h6! ♗xh6!?

Drawing the queen to a post where she's well placed to attack Black but is less effective against the ...b7-b5 break.

The immediate 14...b5 15 ♗xg7 ♔xg7 16 cxb5 axb5 17 ♗xb5 is most unconvincing here. While 14...♗d4 15 ♗xf8 ♘xf8 is inventive – and perhaps good for a five-minute game – it surely can't be enough, e.g. 16 ♘d1 ♕d8 17 ♘e3 ♗d7 18 0-0 b5 and although Black has a 'nice position' White has more wood.

15 ♕xh6 b5 16 h4!?

Going for broke. After 16 cxb5 axb5 17 ♗xb5 ♘e5 18 0-0 Black gets reasonable Benko Gambit type compensation – though the exchange of dark-squared bishops must presumably favour White. Since Black seems to have reasonable chances if he improves on move 19, perhaps this is White's most rational course.

16...f6

If 16...♖d8 17 h5 ♘f8 18 e5 dxe5 19 hxg6 fxg6 20 ♔f2! with a vicious attack.

17 f4

Not 17 h5 g5 18 f4 gxf4 19 g3 f3!

17...♖f7! 18 h5 g5 19 fxg5

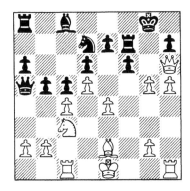

19...♖g7?

Incorrect since now White gets castled after which the knight is unpinned and the g-pawn defended.

Nogueiras and Ruiz Hernandez dismiss 19...fxg5 in *Informator 53* with the comment 20 ♖f1! ♘f6 21 e5! dxe5 22 d6 ♕d8 23 ♘e4! winning. This is wrong in view of 23...♕a5+, but instead of 22 d6 simply 22 ♕xg5+ followed after either 22...♔h8 or 22..♖g7 by 23 ♕xe5 is very good for White.

Instead after 19...fxg5 20 ♖f1 (20 ♕xg5+ ♖g7 21 ♕h4 is also interesting and maybe then 21...h6 to prevent White from playing h5-h6 himself) 20...♘e5! is a much better move, putting the knight where it needs to be. After 21 ♕xg5+ (of course not 21 ♖xf7?? ♘xf7 trapping the queen!) 21...♖g7 is a real mess. Lines like 22 ♕f4 ♗d7 23 h6 ♖xg2! or 22 ♕h4 (eyeing e7) 22...h6 23 ♕f4 b4 24 ♘a4 ♔h7 aren't re-motely clear and could easily end up in Black's favour.

20 gxf6 ♘xf6 21 0-0!

Threatening 22 e5 dxe5 23 d6.

21...b4 22 e5! dxe5 23 ♖xf6

Given as '!!' by Nogueiras and Hernandez, but since the lines aren't quite as clear as they claim I also wondered about 23 d6!? at once:

a) 23...bxc3 24 dxe7:

a1) 24...♕xa2? 25 ♖f2 ♕d2 loses to 26 ♕xf6 (also 26 ♖d1!) 26...♕xc1+ 27 ♗f1 ♗f5 28 ♖xf5 h6 29 ♕f8+ ♔h7 30 ♕xa8 ♕e3+ 31 ♔h1 ♖xe7 32 ♕d8 and wins.

a2) 24...♗b7 is much tougher, though White is better after 25 ♖xf6 ♕c7 26 ♗f3.

b) 23...♗b7!? is also possible immediately, but 24 ♘d5 ♘xd5 (or 24...♗xd5 25 cxd5 with a clear advantage) 25 ♕e6+ ♔h8 26 cxd5 should be very good for White. One nice line goes 26...c4 (26...exd6) 27 dxe7 ♖xg2+? (or 27...♕c5+ 28 ♔h2 ♕xe7 29 ♕xe7 ♖xe7 30 bxc4 with a clear advantage) 28 ♔xg2 ♗xd5+ 29 ♔h2 ♗xe6 30 ♖f8+ ♗g8 31 ♖g1 ♕d5 32 ♗xc4 ♕d2+ 33 ♔h1 and wins.

23...bxc3?

Making it simple for White. Black really had to engage with 23...exf6 24 ♘e4 when:

a) 24...f5 25 ♘f6+ ♔f7 26 ♘e8! and White wins.

b) 24...♗h3 25 ♘xf6+ ♔h8 26 ♘xh7! (26 ♔h2 ♕xa2!) 26...♖xh7! (26...♖xg2+? 27 ♔h1 ♔g8 28 ♖f1! and White wins) 27 ♕f6+ ♔g8 28 gxh3 with a very strong attack.

c) 24...♗f5 25 ♘xf6+ ♔h8 26 ♖f1 ♕xa2 27 ♕e3! ♗h3 28 ♖f2 ♕a1+ 29 ♔h2 ♗c8 30 ♕xc5 ♗b7 31 ♗d3 and White wins (Nogueiras and Hernandez) though Black

can certainly fight a bit, particularly after 31...♕d4 forcing the queens off.

d) 24...♕d8 25 ♘xf6+ ♔h8 26 ♗d3 was marked as winning in *Informator*. But Black has 26...♕f8! 27 ♔h1 ♗f5 (not 27...♗h3? 28 ♘xh7!! ♗xg2+ 29 ♔g1! ♗e4+ 30 ♘g5+ ♔g8 31 ♗xe4 ♕f4 32 ♕xg7+!) 28 ♗xf5 ♖f7 29 ♕xf8+ (29 ♕e3 ♖xf6 30 ♕xe5 ♕h6!) 29...♖fxf8 (29...♖axf8 30 ♘xh7 and White wins) 30 ♘d7 ♖xf5 31 ♘xc5, when White's centre pawns are huge but Black can certainly battle on – my hunch is that he should start with 31...e4, hoping to destabilise matters after 32 ♘xe4?! ♖e8.

24 ♖f2

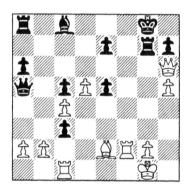

Unfortunately, the game reference in *Informator* ends here and we've been unable to track down the rest. But certainly with a vicious attack and a big structural advantage to boot for no material deficit, White is winning here.

Summary

This is a nice active variation for Black but his biggest problem – and the reason, that, for example, Yasser Seirawan gave up the line – is that White can force a draw and the attempt in Game 22 to avoid it by giving up the queen for two pieces is extremely dubious at best.

In the other lines, Black gets a great deal of counterplay unless White counters exceptionally accurately – as in Game 29. And even then he has a fairly reasonable game.

1 d4 g6 2 e4 ♗g7 3 c4 d6 4 ♘c3 ♘c6 5 d5 ♘d4

6 ♗e3 c5 *(D)* **7 ♘ge2**
    7 dxc6 – *Game 21*
7...♕b6 8 ♘xd4
    8 ♕d2
        8...f5 – *Game 27*
        8...♘f6
            9 ♘xd4 – *Game 28*
            9 f3 – *Game 29*
8...cxd4 9 ♗d2
    9 ♘a4 *(D)*
        9...dxe3 – *Game 22*
        9...♕a5+ – *Game 23*
9...♕a6
    9...♕d8 – *Game 24*
10 ♘xd4 ♗xd4 11 ♘c3 *(D)* **♕b6**
    11...♗d7 – *Game 25*
12 ♘b5 – *Game 26*

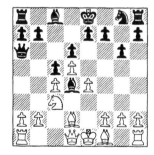

     6...c5   9 ♘a4   11 ♘c3

CHAPTER SIX

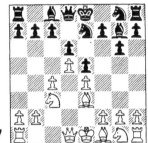

Averbakh Variation with 4...♘c6 5 ♗e3 e5 6 d5 ♘ce7

1 d4 g6 2 c4 ♗g7 3 ♘c3 d6 4 e4 ♘c6 5 ♗e3 e5 6 d5 ♘ce7

This very common line leads to a complex of variations similar to normal King's Indians but with Black arguing that the omission of ...♘f6 is to his advantage since he can play ...f7-f5 at once; it's also sometimes important that on g8 the knight supports ...♗h6.

White must either oppose ...f7-f5 with an immediate g2-g4 (the 'main line') or simply develop, contending that although Black may be pleased to achieve ...f7-f5 so easily, the structure is still quite favourable for White.

a) 7 g4 f5

While 7...f5 is Black's 'principal continuation', it's by no means forced – though the majority of the nearly 200 games in my database with 7 g4 do involve it.

One distinctive plan is to resolve the kingside with 7...♘f6 and if 8 f3 h5 9 g5 ♘d7. This looks just about playable but my feeling is that Black needs either to leave his f-pawn at home for the moment or to continue with ...f7-f5. The superficially good idea of ...f6xg5 to create a weakness on g5 leaves him with very little space – Game 30 is a grisly example of

what can then occur. This line can only sensibly be discussed in terms of structures. White has an alternative idea of playing g5xf6, hoping to have a go at the g6-pawn. But as Barlov-Z.Nikolic in the notes to Game 30 shows, this isn't likely to be so good – the h4-pawn is also weak.

A more positive idea, is to meet 7 g4 with 7...c5. As always, this weakens the d6-pawn in the long term but prevents White's natural queenside expansion with c4-c5. The plus side of this idea is evident in Games 31 and 32.

8 gxf5

The restrained 8 f3 is the subject of Game 33.

8...gxf5 9 ♕h5+

The queen sortie is White's tactical justification of 7 g4. When the line first appeared, Black used to reply 9...♔f8, but after the normal sequence 10 ♗h3 ♘f6 11 ♕f3 f4 12 ♗d2 Black's light-squared weaknesses give White a very pleasant long-term advantage. Slow strangulation is not what Black is looking for from any opening.

The line was resuscitated by new ideas after the bolder

9...♘g6 10 exf5 ♕h4

Here White has a choice between 11

♕xh4 (Game 34) and 11 ♕f3 (Game 35).

b) 7 c5

This is another attempt to take advantage of Black's move order but it is far less well based. Since he can't castle Black is more or less obliged to allow ♗b5+ next move, but ...♔f8 is a more than acceptable response. In Game 36 Black is delighted to be able to exchange dark-squared bishops and then move his king to g7.

c) 7 ♕d2

White aims to stop ...♗h6 and meet ...f7-f5 with f2-f3 and then continuing ♗d3 and ♘ge2 after which he can castle either side – though he often defers the choice for the next few moves. This position is very similar to a normal Sämisch King's Indian. My feeling is that White has preserved the 'advantage of the first move' but no more and there is everything to fight for (see Games 37 and 38).

Game 30
Foisor-Kourkounakis
Nikea open 1985

---

1 d4 g6 2 c4 ♗g7 3 ♘c3 d6 4 e4 ♘c6 5 ♗e3 e5 6 d5 ♘ce7 7 g4 ♘f6 8 f3 c5

The immediate 8...h5 is more flexible. For example, Barlov-Z.Nikolic, Yugoslav Championship, Tivat 1994, continued 9 g5 ♘d7 10 h4 a5 11 ♗h3 f5 12 gxf6!? ♗xf6 when in contrast to the main game, Black has plenty of space on the kingside, though the opening of lines means that he must guard in the short term against a quick attack.

9 h4 h5 10 g5 ♘h7 11 ♘ge2 f6 12 ♘c1 fxg5?! 13 hxg5 0-0 14 ♘d3

Although the g5-pawn is potentially weak, it yields White a nice space advantage. While he can try to play ...b7-b5, Black's natural plan is to use the open f-file to create play on the kingside. But with 14 ♘d3 White has effectively prevented the normal exchange sacrifice ...♖f4. In the

play which follows, both sides feint on the queenside and Black eventually deems it necessary to block it with ...a7-a5.

14...a6 15 a4 b6 16 ♕e2 ♖f7 17 ♗h3 ♕f8 18 ♗xc8 ♘xc8 19 ♖h3 ♘a7 20 ♔d2 ♖e8 21 ♔c2 ♕e7 22 ♕g2 ♘f8 23 ♖hh1 ♕b7 24 b3 ♘d7 25 ♘b1 ♗f8 26 ♘d2 ♗g7 27 ♔d1 ♕b8 28 ♔e2 ♕d8 29 ♖hb1 a5

Now all attention shifts to the kingside where White's space advantage gives him a significant advantage. Black also has a big problem with the a7-knight, which has nowhere sensible to go to. Ideally, Black would like to transfer it to f4 so as to annoy the powerful d3-horse and if exchanged open up the e5-square for its counterpart. In that case Black would have had a perfectly reasonable game, but as it is he is in for a long hard sweat with no foreseeable prospects of active play unless White helps him.

30 ♖g1 ♘f8 31 ♖af1 ♘c8 32 ♔d1 ♘h7 33 ♔c2 ♕e7 34 ♕g3 ♗h8 35 ♖f2 ♕f8 36 ♘b1 ♕g7 37 ♘c3 ♘a7

Black has defended well against the 'natural plan' of eventually effecting f3-f4 to attack d6, but White now begins an excellent manoeuvre to transfer the horse to h4.

38 ♘d1 ♘c8 39 ♗c1 ♕f8 40 ♘e3 ♗g7 41 ♘g2 ♕e7 42 ♘h4! ♘f8 43 ♖e2 ♔h7 44 ♕h2 ♕d7 45 ♘xg6! ♔xg6 46 ♖h1

♔h7 47 g6+ ♘xg6 48 ♕xh5+ ♔g8 49 ♕xg6 1-0

Although Black could presumably have defended better at specific moments, the overall impression is that ...f7-f6xg5 was not a good idea.

Game 31
Polajzer-Davies
World U-26 Ch., Graz 1981

---

1 d4 g6 2 c4 ♗g7 3 ♘c3 d6 4 e4 ♘c6 5 ♗e3 e5 6 d5 ♘ce7 7 g4 c5 8 h4 ♘f6 9 g5?!

Giving the knight access to f4 – exactly what Black is desperately hoping for.

9...♘h5 10 ♗e2 ♘f4 11 ♗f3 0-0 12 ♘ge2 f5 13 ♕d2 ♕a5!?

Although the game swiftly ended in Black's favour, I suspect that 13...a6 may be better, since by opposing queens Black offers his opponent the opportunity to try and exchange them.

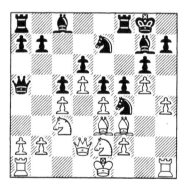

14 0-0-0?!

14 ♘b5 was critical since if White can exchange queens without disaster then he'll still have a good game:

a) 14...♕xd2+ 15 ♔xd2 ♘xe2 16 ♔xe2 is exactly what White wants.

b) But if 14...♘d3+ 15 ♔d1 ♕xd2+ 16 ♔xd2 and neither:

b1) 16...♘xf2 17 ♗xf2 fxe4 18 ♗xe4 ♖xf2 19 ♘xd6 ♘f5 20 ♗xf5 gxf5 21 ♖af1.

b2) Nor is 16...♘xb2 17 ♔c3 ♘a4+ 18 ♔b3 particularly pleasant for Black.

14...♖b8 15 ♘xf4?

Rushing to his doom – 15 ♔b1 looks right.

15...exf4 16 ♗xf4 fxe4 17 ♗xd6 ♖xf3 18 ♗xb8

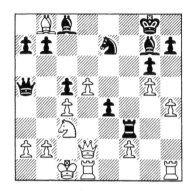

18...♖xc3+! 19 ♔b1

Or 19 bxc3 ♗xc3 20 ♕c2 ♕a3+ 21 ♔b1 ♗f5!

19...e3! 0-1

Game 32
Fedder-Beliavsky
European Junior Ch., Groningen 1970

This fascinating win by the young Beliavsky shows him taking quite big risks on the kingside but then managing to block it very favourably. The rest is a classic demonstration of the overwhelming power of a knight against a hopeless bishop.

1 d4 g6 2 c4 ♗g7 3 e4 d6 4 ♘c3 ♘c6 5 ♗e3 e5 6 d5 ♘ce7 7 g4 c5 8 ♗d3 ♘h6!?

Preparing to move the knight to the excellent f7-square. Apparently 'natural' is 8...f5 9 f3 ♘f6 (Black could also well consider 9...♗h6!? to provoke 10 g5; or perhaps 9...♘h6 analogous to my game with Seirawan below) 10 h3 0-0 11 ♕d2 a6 12 a3 ♗d7 13 b4 ♕c7 14 ♘ge2 ♔h8 15 ♖b1 and White had a pleasant position in

Dlugy-Barreras, Havana 1985.
9 h3 f6! 10 ♕d2 ♘f7

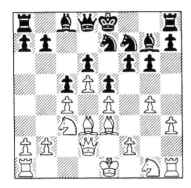

11 ♘ge2 ♗d7 12 ♘g3 a6 13 f3 ♕c8 14 0-0-0 b5 15 h4 0-0 16 ♖dg1 ♖b8 17 ♖h2 bxc4 18 ♗b1

The 'normal' response, keeping the queenside closed and the bishop aimed, albeit through some obstructions, at the enemy king. But if, as I suggest in the next note, White ought to close the kingside then 18 ♗xc4 was certainly to be considered. The only problem would be if Black could generate immediate activity. For example, 18...♖b4 (18...♗b5? 19 ♗b3 doesn't help Black at all) 19 ♗d3 (also conceivably 19 ♕d3 ♗b5 20 b3) 19...♖d4! is certainly a nuisance but White side-steps with 20 ♕e2 and then continues the game – the knights on f7 and e7 are great for defending Black's king but a long way from attacking White's.

18...h6!?

Presumably, this is to be able to meet h4-h5 with ...g6-g5 without worrying about h5-h6, and he may also have been worried about g4-g5 followed by h4-h5. With so many black minor pieces around the king, it's going to be very hard to get a serious attack going, but White's position is clearly perfectly fine here:

a) 19 ♘f5 is the obvious thematic sacrifice but it doesn't seem very sound after 19...gxf5 20 gxf5 (conceivably 20 exf5 but

it's very slow) 20...♔h8 21 ♖hg2 ♖g8.

b) Another way to attack is with 19 g5!?, though again 19...fxg5 20 hxg5 h5 21 ♘xh5!? gxh5 22 g6 ♘h8 isn't very convincing.

c) So perhaps White should settle for a reasonably favourable closure of the king-side with 19 h5, when Black would presumably co-operate with 19...g5, but then White can try slowly to regain the c-pawn perhaps with 20 ♕c2 and ♘g3-f1-d2. The move a2-a3 is also always on the cards, though Black would normally reply ...♖b3 and be more than happy if White played ♗a2 and took it. Black will have a temporary initiative while White is working to regain the pawn, but if he does then in the very long term the game can easily turn in his favour. He is clearly better on the kingside and could, if things went well, having moved his king back towards the centre or kingside, maybe play for b2-b4.

19 ♖hg2 g5 20 ♘f5?

Allowing the e7-knight out. 20 h5 would have been similar to the previous note.

20...♘g6 21 h5??

Now he absolutely had to keep line lines open with 21 hxg5.

21...♗xf5! 22 gxf5?

22 exf5 would at least have freed the e4-square for the bishop.

22...♘f4 23 ♖h2 ♕b7 24 ♘e2 ♕b4 25 ♕c3 ♖b7 26 ♗d2 ♖fb8 27 ♘xf4 exf4 28 ♕xb4 cxb4

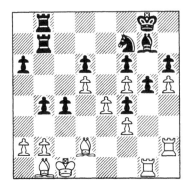

Black should definitely win now.

29 ♗e1 ♘e5 30 ♖h3 ♗f8 31 ♗f2 b3 32 a3 ♗e7 33 ♗d4 ♘d7!

There was obviously no need to allow the exchange of the powerful steed.

34 ♔d2 ♗d8 35 ♖c1 ♗a5+ 36 ♔e2 ♖c8 37 ♖hh1 ♗b6 38 ♖hd1?

He absolutely had to try 38 ♗c3, whatever the consequences, since once the bishops have been exchanged White can happily resign.

38...♗xd4 39 ♖xd4 ♘e5 40 ♖c3 ♖g7 41 ♔f2 ♖c5

Protecting the rook and so stopping 42 ♗d3. Although White's material disadvantage is formally only one pawn, he is effectively a whole bishop down since it can

never escape from b1. Black will break through with ...g5-g4, probably next move, though he could also prepare it by moving the king to b6 first. The only problem then would be that White might – indeed must – at some point play ♖g4 hoping after ...♘xg4 to block the position up. But Black can do things like threatening to bring the king into d4 before capturing and will surely win with accurate play. In any case, presumably over the adjournment, Fedder resigned.

Game 33
Seirawan-Speelman
Elista Olympiad 1998

1 d4 g6 2 e4 ♗g7 3 c4 d6 4 ♘c3 ♘c6

Although the Averbakh is in principle quite a good system, 4...♘c6 wasn't necessarily a particularly good choice against Yasser since, as he reminded me after the game, he played this line extensively until a few years ago. His main objection was the practically forced draw after 5 d5 ♘d4 6 ♗e3 c5 7 ♘ge2 ♕b6 8 ♘xd4 cxd4 9 ♘a4: 9...♕a5+ 10 b4 ♕xb4+ 11 ♗d2 ♕a3 12 ♗c1 ♕b4+ 13 ♗d2 but of course, that wasn't a consideration here. Seirawan now spent some considerable time trying to decide which line he had found most unpleasant to face from the opposite side of the board before plumping for:

5 ♗e3 e5 6 d5 ♘ce7 7 g4 f5 8 f3!?

Avoiding the 'absolute main line' starting 8 gxf5 (see Games 34 and 35).

8...♘h6

This appears to be a novelty – they've almost always played 8...♘f6 here and then mostly 9 h3 0-0. But 8...♘h6 is very logical; Black wants to attack the white kingside pawns and the knight will be well placed on f7 to assault a g5-pawn should White choose to advance it there.

9 ♗e2 ♘f7 10 h4 ♘g8?!

Played very quickly, but in the postmortem we agreed that 10...♗h6 was safer.

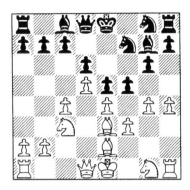

11 exf5!!

After long thought. If 11 ♕d2 fxg4 12 fxg4 ♘f6 13 ♕d1 ♕d7! causes serious trouble.

I'd hardly considered 11 exf5 but as Yasser had understood, the important thing is to open the e4-square for his knight.

11...gxf5 12 ♕d2 ♘f6 13 gxf5 ♗xf5?

Automatic and wrong. After 13...♘h5 Black gets much more play. If Black wants to play 10...♘g8?! then this would still be a reasonable line.

14 ♘h3 e4!?

To avoid being sat on after ♘g5 but very risky with the king in the centre. Yasser now played very well.

15 ♘g5! ♕e7

If 15...exf3 16 ♘xf3 and the knight is en route to d4

16 ♘xf7 ♔xf7

I wanted to play 16...exf3 17 ♘xh8 fxe2 but just didn't believe it, especially after 18 ♗g5.

17 fxe4 ♘xe4 18 ♘xe4 ♕xe4

Now 19 ♖f1? ♖he8! 20 ♗h5+ ♔g8 21 ♗xe8 ♖xe8 is excellent for Black but of course White simply castled.

19 0-0!!

see following diagram

19...♖hg8??

The wrong rook and gross stupidity since I had plenty of time but had used far too little. Black can still fight after 19...♖ag8 20 ♗h5+ when:

a) 20...♔e7 21 ♗g5+ ♔d7 22 ♖f4 and now:

a1) I hardly considered 22...♕d3 but after 23 ♕xd3 (not 23 ♖xf5 ♕xd2 24 ♗xd2 ♗xb2+) 23...♖xd3 24 ♗g4+ ♔e8 25 ♖e1+ Black can block with ...♗e5. However, 26 ♗f6 h5 27 ♗xh8 wins the exchange.

a2) 22...♕d4+ 23 ♕xd4 ♕xd4+ 24 ♖xd4 h6 25 ♖f1 and now:

a21) Now if 25...hxg5 26 ♗f7! gxh4+ 27 ♗xg8 ♖xg8+ 28 ♔h2 is winning.

a22) While if 25...♗h3 26 ♖f7+ ♔c8 27 ♗g4+ ♗xg4 28 ♖xg4 hxg5 then the ending should be winning after either recapture – 29 ♖xg5 looks simpler.

b) 20...♔f8 is better, i.e. 21 ♖xf5+ ♕xf5 22 ♗g5 h6 23 ♖f1 ♕xf1+ 24 ♔xf1 hxg5 25 ♕xg5 (White can't win at once with 25 ♕f2+? ♔e7 26 ♕f7+ ♔d8 27 ♗g4?? since he gets hit by 27...♖f8) 25...♗e5! (not 25...♗xb2 26 ♕d8+ ♔g7 27 ♕xc7+ ♔h6 28 ♗f7) 26 ♕f5+ ♔e7 27 ♕e6+ ♔d8 28 ♗g4 ♖xg4 29 ♕xg4 ♗xb2 and White has good winning chances but it's still a fight.

20 ♗h5+ ♔f8 21 ♖xf5+! ♕xf5 22 ♗g5

And it's all over since if 22...♗f6 23 ♖f1 ♕e5 24 ♕f4. I struggled on for a few more moves.

22...♗e5 23 ♖f1 ♕xf1+ 24 ♔xf1 ♔g7

25 ♗e7! ♔h8 26 ♕h6 ♗g7

Or 26...♖g7 27 ♗f6 ♗xf6 (27...♖f8 28 ♕xg7 mate) 28 ♕xf6 ♔g8 29 ♗g4!

27 ♕e6 ♗xb2 28 ♗f7 ♖g3 1-0

A beautiful game by Seirawan but also one of many reasons why it's taken me a ridiculously long time to complete my part of this book!

> ### Game 34
> ### Meister-Arapovic
> *Augsburg 1989*

1 d4 g6 2 c4 ♗g7 3 e4 ♘c6 4 ♗e3 d6 5 ♘c3 e5 6 d5 ♘ce7 7 g4 f5 8 gxf5 gxf5 9 ♕h5+

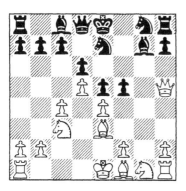

9...♘g6

Almost invariably played nowadays. The old line was 9...♔f8 10 ♗h3 ♘f6 11 ♕f3 and now Black can close the kingside but he remains with chronic light-square problems. For instance, Portisch-Ree, Amsterdam 1967, ground on 11...f4 12 ♗d2 h5 13 ♗xc8 ♕xc8 14 0-0-0 ♗h6 15 ♕d3 ♖g8 16 ♘f3 ♖g2 17 ♕f1 ♖g7 18 ♔b1 c5 19 dxc6 bxc6 20 ♕e2 c5 21 ♘b5 and White went on to win. This type of position is vile for Black whether he can hold or not.

10 exf5 ♕h4 11 ♕xh4

The old move, though 11 ♕f3 is now considered most critical – see the next game.

11...♘xh4 12 ♘b5 ♔d8 13 ♘xa7 ♗xf5 14 ♘b5

The critical position of this variation. Here (instead of the game move) 14...♗e4 15 f3 has been extensively tested:

a) Some old analysis by Boleslavsky in *Konigsindisch bis Grünfeld Verteidigung* continued 15...♘xf3+? (obvious but incorrect) 16 ♘xf3 ♗xf3 17 ♖g1 ♗f6 18 ♗e2 ♗xe2 19 ♔xe2 ♘e7 20 ♖af1 ♗h4 21 ♖g4 ♘g6 22 ♖xh4 ♘xh4 23 ♗g5+ ♔c8 24 ♗xh4 ♖xa2 25 ♖f7 ♖xb2+ 26 ♔f3.

a1) Boleslavsky continued 26...♖xh2 27 ♖xc7+ ♔b8 28 ♗e7 ♖c8 29 ♗xd6 ♖xc7 30 ♗xc7+ ♔c8 31 ♗xe5 ♖h3+ 32 ♔g4 'and White has good winning chances'.

a2) In a correspondence game G.Wilms-G.Tietze, European Championship 1986, Black tried to improve with 26...♔b8, and in fact missed a draw at one point though it was still uphill all the way: 27 ♗g3 ♖b4 28 ♘xc7 ♖xc4 29 ♘b5 ♖d8 30 ♘xd6 ♖c3+ 31 ♔e4 ♖xg3 32 ♖xb7+ ♔a8 33 hxg3 ♖xd6 34 ♖xh7 ♖g6 35 ♖c7 ♖xg3 36 d6 ♔b8 37 ♔xe5 ♖g1? (37...♖h3! takes sufficient checking distance to draw) 38 ♖c2 ♖h1 39 d7 ♖h8 40 ♔d6 ♖h6+ 41 ♔d5 ♖h5+ 42 ♔c6 ♖h6+ 43 ♔b5 1-0.

b) 15...♗xf3! is perfectly playable though. By surrendering the two bishops, Black develops a powerful initiative: 16 ♘xf3 ♘xf3+ 17 ♔d1 e4 (the most dynamic, though 17...♘e7 had also led to success in a correspondence game half a decade earlier: 18 ♗d3 ♔d7 19 ♔e2 ♘d4+ 20 ♘xd4 exd4 21 ♗g5 ♖ae8 22 ♔d2 h6 23 ♗h4 ♖hf8 24 ♖af1 ♗e5 25 ♗g3 ♖g8 26 ♖f3 ♖g7 27 ♗f1 c6 28 ♗h3+ ♔c7 29 ♗e6 ♘g6 30 ♖hf1 ♖ee7 31 b3 ♗xg3 32 ♖xg3 ♘e5 33 ♖f6 ♖xg3 34 hxg3 ♖g7 35 ♖xh6 ♖xg3 36 ♖h7+ ♔b6 37 ♗c8 ♖g2+ 38 ♔d1 ♖xa2 39 ♖xb7+ ♔c5 40 dxc6 d3 41 ♗f5 ♔d4 42 ♗xd3 ♘xd3 0-1 C.Vasile-A.Rades, correspondence 1989-91) 18 ♔c2 ♘e7 19 ♗h3 ♖f8 20 ♘c3?! (this gives Black the opportunity to attack the centre though he had a good game, anyway) 20...♗xc3! 21 ♔xc3 b5! 22 a3 bxc4 23 ♔xc4 ♖a5 24 ♗e6 ♘f5 25 ♗xf5 ♖xf5 26 ♖ad1 ♔d7 27 h4 h5 28 ♖h3 ♘e5+ 29 ♔d4 ♘g4 30 ♔c4 ♘f6 31 ♗g1 ♖axd5 32 ♖xd5 ♘xd5 33 b4 ♘f4 34 ♖h2 d5+ 35 ♔c3 ♘g6 36 ♖h3 ♖f1 37 ♗c5 ♘f4 38 ♖e3 ♘e6 39 ♗a7 ♖f8 0-1 Krivonosov-Poley, Stockholm 1995.

14...♗h6

This nice (temporary) pawn sacrifice is also a good way to play.

15 ♔d2

White can keep the material with 15 ♘c3, but 15...♗xe3 16 fxe3 ♘f6 leaves Black with enormous activity, e.g.

a) 17 ♗e2 ♘e4 18 ♘f3? (18 ♘d1! was correct) led to immediate disaster in K.Osmanovic-N.Kelecevic, Liechtenstein 1987: 18...♘g2+ 19 ♔d1 ♘xe3+ 20 ♔c1 ♘xc3 21 bxc3 ♗e4 22 ♔d2 ♘c2 23 ♖ac1

♖xa2 0-1.

b) 17 h3 ♖g8 18 a3 ♗e4 19 ♘xe4 ♘xe4 20 ♗d3 ♘g2+ 21 ♔f1 ♖f8+ 22 ♘f3 ♖xf3+ 23 ♔xg2 ♖xe3 24 ♖hf1 ♔e7 25 ♗xe4 ♖g8+ 26 ♔f2 ♖xe4 and Black was much better, though White did manage to draw in Zwikker-Lambers, correspondence 1992-93.

15...♗e4 16 f3 ♗xf3 17 ♘xf3 ♘xf3+ 18 ♔e2 ♗xe3 19 ♔xe3 ♘h4 20 ♗h3 ♘g6

Black has an excellent structure, though the open f- and g-files, combined with the annoying knight on b5 and the black king's inability to go to the natural d7-square, mean that White should have reasonable chances too.

21 ♖hg1

In yet another correspondence game Pähtz-Albrecht, 1977, White generated enough immediate activity to force a draw: 21 a3 ♘8e7 22 ♖af1 ♘f4 23 ♗e6 ♘eg6 24 h4 ♘xe6 25 dxe6 ♘f4 26 ♖hg1 ♘xe6 27 ♖f7 ♖c8 28 ♘a7 ½-½ – and this seems a fair reflection of the diagram.

21...♘8e7 22 a3 ♖a4 23 b3 ♖a5 24 a4 ♘f4 25 ♗e6 ♖f8 26 ♖af1 ♖a6 27 ♗g4 ♖f6 28 ♔e4 c6! 29 ♘c3?

29 dxc6 bxc6 30 ♘c3 (30 ♘xd6 ♖xd6 31 ♔xe5 fails to 31...♘d3+ 32 ♔xd6 c5 mate!) was still unclear, since the black central mass isn't stable yet but might fall victim to c4-c5 at some moment. Now, though, Black immediately gains a big

advantage.

29...cxd5+ 30 ♘xd5 ♘exd5 31 cxd5 ♖b6 32 ♗e6 ♖b4+ 33 ♔e3 ♖xb3+ 34 ♔d2 ♖g6 35 ♗f5 ♖b2+ 36 ♔c3 ♖gg2 37 ♗e4 ♖xh2 38 ♖g8+ ♔c7 39 ♖g7+ ♔b8 40 ♖xh7 ♖hd2 41 ♖xf4

The only chance but Arapovic mopped up easily enough.

41...exf4 42 ♖d7 ♖h2 43 ♖xd6 ♖be2 44 ♖e6 ♖e3+ 45 ♔d4 ♖d2+ 46 ♔e5 f3 47 ♔f4 ♖de2 0-1

Game 35
Notkin-Losev
Moscow Championship 1996

These are two serious players getting stuck into this line – it looks better for White to me but well defensible. And if White goes wrong then his opponent can easily emerge with a clear positional advantage – a better pawn structure.

1 d4 g6 2 c4 ♗g7 3 e4 d6 4 ♘c3 ♘c6 5 ♗e3 e5 6 d5 ♘ce7 7 g4 f5 8 gxf5 gxf5 9 ♕h5+ ♘g6 10 exf5 ♕h4 11 ♕f3

Since White has not enjoyed much success with 11 ♕xh4, the focus has therefore shifted to the great complications introduced by 11 ♕f3. This is a very dangerous line, particularly for Black, but if he can weather the initial storm then he does have the better pawn structure in the long term.

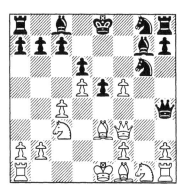

11...♘6e7

11...♘f4 is unsatisfactory after 12 ♘h3 and either:

a) 12...♘xh3 13 ♗xh3 ♘f6 14 ♕g3 ♕xg3 15 hxg3 h5 16 0-0-0 a6 17 f3 with a clear advantage for White in A.Shariazdanov-S.Kosanski, Djakovo 1994.

b) 12...♗xf5 13 ♘xf4 exf4 14 ♕xf4 ♕xf4 15 ♗xf4, as in Psakhis-Ranola, Yves Balaguer open 1987.

12 ♘b5

A logical test of Black's idea, but 12 ♗d3 is even sharper, e.g. 12...♘h6 13 f6 ♖f8 14 ♘e4 ♗xf6 15 ♘xf6+ ♖xf6 16 ♕g3 ♕h5 (certainly not 16...♕xg3? 17 hxg3, repairing White's pawn structure, while 16...♘ef5? lost material to 17 ♕xh4 ♘xh4 18 ♗g5 in C.Flear-D.Baudot, Mondorf open 1991) and now:

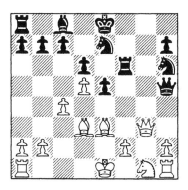

a) 17 ♗xh7 ♘g4 looks ridiculous.

b) 17 ♕g7? loses much too much time due to 17...♘g4 18 ♕h8+ ♖f8 19 ♕xh7 ♕xh7 20 ♗xh7 ♗f5 21 ♗xf5 ♘xf5 22 ♘h3 ♘fxe3 23 fxe3 ♘xe3 with a big advantage in Timson-Pineault, correspondence 1992.

c) The splendid game Petursson-Michalet, St Martin open 1992, concluded 17 ♗e2 ♕f5 18 ♘f3 ♘g4 19 ♘h4 ♕e4 20 ♖g1 ♘xe3 21 fxe3 ♗f5 22 ♕g5 ♖f8 23 ♗h5+ ♔d7 24 ♘xf5 ♖xf5 25 ♗g4 ♖g8! 26 ♗xf5+ ♘xf5 27 ♕xg8 ♕xe3+ 28 ♔f1 ♕f3+ 29 ♔e1 ½-½.

d) 17 ♕g5 ♕f7 18 0-0-0 ♝f5 19 ♝e2 and now instead of 19...0-0-0 20 ♕h4 losing the exchange in Sashikiran-Ranola, Calcutta 1998, 19...♖g6 20 ♕h4 ♞g4 was a possible alternative.

12...♔d8

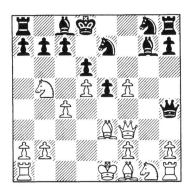

Black has an excellent pawn structure but must suffer White's initiative at least in the short term.

13 ♞h3

13 ♕g2 is also dangerous, e.g. 13...♝h6 14 ♞f3 and now:

a) 14...♕e4 looks wrong since the tactics all now favour White. A game played at the Internet Chess Club by Email but impressive for all that ended 15 ♞g5 ♕xg2 16 ♝xg2 ♝xg5 17 ♝xg5 ♝xf5 (17...a6 18 f6!) 18 c5 ♝d3 19 ♞xd6 cxd6 20 cxd6 ♖c8 21 dxe7+ 1-0 Claridge-Meadows, 1995.

b) 14...♕f6 15 h4 (15 0-0-0 is also possible: 15...♞xf5 16 ♝xh6 ♞gxh6 17 ♞d2 and now 17...♖g8 looks a good idea) 15...♞xf5 (15...♝xe3 16 fxe3 ♞xf5 is critical and probably correct) 16 ♝g5 ♝xg5 17 hxg5 ♕g7 18 ♞c3 ♞ge7 19 ♞e4 ♞g6 20 0-0-0 ♞f4 21 ♕h2 ♞e7 22 ♞f6 ♝f5 23 ♕g3 ♞eg6 24 ♞h4 ♞xh4 25 ♕xh4 ♔e7 26 ♖e1 ♔f7 27 ♞g4 ♝xg4 28 ♕xg4.

see following diagram

28...♔g8? (after successfully resisting sustained pressure Black cracks; it must be correct to keep the rooks connected with

28...♖af8!, preparing to play 29...♔e7) 29 ♖h6 ♖f8 30 ♔b1 ♕f7 31 ♖f6 ♕e8 32 ♖xf4 1-0 Naumann-Boehm, Germany 1994.

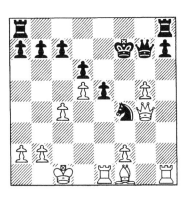

13...♝h6 14 ♖g1 ♝xe3 15 ♕xe3 ♞xf5 16 ♕g5+ ♞f6 17 0-0-0 a6 18 ♞c3 ♖g8

18...♖f8!? and if 19 ♕xh4 ♞xh4 20 ♞g5 ♔e7 looks like an improvement since in the game White gets a serious initiative.

19 ♕xh4 ♞xh4 20 ♖xg8+ ♞xg8 21 ♞g5 ♞f6 22 ♝d3 h6

If 22...♔e7 23 ♞xh7 ♞xh7 24 ♝xh7 ♝f5 25 ♝xf5 ♞xf5 White maintains his extra pawn for the moment. Since Black's structure is so good, this might be the moment for 26 f4!?

23 ♞f7+ ♔e7 24 ♞xh6 ♝d7 25 ♖g1 ♖h8 26 ♖g7+ ♔e8 27 ♝g6+ ♞xg6 28 ♖xg6 ♞h5 29 ♞e4 ♔f8 30 c5

If 30 ♞f6 ♞xf6 31 ♖xf6+ ♔e7 32 ♖g6 ♝e8 33 ♖e6+ ♔d8 34 ♔d2 ♖f8 35 ♔e3 ♖f4 Black looks fine.

30...♝e8 31 ♖e6 ♝d7 32 cxd6 ♝xe6 33 dxe6 cxd6 34 ♞f5 d5 35 ♞ed6 ♞f6 36 e7+ ♔g8 37 e8♕+!?

Releasing the tension. White now emerges with some advantage but it looked more dangerous to keep the pawn on, e.g. 37 h4 ♔h7 38 h5 ♖g8 39 ♔d2 ♖g5 40 ♞e3! (40 h6 ♔g6) 40...e4 41 e8♕ ♞xe8 42 ♞xe8 d4 43 ♞f6+! ♔g7 44 ♞eg4 with good winning chances.

37...♞xe8 38 ♞xe8 ♔f7 39 ♞c7 d4 40 ♔d2 ♖xh2 41 ♞d6+ ♔g6 42 ♞e4 ♔f5

43 ♔d3 ♖h3+ 44 ♘g3+ ♔g4 45 ♘e6 b6 46 a4 ♖h6 47 ♘c7 ♔f3 48 ♘xa6 ♔xf2 49 ♘e4+ ♔e1 50 ♘b4 ♖h3+ 51 ♔c4 ♔e2 52 ♘d5 ♖h4 53 ♘g3+ ♔f2 54 ♘f5 ♖g4 55 b4 ♔e2 56 ♘f6 ♖g5 57 ♘e4 ♖g4 58 ♘f6 ♖g5 59 ♘e4 ♖g4 60 ♘f6 ♖g5 61 ♘e4 ♖g4 ½-½

Game 36
Urban-Krasenkov
Polish Ch., Lubniewice 1995

1 d4 g6 2 c4 ♗g7 3 ♘c3 d6 4 e4 ♘c6 5 ♗e3 e5 6 d5 ♘ce7 7 c5!?

A different attempt to exploit Black's move order.

7...f5 8 cxd6 cxd6 9 ♗b5+ ♔f8!

Of course Black shouldn't exchange his excellent light-squared bishop but rather happily moves the king towards safety on g7.

10 f3 ♗h6 11 ♗xh6+

Of course 11 ♗f2?! is legal but it hardly tests Black's play.

11...♘xh6 12 ♕d2 ♘f7

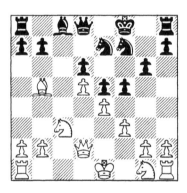

Essentially, Black has a very good game in this position with excellent play on the dark squares, unless White can do something instantly. The only way to destabilise the black position is 13 f4!? but this also weakens White's position. If, at the cost a pawn, White could get control of e5 or even force ...d6xe5 in response to f4xe5

then the black position might crumble. But I think that Black can defend and defend well:

a) 13...exf4 14 ♕xf4 g5 15 ♕d2 f4 16 h4 ♘g6 looks possible, though Black's position is somewhat compromised in return for the e5-square.

b) 13...♔g7 14 ♘f3 fxe4 15 ♘xe4 ♗f5 and now:

b1) 16 ♘eg5 ♘xg5 17 ♘xg5 ♕b6 18 ♗d3 (18 fxe5 ♕xb5 19 exd6 ♘xd5 20 ♕d4+ ♘f6 wins, while 18 ♗e2 h6 19 ♘e6+ ♗xe6 20 dxe6 ♖hf8 should be fine for Black) 18...♗xd3 19 ♘e6+ ♔f7 20 ♕xd3 ♕a5+!

b2) 16 ♘c3! is much better, i.e. 16...a6 17 ♗e2 ♖e8 18 fxe5 dxe5 19 0-0 ♕d6 and Black is developed but he's lost his beautiful structure.

c) 13...fxe4!? is the most combative of all, denying the king's knight access to the f3-square from which he can fight for e5, while if White recaptures then his opponent will have a potentially very useful tempo on the bishop with ...♕b6 and on the knight with ...♗f5. For example, 14 fxe5 (if 14 ♘xe4 ♗f5 15 ♘c3 exf4 16 ♘f3 ♕b6 17 ♕xf4 ♘xd5 18 ♘xd5 ♕xb5 19 ♕d4 ♖e8+) 14...♘xe5 15 ♕h6+ (15 ♕g5 ♔g7 16 ♘xe4 ♘f5 is worse, while if 15 ♘xe4 ♗f5 16 ♕h6+ ♔g8 17 ♘f6+ ♔f7 18 ♘xh7 ♕a5+ and wins) 15...♔g8 16 ♘xe4 ♘f5! Now White will go backwards and Black emerges with the advantage.

13 ♘ge2 ♔g7!?

13...f4 14 h4 h6 15 g3 g5 16 hxg5 hxg5 17 0-0-0 ♖xh1 18 ♖xh1 ♘g6 was played in the classic game Koraksic-Ivkov, Zemun 1980. Without worrying about the details, here is how Ivkov exploited his space advantage: 19 gxf4 gxf4 20 ♘g1 ♕f6 21 ♗f1 ♔g7 22 ♕h2 ♗d7 23 ♕f2 a6 24 ♖h5 ♖h8 25 ♖xh8 ♘gxh8 26 ♗h3 ♗xh3 27 ♘xh3 ♘g6 28 ♔d2 ♕d8 29 ♕g2 ♕b6 30 ♔c2 ♕e3 31 ♘f2 ♕e1 32 ♘b1 ♔f6 33 ♘d3 ♕g3 34 ♕h1 ♘h4 35 ♘d2 ♘g5 36 ♘e1

♘h3 37 ♘f1 ♕f2+ 38 ♘d2 ♘g1 39 ♘d3 ♕g3 40 ♘f1 ♕g2+ 41 ♕xg2 ♗xg2 42 ♘d2 ♘e3+ 43 ♔c1 ♘e2+ 44 ♔b1 ♘d4 45 ♔c1 ♘e2+ 46 ♔b1 ♔g5 47 ♘b3 ♘c4 48 ♔c2 ♘g1 49 ♘e1 ♔h4 50 ♔c3 b5 51 ♘c1 ♔g3 52 b3 ♘a5 53 ♔d3 ♔f2 54 ♘c2 ♘b7 55 ♘b4 ♘c5+ 56 ♔c3 ♔xf3 57 ♘cd3 ♘xe4+ 58 ♔c2 a5 59 ♘c6 ♔e3 60 ♘xa5 ♘e2 61 ♘c6 ♘d4+ 62 ♘xd4 ♔xd4 63 a4 bxa4 64 bxa4 ♘c5 65 ♘b2 f3 0-1.

14 ♗d3 ♗d7 15 0-0-0 ♖b8 16 ♔b1 b5 17 ♖c1 ♕b6

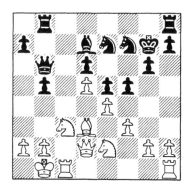

18 ♘d1?!

He should have tried to stir things up with 18 h4 and if 18...f4 19 h5 g5 20 g4 fxg3 21 h6+!; or conceivably 18 f4!?, though it looks way too late to be seriously effective.

18...f4! 19 ♖c2

If 19 g3 g5 20 gxf4 exf4! 21 h4 h6 22 hxg5 hxg5 23 ♖g1 ♘g6 24 ♕c3+ ♘ge5!; or 19 g4 h5!

19...g5

With a secure space advantage on the kingside, Black already has a big advantage.

20 ♘c1 ♘g6 21 ♕f2 ♕xf2 22 ♘xf2 ♖bc8 23 ♖d1

Or 23 ♖xc8 ♖xc8 24 ♘b3 ♘h4! 25 ♖g1 h5 26 ♗e2 ♔f6 27 g3 ♘g6 etc. White can't resolve the kingside satisfactorily and so must suffer.

23...♖xc2 24 ♔xc2 h5 25 h3 g4! 26

hxg4 hxg4 27 ♘xg4 ♗xg4 28 fxg4 ♘g5

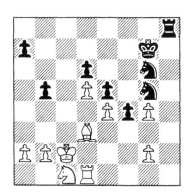

29 ♘b3

Or 29 ♗xb5 ♖h2 30 ♖d2 ♘xe4 31 ♖e2 ♘g3 32 ♖f2 e4 and Black is winning.

29...♖h2 30 ♖d2 ♘h4 31 ♔c3 a5! 32 a4

If 32 ♘xa5 b4+ 33 ♔c2 (33 ♔xb4 f3!) 33...♘xg2 34 ♔b3 ♘f3 35 ♖f2 ♘ge1 36 ♖xh2 ♘xh2 37 ♗e2 f3 38 ♗xf3 ♘hxf3 39 ♔xb4 ♘d3+ 40 ♔c4 ♘f2 and Black should presumably win, though the a-pawn is a problem.

32...bxa4 33 ♘xa5 ♔f6 34 ♘c4 ♔e7 35 ♔b4 ♘xg2 36 ♔xa4 f3 37 ♘e3 ♔f6

38 ♘f5

If 38 b4 ♖h3! 39 ♘f5 ♘f4 40 ♘xd6 ♘xd3 41 ♖xd3 f2 42 ♖d1 ♖e3 43 ♖f1 ♘h3 44 b5 ♖e1 45 ♖xf2+ ♘xf2 46 b6 ♖b1 47 ♘b5 ♘xe4 48 b7 ♘c5+ wins.

38...♖h8 39 ♘xd6 ♘e1 40 ♗b5?

Losing. 40 ♔b3!? ♘xd3 41 ♖xd3 f2 42

罝d1 罝d8 43 罝f1! 罝xd6 44 罝xf2+ would have made a fight of it.

40...罝d8 41 ♘e8+

If 41 ♘f5 ♘xe4 the white position soon disintegrates.

41...♔f7 42 d6 罝xe8 43 ♗xe8+ ♔xe8 44 罝h2 ♘xe4 45 罝h5 ♘d3 46 罝f5 f2 0-1

Game 37
Moiseenko-Popov
Chigorin Memorial 1995

1 d4 g6 2 c4 ♗g7 3 ♘c3 d6 4 e4 ♘c6 5 ♗e3 e5 6 d5 ♘ce7 7 ♕d2

In contrast to previous games, White simply continues his development.

7...f5 8 f3 ♘f6 9 0-0-0 0-0 10 h3 f4 11 ♗f2 ♘h5 12 ♘ge2 ♗f6 13 ♔b1 ♔h8

13...♗d7 is also possible, intending ...♘c8 and often to recapture later on d6 with the knight.

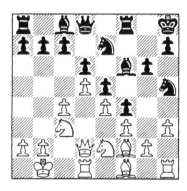

14 ♘c1 ♘g8 15 c5 罝f7 16 ♗c4 ♗h4 17 ♘b3

White is more or less forced to allow the exchange of dark-squared bishops, since if 17 ♗g1 ♘g3 18 罝h2 the rook looks extremely odd. In order to avoid this, White would have liked to have arranged to move his king's rook beforehand, but Black's purposeful play meant that from move 15 onwards, he was always ready to offer this favourable exchange.

17...♗xf2 18 ♕xf2 ♘g3 19 罝he1 ♘f6 20 c6!? b6 21 ♕c2 ♔g7 22 ♘d2

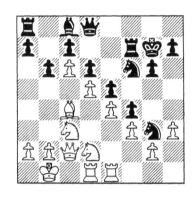

22...a5?!

I don't like this weakening so early and would prefer to play 22...a6 if possible:

a) One thematic idea for White is then to arrange to sacrifice on b5, but something like 23 b4 g5 24 a4 h5 25 a5 b5 26 ♘xb5 axb5 27 ♗xb5 罝b8 28 ♕c4 g4 29 hxg4 hxg4 30 ♔a2 ♕h8 31 ♔a3 ♕h2 looks very good for Black.

b) 23 ♘e2 ♘fh5 24 ♘f1 ♕g5 (24...♘h1!?) 25 ♘fxg3 ♘xg3 26 ♘xg3 ♕xg3 27 ♕e2 g5 28 罝d3 h5 29 罝a3 ♔f6 looks fairly thematic and quite good for Black.

c) 23 ♕d3 g5 24 罝c1 and now:

c1) 24...♕h8?! 25 ♘e2 is much less clear, e.g. 25...♘xe2 (after 25...♘hf5 26 ♘f1 ♘xf1 27 罝xf1 Black can't play for ...g5-g4 without allowing White to play g2-g3 at some moment) 26 ♕xe2 h5 27 罝g1 ♔f8 28 罝c3 ♔e7 29 罝a3 g4 30 h4 罝g7 31 g3! and the kingside is opening before Black is ready.

c2) 24...h5 looks right immediately, when 25 ♘e2 ♘xe2 26 罝xe2 g4 27 hxg4 hxg4 28 fxg4 ♗xg4 (not 28...♘xg4 29 g3!) 29 罝f2 b5 30 ♗b3 ♘h5 is nice for Black – ...b6-b5 is weakening but the kingside is very good and ...♕b8-b6 looks possible, while most importantly g2-g3 has been prevented.

23 ♕d3 ♔f8 24 ♖c1 g5 25 ♘e2 ♖g7 26 ♖c3 ♘xe2 27 ♕xe2 ♗e7 28 ♖a3 ♖b8 29 ♘f1 h5 30 ♘h2 ♕h8 31 ♗a6 ♕h7 32 ♗xc8 ♖xc8 33 ♕a6 ♖gg8 34 ♖d3 ♖a8 35 ♕c4 g4 36 hxg4 hxg4 37 ♘xg4 ♘xg4 38 fxg4 ♖xg4

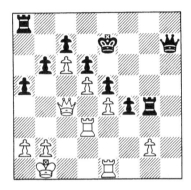

Despite getting in his thematic kingside break, Black still isn't clearly better since he must always guard against a queenside invasion starting ♕a6; and much more crucially, White's coming control of the h-file combined with the light-square control on e6 and d7 renders Black's king position always potentially vulnerable.

39 ♖h3 ♕f7 40 ♕e2 ♖ag8 41 ♖g1 ♕g6 42 a3 f3?!

42...♔f6 looks sensible, though White would reply 43 ♖h2 and hold the position for the moment.

43 ♕xf3 ♖xe4 44 ♔a2 ♖f4 45 ♕h5 ♕xh5 46 ♖xh5 ♖fg4 47 ♖h7+ ♖8g7 48 ♖xg7+ ♖xg7 49 ♔b3 b5 50 g4 ♔f6 51 a4 bxa4+ 52 ♔xa4 e4 53 ♔xa5 ♔e5

Here White, who was rated 190 points less than Black, agreed to a draw. Of course, it's extremely messy but my feeling is that Black was indeed 'pulling rank', though if e.g. 54 b4 ♔xd5 55 b5 e3 56 ♔a6 ♔e4 (56...♔c5 57 b6 cxb6 58 ♖c1+ ♔d4 59 c7 ♖xc7 60 ♖xc7 wins easily) 57 b6 cxb6 58 ♔xb6 d5 59 c7 ♖g8 60 ♔b7 d4 61 g5 d3 62 g6 d2 63 g7 e2 64 c8♕ ♖xc8 65 ♔xc8 e1♕ 66 g8♕ ♕c1+ 67 ♔b7 ♕b2+ 68 ♔a6

I guess Black will probably draw.

This game is interesting in that Black appears to do everything right but at the end he may be worse. Perhaps it was wrong to play 22...a5, but presumably Black was worried that if ...a7-a6 White plays a2-a4-a5 and if ...b7-b5 White arranges to 'sacrifice' on b5.

> ## Game 38
> ### Istratescu-Chernin
> *FIDE World Ch., Groningen 1997*

1 e4 g6 2 d4 ♗g7 3 c4 d6 4 ♘c3 ♘c6 5 ♗e3 e5 6 d5 ♘ce7 7 ♕d2 f5 8 f3 ♘f6 9 ♗d3 a6?!

The difficulty about this game from Black's (and an annotator's) point of view, is that he loses after seemingly doing very little wrong. Perhaps 9...a6?! is his first bad decision since the weakness on b6 later turns out to be very serious.

Another idea is 9...c5!?, trying to block the queenside. Kraidman-Gausel, Gausdal 1983, continued 10 dxc6!? (the critical response, attempting to take immediate advantage, but if Black defends accurately then it seems he should emerge with a very reasonable position so 9...c5!? looks like an excellent idea) 10...bxc6 11 ♘ge2 0-0 12 ♖d1 ♗e6 13 0-0 ♔h8 and Black had a perfectly satisfactory position.

10 h3 f4

The position is now rather similar to the Advance variation of the French Defence, reflected about the line dividing king and queenside. In that opening, Black fixes a weakness on g3 (b3 in the French) but I don't like Chernin's decision in a couple of moves to advance his g-pawn. I would rather prefer to see Black aim towards ...♗h4, trying to exchange bishops.

11 ♗f2 0-0 12 ♘ge2 g5?! 13 0-0-0 ♘g6

Despite the presence of their respective kings, both sides start play on the flank where they have more space.

14 c5 ♗d7 15 ♔b1 ♕e7 16 cxd6 cxd6 17 ♘c1 ♖fc8 18 ♘b3 ♕d8 19 a4!

Aiming to fix the weakness on b6.

19...♗f8?!

If 19...b5!? 20 axb5 axb5 21 ♘a2!, Black will find it hard to generate any real play on the queenside, while the weakness on c6 beckons the white knight. But perhaps Black could play 21...b4!?, preventing a blockade and hoping to start an attack. In any case, I think he must do something, however risky, since waiting on the queenside ultimately leads to total disaster.

20 a5 ♗e7 21 ♖c1 ♗e8

As Baburin pointed out in *ChessBase magazine* the immediate 21...h5?! would allow 22 g4! when 22...fxg3 23 ♕xg5 gxf2 24 ♕xg6+ is good for White.

22 ♘a2 ♕d7 23 ♕b4 ♔g7 24 ♖hd1 h5 25 ♘d2 ♖xc1+ 26 ♖xc1 ♖c8

27 ♘c4!

Much better than exchanging the last pair of rooks. Now the ever-present threat of ♘b6 is seriously embarrassing.

27...g4 28 hxg4 hxg4 29 ♘c3 ♖c7 30 ♗b6 ♖c8 31 ♗a7 ♖c7 32 ♗b6 ♖c8 33 ♗f2 ♖c7 34 b3! ♗f8 35 ♗b6 ♖c8 36 ♗a7 ♕e7

Not 36...♖c7? 37 ♗b8 ♖c5 38 ♕b6 and the d6-pawn falls.

37 ♘b6 ♖d8

If 37...♖c5 White could if he wished switch his rook to the h-file, leaving the rook stranded on c5 and vulnerable to all sorts of attacks by minor pieces. But with this surrender of the c-file he gives White a clear-cut winning plan.

38 ♘ca4 ♘h4 39 ♘c8! ♕d7 40 ♘ab6 ♕f7 41 ♗b8 gxf3 42 gxf3

42...♔g8

If 42...♘xf3 White could play 43 ♗c7 anyway. though I imagine that Chernin moved the king first because of the other possible threat of 43 ♖c7.

43 ♗c7! ♖xc8 44 ♘xc8 ♘xf3 45 ♗xd6 ♗h6 46 ♘e7+ ♔h7 47 ♘f5 ♗g5 48 ♖h1+ ♔g6 49 ♕c3 ♘g4 50 ♗e2 ♘fh2 51 ♗xg4 ♘xg4 52 ♕h3 ♘f6 53 ♘e7+ ♔g7 1-0

Chernin resigned before 54 ♕h8 mate. A model game by Istratescu and a warning of what to avoid when playing Black.

Summary

Although 7 g4 is supposed to be the 'main line' I'm not utterly convinced by it and indeed Yasser Seirawan, who, it must be remembered played this line for many years as Black, avoided it in his superb win against me in Game 33.

White's other approaches are simply to develop when presumably his space advantage should, in theory, give him a miniscule edge; but in practice it's just a game. And after the immediate 7 c5!? I feel that Black's resources should also be sufficient.

1 d4 g6 2 c4 ♗g7 3 ♘c3 d6 4 e4 ♘c6 5 ♗e3 e5 6 d5 ♘ce7 *(D)*

7 g4
>7 c5 – *Game 36*
>7 ♕d2 f5 8 f3 ♘f6
>>9 0-0-0 – *Game 37*
>>9 ♗d3 – *Game 38*

7...f5 *(D)*
>7...♘f6 – *Game 30*
>7...c5
>>8 h4 – *Game 31*
>>8 ♗d3 – *Game 32*

8 gxf5
>8 f3 – *Game 33*

8...gxf5 9 ♕h5+ ♘g6 10 exf5 ♕h4 *(D)* **11 ♕f3**
>11 ♕xh4 ♘xh4 – *Game 34*

11...♘6e7 – *Game 35*

6...♘ce7

7...f5

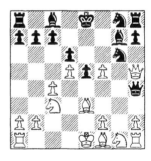

10...♕h4

CHAPTER SEVEN

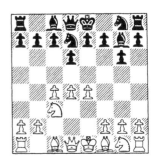

Averbakh Variation with 4...♘d7

1 d4 g6 2 e4 ♗g7 3 c4 d6 4 ♘c3 ♘d7

Whereas the system with 4...♘c6 in the previous two chapters is immediately forcing, this chapter deals with initially calmer systems in which Black plays a more or less normal King's Indian but with the big difference that the g8-knight either goes to h6 or e7 or occasionally even stays at home for some time.

The obvious upside to this flexible approach is that by not blocking the f-pawn, Black keeps the possibility of an immediate ...f7-f5; but on the other hand by failing to put pressure on White's e-pawn, Black gives his opponent a very free hand. This can even be an advantage since that freedom can easily turn into rope with which White can twist himself in knots, but if White reacts well then his opponent is likely to come under some pressure, at least in the early stages.

Move Orders

These are very complex in this family of systems. If Black can get in all his moves, then he will usually have rather a good game. This will particularly be the case if he achieves ...f7-f5 either before or after putting the knight on f7 where it protects the d6-square and the e5-pawn, making it

hard for White to attack the black centre. A knight on h6 may have the added bonus of threatening to harass the white dark-squared bishop if it comes to e3. White's task is, depending on the exact sequence, to find the appropriate spoke to put into his opponent's intentions.

The Question of ...c7-c6

Normally Black will play 4...♘d7 followed by 5...e5 and then only later if at all ...c7-c6. It is of course possible, though, to play 4...c6 and this does have one advantage in that then 5 f4 can be quite well met by 5...♕b6 – see Chapter 8, Game 48, whereas after 4...♘d7 4 f4 is less risky for White (see the notes to that game). Nevertheless, I would generally be very pleased to see a move as committal as 5 f4 so early, so unless he has very strong feelings on this, Black would be better advised to develop the knight first with 4...♘d7. Play normally continues:

5 ♘f3 e5 6 ♗e2

Here Black would like to play 6...♘h6, when White's critical reaction, is, of course, 7 h4 (Game 39). Unfortunately, it also looks very good and White has a huge plus score, at least in my database. So Black must either wait for his opponent to castle before developing the horse to h6 with 6...c6 (Games 40 and 41) or settle for 6...♘e7 (Games 42-47).

Game 39
Legky-Vujadinovic
Vrnjacka Banja open 1989

1 d4 g6 2 c4 ♗g7 3 ♘c3 d6 4 e4 e5 5 ♘f3 ♘d7 6 ♗e2 ♘h6?!

If he can get away with it, this is the move that Black wants to play. Unfortunately:

7 h4!

is not only obvious but also rather unpleasant.

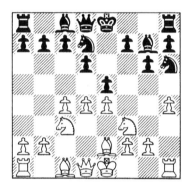

7...f6 8 h5

In order to avoid 8...♘f7, White can also play 8 ♗xh6 ♗xh6 9 h5, and this is almost reason enough to ditch 6...♘h6 on its own. After 9...c6 10 d5 ♕e7 11 ♘h4 Black has tried:

a) 11...♘f8 12 ♗g4 ♗xg4 13 ♕xg4 ♕d7 14 ♕f3 ♗g5 15 g3 0-0-0 16 ♔f1 ♔b8 17 ♔g2 ♖g8 18 ♖ad1 cxd5!? 19 ♖xd5!? was played in Knaak-Peev Leipzig 1977 (and in fact led to quite a quick win with 19...♘e6 20 ♘b5 a6 21 ♘xd6 ♕c6 22 ♕d3 ♘c5 23 ♕d1 ♗xh4 24 ♖xh4 ♘e6 25 hxg6 hxg6 26 ♖h7 ♘c7 27 ♘xb7 ♖c8 28 ♘a5 ♕b6 29 b4 ♔a8 30 ♖d6 1-0).

b) In Ftacnik-Tibensky, Trnava 1980, Black tried to improve with 11...♗g5 but

after 12 g3 a5 13 ♔f1 ♘c5 14 ♘f3! ♗h6 15 ♔g2 ♔f7 16 ♘h4! he couldn't now play 16...♗g5? in view of 17 hxg6+ hxg6 18 ♘xg6! So he still had to allow the exchange of light-squared bishops with 16...♗d7 and after 17 ♗g4 ♗g5 18 ♗xd7 ♕xd7 19 ♘f3! ♗h6 20 ♕e2 ♔g7 21 ♖h3 ♖af8 22 ♖ah1 f5 23 ♘h2 fxe4 24 hxg6 hxg6 25 ♘g4 ♗g5 26 ♖xh8 ♖xh8 27 ♖xh8 ♔xh8 28 ♘xe4 ♘xe4 29 ♕xe4 White has reached an archetypal ending which is vile for Black and Ftacnik duly ground his way to victory in 30-odd more moves.

8...c6

8...g5? 9 d5 a5 10 ♗e3 ♘c5 11 ♕d2 0-0 12 ♘h2 ♗d7 13 g4! was repulsive in Züger-Baumhus, Gelsenkirchen 1991, but of course Black can play 8...♘f7 at once, when 9 d5 c6 would transpose back into this game and he avoids 9 ♗xh6 now, transposing to the lines above.

9 d5!?

It is reasonable to close the centre since it re-emphasises White's advantage on the light squares, but it's also quite possible to exchange on e5 to open up the position before Black gets developed.

9...♘f7 10 ♘h4! ♘f8 11 g3!? c5!?

But here he should have offered the positionally desirable exchange of bishops with 11...♗h6, when 12 f4 exf4 13 gxf4 g5! offers counterplay.

12 ♗e3 f5!?

12...♗h6!? was also possible here, though 13 f4! exf4 14 gxf4 g5 15 ♘g2 gxf4 16 ♗xf4 ♗xf4 17 ♘xf4 ♘e5 18 ♖g1 is more comfortable for White – it looks better to hit out in the more fluid position with the pawn on c6.

13 exf5

Certainly not 13 ♕d2?? f4 14 gxf4 exf4 15 ♗xf4 g5!

13...gxf5 14 ♕c2 ♕f6 15 g4!

A powerful thrust, seizing control of e4.

15...fxg4 16 ♘e4

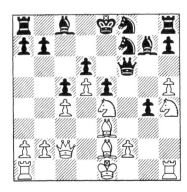

be followed by ♗g5 and ♕a4!

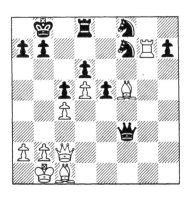

16...♕d8

Designed against 17 b4, which could now be met by 17...cxb4 18 c5 ♕a5!, whereas after 16...♕e7?! 17 b4! Black has to resign himself to 17...b6! (not 17...cxb4 18 c5 dxc5? 19 ♗b5+ ♗d7 20 ♘f5 winning) when 18 bxc5 bxc5 19 ♖b1 is pretty nasty.

17 0-0-0 ♗f6 18 ♘xf6+ ♕xf6 19 ♖dg1 ♖g8 20 ♗d3 ♗d7 21 ♘f5!

Much better than 21 ♗xh7?! ♘xh7 22 ♕xh7 0-0-0 with counterplay.

21...0-0-0 22 f3 g3 23 ♖h3 g2?

A mistake which allows White to remove the pawn while keeping his coordination. Instead 23...♔b8! 24 ♖hxg3 ♖xg3 25 ♘xg3! (or 25 ♖xg3 ♗xf5 26 ♗xf5 ♕h4 27 ♖g1 ♕xh5) 25...♕xf3 26 ♕d2 gives White good play for the pawn but nothing immediate.

24 ♖h2 ♔b8 25 ♖hxg2 ♖xg2 26 ♖xg2 ♗xf5 27 ♗xf5 ♕h4 28 ♔b1!

Not 28 ♖g7?? ♕e1+.

28...♕xh5 29 ♖g7 ♕xf3 30 ♗c1!

---

see following diagram

Despite his extra pawns, Black is in terrible trouble since he can hardly move.

30...♘h8!

Forced for if 30...♕h5 31 ♗e6! ♘h6 32 ♕b3.

31 a3!

Threatening to move the king to a2 to

31...♘fg6! 32 ♔a2 ♖f8!

32...♘f4 lost at once to 33 ♗xf4 exf4 (or 33...♕xf4 34 ♕b3) 34 ♕a4 en route to b5.

33 ♗e6 ♕f6 34 ♗h6 ♘e7 35 ♖xh7 ♖d8 36 ♗g7 ♕g6 37 ♕h2

Perhaps Black could have done better over the last few moves – which I presume were played in time trouble – but now White is clearly winning.

37...♕d3

Or 37...♘f7 38 ♗xf7 ♕xf7 39 ♗e5 ♕g6 40 ♖xe7 dxe5 41 ♕xe5+ etc.

38 ♗xh8

38 ♖xh8 was simpler.

38...♘g6 39 ♗f6 ♖f8 40 ♗g5??

Spoiling it on the last move before the time control. Instead 40 ♖f7! ♖h8 41 ♕xh8+! ♘xh8 42 ♖f8+ ♔c7 43 ♗d8+ ♔b8 44 ♗b6 was mate!

40...♕xc4+ 41 b3 ♕f1! 42 ♗e3 c4??

Returning the compliment. Legky gives some long analysis to show that 42...♕e1! 43 ♖h3 ♖f1 gives excellent drawing chances.

43 ♖xb7+!

Now it's over again.

43...♔a8

Or 43...♔xb7 44 ♕h7+ etc.

44 ♖xa7+ ♔b8 45 ♖b7+ ♔a8 46 bxc4 ♕xc4+ 47 ♖b3 ♖b8 48 ♕b2 ♘f4 49 ♗d7! ♖xb3 50 ♕xb3 ♕e2+ 51 ♕b2

♕c4+ 52 ♔a1 ♘xd5

If 52...♕xd5 53 ♕c1!

53 ♗b5 ♕c3 54 ♕xc3 ♘xc3 55 ♗c6+ ♔b8 56 ♗b6! 1-0

A hard fight in which Black also missed some chances, but White has so many pleasant options in the opening that the whole line is very dubious.

Game 40
Stohl-Berezovics
Mlada Boleslav 1993

---

1 d4 d6 2 ♘f3 g6 3 c4 ♗g7 4 ♘c3 ♘d7 5 e4 e5 6 ♗e2 c6

A safe move, waiting for White to castle before playing the knight to h6. 6...f6 and 6...a5 have also been played, though to my slight surprise I found no instance of 6...a6. Then after 7 0-0 Black would like to play 7...♘h6, but this still runs into 8 c5.

7 0-0 ♘h6

Black's alternatives here are considered in the next main game.

8 c5!

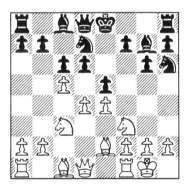

Following some fairly desperate defence against David Goodman in an Islington open some 25 years or so ago, I'd always believed that 8 c5! more or less refuted this move order. However, the notes below suggest that Black does have reasonable chances. This is important for the assessment of the whole line with 4...♘d7, since if Black can play this way, then he is imposing himself on the opening, whereas the various attempts to avoid 8 c5 are somewhat less satisfactory.

All the early games featured 8...dxc5 9 dxe5 which does indeed seem to be pretty dicey, though far from totally clear, viz. 9...0-0 (not 9...♘g4? 10 e6! fxe6 11 ♘g5 winning) 10 h3 ♔h8 (10...♕e8 11 ♗f4 ♔h8 12 ♕d6 ♕e6 13 ♖ad1 ♕xd6 14 exd6 f6 15 a4 b6 16 ♗c4 ♘f7 17 ♖fe1 ♗b7 18 ♗xf7 ♖xf7 19 e5 fxe5 20 ♗xe5 was grim in Kumaran-Fries Nielsen, Lyngby open 1990 - White won in a dozen more moves) 11 ♗f4 and now:

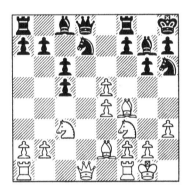

a) 11...♕e8 12 ♕d2 ♘g8 13 ♕d6 ♕e6 (Black has the extra move here ...♘g8 as compared to Kumaran-Fries Nielsen, but as a result the knight is further from f7) 14 ♖ad1 h6 15 ♖d2 ♖e8 16 ♕c7 ♕e7 17 ♖fd1 ♘f8 18 ♕d6 ♘e6 19 ♗e3 ♕xd6 20 exd6 ♗d7 21 ♗c4 b6 22 ♘e1 ♘d8 23 f3 a5 24 ♗f1 a4 25 a3 ♘b7 26 ♗c4 ♖f8 27 f4 b5 28 ♗a2 b4 29 ♘e2 ♖fe8 30 ♘g3 b3 31 ♗b1 h5 32 e5 was played in the earliest game I've found in this line, Petran-Ivanovic, Zalaegerszeg 1977 - White went on to win.

b) 11...♘g8 12 ♕d6 ♕e8 13 a4 h6 14 ♖fd1 g5 15 ♗g3 ♘e7 16 a5 ♘g6 17 a6 ♘dxe5 18 axb7 ♗xb7 19 ♕xc5 ♘xf3+ 20 ♗xf3 ♗e5 21 ♖xa7 ♖xa7 22 ♕xa7 ♗c8 23

♗xe5+ ♘xe5 24 ♗e2 was utterly grim for Black in Uhlmann-Ciocaltea, Bucharest 1978, though he did draw after 117 moves of torture!

c) Vegh-Lau, Budapest 1978, ended 11...♕e7 12 ♕d6 ♖e8 13 ♕xe7!? ♖xe7 14 ♖ad1 ♘g8 15 ♗g5 ♖e8 16 ♗c4 ♘xe5 17 ♘xe5 ♗xe5 18 ♗xf7 ♖f8 19 ♗b3 b6 20 ♖d2 ½-½, but even at the end White looks slightly more comfortable; and 13 ♖ad1 looks much more critical on the way.

8...exd4!

A new idea which may possibly resuscitate Black's move order. Immediately sacrificing a pawn, he allows White a powerful but potentially surroundable extra unit on d6 but avoids the cramping effect of a white pawn on e5 and hopes to use his superiority on the dark squares to good effect.

9 ♗xh6 ♗xh6 10 ♕xd4 0-0 11 cxd6

Not 11 ♕xd6?! when 11...♕a5 surrounds the c5-pawn immediately.

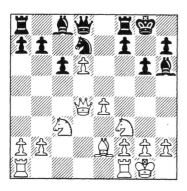

11...♗g7?!

In his notes in *Informator 58*, Stohl suggests that this is inaccurate, preferring the immediate 11...♕b6 when there are two main lines:

a) 12 ♖fd1 ♕xb2!? 13 ♘d5 ♕xd4 14 ♘e7+ ♔h8 15 ♘xd4 ♘c5!?, which he rightly assesses as unclear. If White can support the d6-pawn, even perhaps at the cost of the exchange, then he may obtain a

wonderful game, but if Black can surround it he will be in the driving seat. This line could also be played after 12 ♖ad1 and needs testing before a verdict can be reached. Perhaps White should play 16 ♘b3, when 16...♘xe4? fails to 17 d7 while 16...♘xb3 17 axb3 ♗d7 clarifies matters somewhat, making it fairly easy for White to support his big pawn.

b) 12 ♕xb6 axb6 13 ♖fd1 ♗g7 14 a3 b5 leaves White a large and fairly safe pawn up at the moment but Black does have play both against it and on the dark squares and a-file; and the queenside pawn structure is much in his favour.

Personally, I'm a little sceptical of these two lines but it's up to you, the reader. If you like them then this line may be just right for you since there's a very reasonable chance anyway that White won't play 8 c5 and in that case Black has got exactly what he wanted out of the line.

12 ♕d2

If 12 ♕e3 ♕b6! is even better.

12...♘c5

13 ♖ad1

Stohl also gives 13 e5!? ♘d7 (if 13...♗g4?! 14 ♘d4! is strong with f2-f4 to come or 13...♖e8 14 ♕f4, teeing up against f7) 14 ♖ad1 with the advantage.

13...♗xc3?!

Regaining the pawn but at too great a cost. Instead 13...♖e8 14 ♖fe1 ♗g4 (not

14...♘xe4? 15 ♘xe4 ♖xe4 16 d7) 15 h3 ♗xf3 16 ♗xf3 ♗e5 17 b4 is good for White, but at least Black has some dark-square control.

14 ♕xc3

14 bxc3 ♘xe4 15 ♕d4 ♘f6 16 c4 was also good.

14...♘xe4 15 ♕d4 ♘f6 16 ♗c4 ♗g4 17 ♖d3?!

Stohl recommends 17 ♖fe1 ♗xf3 18 gxf3 ♖e8 19 ♖xe8+ ♘xe8 20 d7 ♘f6 21 b4 as cleaner.

17...♗f5 18 ♖e3 ♗e4!

If 18...c5 19 ♕xc5 ♘e4 20 ♕b4 ♕xd6 (not 20...♘xd6? 21 ♖d1) 21 ♕xb7 wins a pawn, while the more ambitious 19 ♕d1!? may be even better, intending 19...♘e4 20 d7 ♘f6 21 ♘e5 ♘xd7 22 ♘xf7 ♖xf7 23 g4! ♕g5 24 ♖g3 winning material.

19 ♘g5!?

19 ♖xe4 ♘xe4 20 ♕xe4 ♕xd6 is very good for White but this seems to win.

19...♗d5

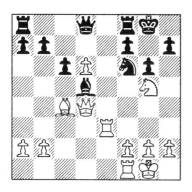

20 ♗xd5 ♘xd5

After 20...cxd5 21 ♖f3 h6! (21...♘h5 22 ♕xd5 or 21...♘e4 22 ♘xh7) 22 ♖xf6 hxg5 23 h4! gxh4 24 ♖e1 ♖e8 25 ♖xe8+ ♕xe8 26 ♕xd5 ♔g7 27 ♖f4 White should win.

21 ♘xh7! ♘xe3 22 ♘f6+ ♕xf6!

Not 22...♔h8 23 fxe3 and White will soon deliver mate.

23 ♕xf6 ♘xf1 24 ♔xf1 ♖ad8 25 ♕e7

Through stormy complications White

has preserved the powerful passed pawn on d6 which now ensures victory.

25...b6

Black can't get play with 25...♖fe8 26 ♕c7 ♖c8?, hoping for 27 ♕xb7 ♖b8, in view of 27 d7! winning immediately.

26 ♕c7 c5 27 d7 ♖a8 28 ♔e2 ♖fd8 29 ♔e3 ♔f8 30 ♕d6+ ♔g8 31 ♔e4 b5 32 ♔e5 a5 33 ♕e7 c4 34 ♔f6

34...♖f8

Or 34...♖a6+ 35 ♔g5 ♖aa8 36 ♔h6 b4 37 ♕e5 ♔f8 38 ♔h7! ♖xd7 39 ♕h8+.

35 ♕c5 ♖ab8 36 ♔e7 ♔g7 37 a4 bxa4 38 ♕xc4 f6 39 ♕d5! ♖bd8 40 ♕xa5 ♖b8 41 d8♕ ♖fxd8 42 ♕xd8 1-0

A depressing game for Black, but the note on move 11 suggests a line which just might allow him to employ a move order which, but for 8 c5, would be highly desirable.

Game 41
Schlosser-Chiburdanidze
Lippstadt 1995

---

1 c4 c6 2 e4 g6 3 d4 ♗g7 4 ♘c3 d6 5 ♘f3 ♘d7 6 ♗e2 e5 7 0-0

Via an unusual move order we've now reached a familiar position. Dissatisfied with the ramifications of the game above, some of the top Georgian women looked for an alternative move order and came up with:

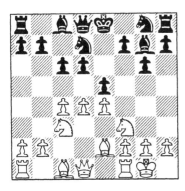

7...f6?!

7...♕c7 is another way of trying to do this, though Black doesn't normally want his queen on c7 in these positions. In the chaotic game Knaak-Ciocaltea, Halle 1974, Black did manage to set up his stall but at the cost of some time. Later White gave up his queen for two pieces and eventually won. It's not very relevant here but it's sufficient fun that I'll give all the moves: 8 ♖b1 ♘h6 9 b4 f6 10 d5 ♘f7 11 ♕c2 0-0 12 ♖d1 c5 13 ♘b5 ♕d8 14 ♗e3 b6 15 a3 a6 16 ♘c3 f5 17 exf5 gxf5 18 ♕xf5 cxb4 19 axb4 e4 20 ♘xe4 ♘c5 21 ♕f4 ♘e5 22 bxc5 ♖xf4 23 ♗xf4 ♗f5 24 ♘xd6 ♘xf3+ 25 ♗xf3 ♗xb1 26 ♖xb1 ♕f6 27 ♗g3 bxc5 28 ♗g4 ♖f8 29 ♗e6+ ♔h8 30 h4 a5 31 ♖b7 a4 32 ♘f7+ ♖xf7 33 ♗xf7 h5 34 ♖b8+ ♔h7 35 ♗g8+ ♔g6 36 d6 a3 37 d7 a2 38 d8♕ a1♕+ 39 ♔h2 ♕xd8 40 ♖xd8 ♗d4 41 ♖d7 ♕f1 42 ♗f7+ ♔f6 43 ♗d5 ♔g6 44 ♖f7 ♕e1 45 ♖f3 ♔g7 46 ♗f7 ♕f1 47 ♗d5 ♕e1 48 ♖f4 ♕e2 49 ♖e4 ♕d1 50 ♖e7+ ♔f6 51 ♖e6+ ♔g7 52 ♗f4 ♗xf2 53 ♗e5+ 1-0.

8 d5!

In conjunction with his next move, this puts a serious question mark over Black's move order. Instead in Zsu.Polgar-Gaprindashvili, Shanghai Women's Candidates 1992, White got nothing much after 8 ♗e3 ♘h6 9 dxe5 dxe5 10 ♘d2 ♕e7 11 a3 0-0 12 b4 ♖d8 13 c5 ♘f8 14 ♗c4+ ♗e6 15 ♕e2 ♖d7 16 ♘b3 ♗xc4 17 ♕xc4+

♕e6 18 ♕xe6+ ♘xe6 19 ♖fd1 ♖ad8 20 ♖xd7 ♖xd7 21 ♖d1 ♖xd1+ 22 ♘xd1 ♘f7 23 ♔f1 ♗f8 24 f3 ½-½.

8...c5 9 ♘b5!

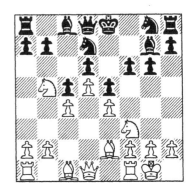

Most annoying, though it does seem surprising that this crude move can lead to such trouble for Black.

9...♔e7

The alternatives are also unappetising:

a) If 9...♘b6 10 b4 a6 (or 10...cxb4 11 ♗e3 ♗h6 12 ♘xd6+ ♕xd6 13 c5 with a clear advantage) 11 bxc5 dxc5 12 ♘c3 White had much the better structure in Chiburdanidze-Gaprindashvili, Kuala Lumpur 1994, and went on to win.

b) 9...♘b8 is also met by 10 b4 and if 10...a6 11 ♕a4!

c) 9...♗f8 looks sensible, but after 10 ♘e1 (10. a3 a6 11 ♘c3 ♘h6 12 b4 ♘f7 13 ♘e1 ♗e7 14 ♘d3 0-0 15 ♖b1 ♕c7 16 bxc5 dxc5 17 ♗g4 ♘d6 was less immediately traumatic in Ioseliani-Gaprindashvili played in an earlier round at Belgrade 1996, though White still won eventually) 10...a6 11 ♘c3 ♗g7 12 ♗g4 f5 13 ♗h3 f4 14 ♘d3 ♘e7 15 ♖b1 0-0 16 b4 cxb4 17 ♖xb4 ♕c7 18 ♗xd7 ♗xd7 19 ♕b3 f3 20 ♖xb7 ♕c8 21 g3 ♘f5 22 exf5 ♗xf5 23 ♘e1 e4 24 ♗b2 ♗h6 25 ♘xe4 Black had been utterly blown away in Matveeva-Gaprindashvili, Belgrade 1996, and resigned here.

10 a3 ♗h6 11 b4 b6 12 ♗b2 ♗g7 13

♕a4 ♗b7 14 ♘e1

Of course not 14 ♘xa7?? b5!

14...♘h6 15 ♘d3 a6 16 ♘c3

16...g5

To prevent 17 f4. Black's position is now rather repulsive but proves to be much more resilient than it appears at first sight.

17 ♕b3 ♕c7 18 ♗c1 ♖hb8 19 ♗e3 ♗c8 20 ♖fb1 ♔f7 21 a4?!

Allowing counterplay with ...a6-a5.

21...♗f8 22 ♕a3 a5! 23 ♘b5 ♕d8 24 bxa5 bxa5 25 h4 ♔g6 26 ♕c1 ♗e7 27 ♘e1 ♘f8 28 ♘f3 ♘f7 29 ♕d1 ♔g7 30 hxg5?!

Helping Black by freeing f6 for her pieces.

30...fxg5 31 ♘h2 ♘d7! 32 ♗g4 ♘f6 33 ♗xc8 ♖xc8 34 ♕c2 h5

Finally getting some counterplay.

35 ♖b3 ♕d7 36 ♗d2 g4 37 ♖ab1 ♘h7 38 ♘f1 h4 39 ♘d4 exd4 40 ♖xb8 ♖xb8 41 ♖xb8

Although Chiburdanidze has lost the exchange, she now gets serious counterplay against the enemy king.

41...♘hg5 42 ♗f4 ♗f6 43 ♕e2 ♗e5 44 ♗xg5 ♘xg5 45 ♘h2 g3 46 fxg3 hxg3 47 ♘f3 ♕g4 48 ♖b7+ ♔h6 49 ♖e7

see following diagram

49...♘xe4?!

Perhaps she 'ought' to have played

49...♗g7, but in practice you should take pawns like this unless it's absolutely obviously why not.

50 ♖e6+ ♔g7

If 50...♘f6 51 ♕d2+ is easy.

51 ♕b2 ♘f6 52 ♕b7+!?

The more forcing 52 ♖e7+ was also good when:

a) 52...♔g6? 53 ♖xe5!

b) 52...♔h6 53 ♕b8 ♕f4 54 ♕h8+ ♔g6 55 ♘h4+ ♔g5 56 ♖g7 mate.

c) So Black should try 52...♔f8, though even 53 ♖xe5!? dxe5 54 ♕b8+ ♔g7 55 ♕xe5 ought to be enough.

52...♔h6 53 ♕c8?

But here he should have played 53 ♕a8! and if 53...♕f4 54 ♕xa5.

53...♕f4! 54 ♕f8+ ♔g6 55 ♕e8+ ♔f5 56 ♖xf6+

Forced. But now it's just a draw.

56...♗xf6 57 ♕e6+ ♔g6 58 ♕g8+ ♔h6 59 ♕f8+ ♔g6 60 ♕g8+ ♗g7 61 ♕e6+ ♔h7 62 ♕h3+ ♔g8 63 ♕c8+ ½-½

Although Chiburdanidze suffered in this game, her eventual escape shows that such positions have great resilience, however foul they appear to the casual eye.

Game 42
Atalik-Gelashvili
Greek Team Ch., Poros 1998

---

1 d4 d6 2 ♘f3 g6 3 c4 ♗g7 4 ♘c3 ♘d7

5 e4 e5 6 ♗e2 ♘e7 7 h4!?

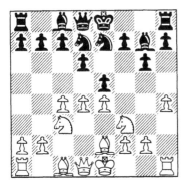

This is less effective than with the black knight on h6, since there's no immediate target and with the g5-d8 diagonal presently blocked Black can usually play ...f7-f5 without, at any rate, worrying about ♗g5. Indeed ...f7-f5 as fast as possible is Black's correct plan and sufficient to get a reasonable game. The point is that once the knight can move to f5 Black gets space for his pieces, otherwise he can end up revoltingly cramped.

7...exd4?!

Black should react to White's thrust for if he simply castles he comes under a strong attack e.g. Ernst-J.Johansson, Malmo 1992, ended in serious bloodshed after 7...0-0 8 h5 exd4 9 ♘xd4 ♘c6 10 ♗e3 ♖e8 11 hxg6 hxg6 12 ♕d2 ♘de5 13 ♗g5 f6 14 ♗h6 ♗h8 15 ♗e3 ♘xd4 16 ♗xd4 ♗g7 17 0-0-0 ♗e6 18 b3 c6 19 f4 ♘f7 20 g4 g5 21 f5 ♗c8 22 ♖h3 a6 23 ♖dh1 b5 24 ♖h7 b4 25 ♘d1 c5 26 ♗b2 ♗b7 27 ♗f3 ♘e5 28 ♕h2 d5 29 ♗xe5 1-0.

However, 7...h5 8 d5 a5 is quite playable for Black and now:

a) 9 ♘g5 ♘c5 10 f3 f6 11 ♘h3 ♘g8 12 ♗e3 ♗h6, as in Atalik-Baum, Groningen open 1998, when by exchanging the dark-squared bishops Black gets a potentially good structure at the cost of a very little time.

b) White can also prepare the standard queenside play with 9 a3 to be followed by ♖b1 and b2-b4 – the inclusion of h2-h4 and ...h7-h5 certainly doesn't commit White to attack there, but by creating a potential outpost on g5 if Black plays ...f7-f5 may instead serve to stifle Black's play on that side of the board. Rogozenko-Badea, Brasov 1998, continued 9...♘f6 10 ♘g5 ♗d7 11 b3 0-0 12 ♖b1 ♘c8!? (maybe 12...♘h7) 13 b4 axb4 14 axb4 c6 15 0-0 cxd5 16 ♘xd5! ♘xd5 17 cxd5 and here Black fell for 17...b5? 18 ♗xh5!, but of course 17...♗f6 would lead to a normal game – Rogozenko suggests then 18 ♗e3 or 18 b5!?

But the right reaction appears to be 7...h6, as in the following two games.

8 ♘xd4 ♘c6 9 ♗g5!

Very disruptive.

9...♗f6

The self-pin 9...♘f6 is also very dodgy. Volkov-Zhelnin, Sochi 1997, continued 10 ♘d5 ♗d7? (if 10...a6 11 h5 h6 12 ♗xf6 ♗xf6 13 ♘xf6+ ♕xf6 14 ♘xc6 bxc6 15 hxg6 fxg6 16 ♕d2 gives White a clear advantage, but Volkov suggests 10...♗e6 or 10...h6) 11 ♘b5 ♖c8 12 ♘xa7! ♘xa7 13 ♕d4 ♘c6 14 ♕xf6! ♗xf6 15 ♗xf6 ♘e7 and here White continued 16 h5, which after 16...c6 is presumably good but messy. Instead simply 16 ♗xe7 ♕xe7 17 ♘xe7 ♔xe7 18 h5 leaves White a clear pawn up for absolutely no compensation.

10 ♘d5 ♗xg5

Black would prefer to avoid this exchange, and in H.Olafsson-Zilberman, Manila Olympiad 1992, he obtained reasonable play for a pawn after 10...h6 11 ♗xf6 ♘xf6 12 ♘b5 ♘xd5 13 cxd5 a6 14 dxc6 axb5 15 cxb7 ♗xb7 16 ♗xb5+ c6 17 ♗d3 0-0 18 ♕d2 h5 in the form of a lead in development, open lines and several potentially loose white pawns to attack, including one on h4 which either has to advance or requires further time to defend. They continued 19 ♕g5 ♕b6 20 ♕f6 ♗a6

21 ♗xa6 ♕xa6 22 ♕xd6 ♕c4 23 f3 ♖fd8 24 ♕e5 ♖xa2 (but maybe 24...♕c2 here) 25 ♖xa2 ♕xa2 26 0-0 ♖d2 27 ♖c1 ♖xb2 28 ♔h1 ♖b1 29 ♕e8+ ♔h7 30 ♕xc6 and White subsequently reached a rook ending with four pawns against three, though the game was still eventually drawn. But near the beginning of this sequence 14 ♕a4 looks even stronger since 14...axb5 15 ♕xa8 ♘d4 16 ♗d3 0-0 is pretty unconvincing for Black.

11 hxg5 ♘e7

11...0-0 12 ♘b5! ♕xg5 13 ♕c1 ♕xc1+ 14 ♖xc1 is most unpleasant. Garcia Palermo-Carruez, Zaragoza 1993, continued just three more moves: 14...♘c5 15 ♘bxc7 ♖b8 16 ♘f6+ ♔g7 17 ♘ce8+ 1-0.

12 ♕d2 ♘xd5 13 exd5

13 cxd5 also looks good.

13...♘c5 14 b4 ♘a4 15 ♕f4 ♕e7 16 ♔d2! ♕e5 17 ♕xe5+ dxe5 18 ♘b5 ♔d8 19 ♗d1 ♘b6 20 ♗b3 a6 21 ♘c3 a5

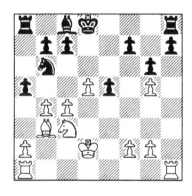

22 bxa5

Although White now wins a pawn by doubling on the h-file, this move seriously spoils his queenside structure so 22 a3! may be even better.

22...♖xa5 23 ♖ae1 ♘d7 24 ♖h4 b6 25 ♖eh1 ♗a6 26 ♖xh7 ♖xh7 27 ♖xh7 ♔e7 28 ♘e4 ♘c5 29 ♘f6?!

This looks wrong since after Black's next move he gets serious play on the queenside. So perhaps 29 ♔e3, say, though

it would still be tough to win.

29...b5 30 cxb5 ♘xb3+ 31 axb3 ♖xb5 32 ♔c3 ♖c5+ 33 ♔b4 ♖b5+ 34 ♔a4 ♖b8 35 ♘g4 ♗b7 36 ♘xe5 ♖a8+!

Not 36...♗xd5 37 ♖xf7+!

37 ♔b4 ♗xd5 38 f4 c6 39 ♘xg6+ ♔e6 40 ♘e5 ♖b8+ 41 ♔a5 ♔f5 42 b4 ♔xf4 43 ♘xf7 ♔f5 ½-½

Game 43
Zviaginsev-Makarov
President's Cup, Elista 1998

---

1 ♘f3 g6 2 d4 ♗g7 3 c4 d6 4 ♘c3 ♘d7 5 e4 e5 6 ♗e2 ♘e7 7 h4 h6 8 ♗e3?!

This seems quite inconsequent since not only does it not prevent Black's ...f7-f5 break, but the break is even encouraged by presenting the bishop as a possible target for ...f5-f4. The critical 8 h5 is the subject of the next main game.

8...f5!

In the blitz game Sosonko-Ljubojevic Brussels 1987, Black wrongly passed up this opportunity with 8...0-0?! After 9 ♕d2 ♔h7 10 0-0-0 c6 11 dxe5 dxe5 12 ♕d6 White was doing well and the further 12...♘g8 13 c5 ♖e8? led to 14 ♘g5+ hxg5 15 hxg5+ ♘h6 16 gxh6 ♗f8. The rest is of interest, only as a cautionary tale as to what Black should avoid: 17 ♕d3 ♕a5 18 ♕c4 ♖e7 19 ♖d6 b5 20 ♕b3 b4 21 ♘a4 ♗a6 22 ♗xa6 ♕xa6 23 ♖hd1 ♕b7 24 ♗g5 f6 25 ♗xf6 ♗xh6+ 26 ♔b1 ♘xf6 27 ♖xf6 ♗g5 28 ♖fd6 ♔g7 29 ♕g3 ♗f6 30 ♕g4 ♖f8 31 ♖d7 ♕c8 32 ♕e6 ♖fe8 33 ♖xe7+ ♗xe7 34 ♖d7 ♔f8 35 b3 ♗xc5 36 ♕f7 mate.

9 dxe5 dxe5 10 g3

Aimed against ...f5-f4. In Ivanisevic-Popovic, Yugoslav Championship, Belgrade 1998, White allowed this with 10 b4 but Black still followed the same recipe of exchanging on e4 to free f5 for the knight and later opening things up with ...e5-e4, i.e. 10...fxe4 11 ♘xe4 ♘f5 12 c5 ♕e7 13 ♕c2 ♘f6 14 ♖d1 0-0 15 ♗c4+ ♔h8 16 ♘xf6 ♗xf6 17 ♗d5 a5 18 a3 axb4 19 axb4 e4 with an advantage for Black.

10...0-0 11 ♕d2

11 c5 f4!? 12 gxf4 exf4 13 ♗d4 is unclear – if Black can get control of the dark squares then he'll be doing well, but for example 13...♘c6 14 ♕b3+ ♔h8 15 ♗xg7+ ♔xg7 16 ♘d5 gives White a dangerous initiative. So probably Black would meet 11 c5 with 11...fxe4, as well.

12 ♘xe4 ♘f5 13 c5 ♘xe3 14 ♕xe3 ♕e7 15 ♘h2 ♘f6

Black is very active and despite White's strongpoint on e4, he has a good game.

16 ♘xf6+ ♕xf6 17 ♘g4 ♗xg4 18 ♗xg4

18...e4!

After this thematic advance, White is in some trouble and Zviaginsev later had to defend himself very carefully to hold the balance.

19 0-0 ♖ae8 20 b3 h5 21 ♗h3 ♔h7 22 ♖ad1 ♖f7 23 ♗g2 ♗h6 24 ♕d4 ♕xd4 25 ♖xd4 e3 26 fxe3 ♖fe7 27 ♔h2 ♗xe3 28 ♖c4 c6 29 b4 ♔g7 30 a4 a6 31 ♖b1 ♖d8 32 ♖e4 ♖xe4 33 ♗xe4 ♖d2+ 34 ♔h3 ♖d4 35 ♗g2 ♖d3 36 ♗f3 ♗d4 37 ♔g2 ♖d2+ 38 ♔h3 ♖f2 39 ♖d1 ♗e5 40 ♖d3 ♔f6 41 b5 axb5 42 axb5 cxb5 43 ♗xb7 ♖c2 44 ♖f3+ ♔e7 45 ♗e4 ♖xc5 46 ♗xg6 ♗d6 47 g4 hxg4+ 48 ♔xg4 b4 49 h5 ♖c4+ 50 ♔f5 ♖c5+ 51 ♔e4 ♖g5 52 ♔d4 ♖g1 53 ♔d5 ♖d1+ 54 ♖d3 ♖g1 55 ♖f3 ♖g5+ 56 ♔c4 ♖c5+ 57 ♔b3 ♖a5 58 ♔c4 ½-½

Game 44
Burgess-P.H.Nielsen
Aarhus open 1989

---

1 d4 g6 2 e4 ♗g7 3 c4 d6 4 ♘c3 ♘d7 5 ♗e2 e5 6 ♘f3 ♘e7 7 h4 h6 8 h5 g5 9 d5

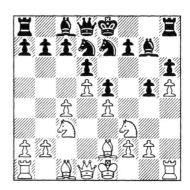

9...f5!

Essential, since if White gets in g2-g4 then he will secure a stable kingside structure in which he has eventual access to f5, while there is no route for a black knight to reach f4. This structure gives White excellent long-term winning chances by eventually opening the queenside, though it need not be quite as horrible for Black as the copybook game Mallet-Yanofsky, Skopje Olympiad 1972: 9...♘f6? 10 ♘h2 c5 11 a3 a6 12 ♘f1 ♘fg8 13 g4 ♘f6 14 ♘e3 ♗d7 15 f3 ♕c7 16 ♗d2 0-0 17 ♔f2 ♖fb8 18 b4 b5 19 bxc5 dxc5 20 cxb5 axb5 21 a4 bxa4 22 ♘xa4 ♘c8 23 ♕c2 ♗f8 24 ♘b2 ♘d6 25 ♘bc4 ♘b5 26 ♗a5 ♕b7 27 ♖hb1 ♗e8 28 ♘f5 ♖a6 29 ♗c3 ♖ba8 30 ♖xa6 ♖xa6 31 ♘xe5 c4 32 ♘xc4 ♕a7+ 33 ♔g2 ♘xc3 34 ♕xc3 ♕c5 35 ♖a1 ♖xa1 36 ♕xa1 ♗b5 37 ♕xf6 ♗xc4 38 ♗xc4 ♕xc4 39 ♕d4 ♕c2+ 40 ♕f2 ♕c7 41 ♕b2 ♕d8 42 d6 1-0.

10 exf5!?

The alternative is 10 g4, when I've found a couple of games, both of which ended in quick draws:

a) 10...fxg4 11 ♘h2 ♘f6 12 ♘f1!? (but of course White can play 12 ♘xg4) 0-0 13 ♘g3 a6 14 ♗e3 ½-½ P.H.Nielsen-Dunnington, Gausdal 1990.

b) 10...fxe4 11 ♘xe4 ♘f6 12 ♘xf6+ ♗xf6 13 ♘d2 0-0 14 ♘e4 ♖f7 15 ♗e3 ♗g7 16 ♕d2 b6 17 f3 ♗b7 18 ♖d1 ♕d7 19 0-0 ♖d8 20 b3 ♔h8 21 ♔g2 ½-½ Keitlinghaus-Lau, German Championship 1989.

While neither of these games tells us much, they do show that White players aren't nearly as happy with the kingside in this fairly tense state (as compared to Malich-Yanofsky above) and feel that the advantage of the e4-square is counterbalanced by the need to hold the kingside.

10...♘xf5 11 ♘e4 ♘f6

It's just possible that Black should castle here first, so that if 11...0-0 12 ♘fxg5 hxg5 13 ♗xg5 (not 13 h6? ♗xh6 14 ♖xh6 ♘xh6 15 ♗xg5 ♘f6!) 13...♕e8, intending 14 h6 ♗f6 leaving the h8-square for the king. But I can't believe that the coming sacrifice is more than adequate for White.

12 ♘fxg5!

The point of 10 exf5 and already almost 'morally forced', though not hugely convincing.

12...hxg5 13 ♗xg5

---

see following diagram

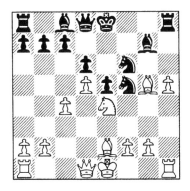

13...♘xe4!?

A delightful riposte but White does now obtain a nominal material advantage. Instead if:

a) 13...♘h6 14 ♕c1 (not 14 ♕d2? ♘xe4; while 14 ♕b3 ♗f5 15 ♘xf6+ ♗xf6 16 ♗xf6 ♕xf6 17 ♕xb7 0-0 gives Black a dangerous initiative) and White has dangerous pressure, e.g. 14...♘hg8 15 h6 (15 ♕e3 ♗f5) 15...♕d7 (not now 15...♗f5? 16 ♗h5+!) 16 ♘g3 ♗f8 17 ♗d3 ♕f7 18 h7 ♘xh7 19 ♕c2 ♘xg5 20 ♖xh8 is unclear.

b) But the apparently risky 13..♕e7 may be best, when after 14 h6 ♕f8 15 ♗h5+ ♘xh5 16 ♕xh5+ ♕f7 Black seems to emerge with the advantage.

14 ♗xd8 ♔xd8 15 ♗d3?

White should act quickly before his opponent can get fully co-ordinated, but 15 ♕c2 looks much better and if for example 15...♘c5 16 g4 ♘d4 17 ♕g6, as although the knight is beautifully placed on d4 the queen's penetration decides immediately.

15...♘c5! 16 ♗xf5? ♗xf5 17 g4 ♘d3+ 18 ♔f1 ♗e4 19 ♖h3

Certainly not 19 f3? ♖f8 20 ♖h3 ♘f4.

19...♘f4 20 ♖g3 ♗f6

With the knight powerfully ensconced on f4, Black has quite a good game though he must still watch the white kingside pawns carefully.

21 ♕b3

Not 21 g5?? ♖xh5!

21...b6 22 ♖e1 ♗h7

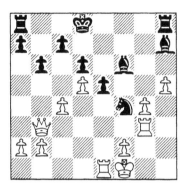

23 c5?!

Trying to generate play against the black king. But this was the moment for 23 g5! when:

a) Black would probably retreat 23...♗e7 24 g6 ♗g8. Now the h5-pawn is doomed but White can and must try to exploit his opponent's temporary discoordination with 25 ♖e4! when if 25...♖xh5 26 ♖xf4 exf4 27 ♖g4 looks very good, since the bishop is trapped on g8 and it's impossible to get the a8-rook into play.

b) So perhaps Black might try 23...♗xg5 24 ♖xg5 ♗d3+ 25 ♔g1 ♘h3+ 26 ♔g2 ♘xg5 27 ♕xd3 ♔e7 which looks better for White, though Black might be able to hold, e.g. 28 f4 ♘f7 29 ♕f5 ♖ag8+ 30 ♔h3 ♖h6 31 ♔h4 ♖f6 32 ♕e4 ♔d8 33 ♖f1 ♘h6 34 f5 ♔e7 35 b4 ♖gf8 36 ♔g5 ♘xf5 37 ♖xf5 ♖xf5+ 38 ♕xf5 ♖xf5+ 39 ♔xf5 ♔f7 with equality.

23...bxc5 24 ♕b7 ♖c8 25 ♖d1 c4

see following diagram

26 ♖a3?

Chasing the enemy king but Black will be first. 26 g5 ♗e7 g6 ♗g8 was still correct.

26...♗d3+ 27 ♔g1 ♖g8 28 f3 e4! 29 fxe4 ♗d4+ 30 ♔h2 ♖xg4 31 ♖axd3 cxd3 32 h6 ♗f2 0-1

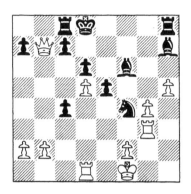

Game 45
Lautier-Yusupov
Belgrade 1991

1 c4 e5 2 ♘c3 d6 3 ♘f3 g6 4 d4 ♘d7 5 e4 ♗g7 6 ♗e2 ♘e7 7 d5

Usually one should maintain a centre until forced to do otherwise, since the very act of forcing developments will often cost the 'defender' time. But of course it's quite legal to release the tension.

7...0-0!?

Inviting, indeed practically forcing White to attack with 8 h4 since if 8 0-0 he would simply be a tempo down in a normal King's Indian – Black has already played the knight to d7, whereas in a KID after 1 d4 ♘f6 2 c4 g6 3 ♘c3 ♗g7 4 e4 d6 5 ♘f3 0-0 6 ♗e2 e5 7 0-0 ♘c6 8. d5 ♘e7 it's still on f6, though 8 ♗e3 or 8 g4!? are possible.

Instead 7...f5!? is just about conceivable and if 8 exf5 gxf5 (if 8...♘xf5 9 ♘e4 White's control of the e4-square gives him a comfortable edge) 9 ♘g5 ♘f8!, preparing to block 10 ♗h5+ with 10...♘eg6 – but the whole thing is very uncomfortable for Black at least in the short term and instead 10 f4 looks quite good for White too.

In any case Black absolutely mustn't play 9...♘f6? 10 ♗h5+, when if 10...♘g6 11 ♘xh7! while 10...♔f8 11 ♗f7! is perfectly vile.

Another plausible idea is the waiting move 7...a5 and if 8 h4 h5, transposing to the note to Black's seventh move in Game 42.

8 h4! ♘f6

Slightly submissive. 8...f5 is crucial, though a couple of games by Cvetkovic don't place it in a very good light. In a game in Yugoslavia in 1986 against Minic he tried 9 ♘g5!? ♘c5 10 ♗e3!? and was rewarded by 10...♘xe4?! 11 ♘gxe4 fxe4 12 g4! with a very nice edge, but 10...h6! 11 ♗xc5 hxg5 12 ♗a3 (if 12 ♗e3 f4 13 ♗c1 gxh4 14 ♖xh4 ♘f5!) 12...gxh4 13 ♖xh4 fxe4 (not 13...♘c6? 14 dxc6) 14 ♘xe4 ♘f5 15 ♖h2 ♘d4 16 ♕d3 would have been quite unclear.

Two years later Cvetkovic-Strikovic also in Yugoslavia went 9 h5 ♘c5 (9...♘f6 10 hxg6 hxg6 11 exf5 gxf5 12 ♗g5 would leave a lot of air around the black king – presumably White could also try this against 9...♘c5) 10 ♘g5 h6 11 b4! ♘xe4 (if 11...♘a6 12 ♘e6 ♗xe6 13 dxe6 Black has lots of light-square weaknesses – Cvetkovic in *Informator 45* assesses this as a large advantage to White which is probably true, though lines like 13...♘xb4 14 hxg6 f4 are far from absolutely clear to me) 12 ♘gxe4 fxe4 13 hxg6 ♘xg6 14 g3 ♗f5 15 ♗e3 ♘h8!? (perhaps 15...♕f6) 16 ♗g4 ♕d7 17 ♗xf5 ♕xf5 18 ♕h5! ♘g6 19 ♕xf5 ♖xf5 and now the simple 20 ♘xe4 would have yielded a clear advantage – White played the messier 20 ♗xh6 and subsequently won anyway.

9 ♗e3

Threatening to become well organised after 10 ♘d2, so Black is obliged to try and create some confusion.

9...♘g4 10 ♗d2

A very critical position. Unless Black can generate counterplay in the next few moves (which will normally involve playing ...f7-f5 – desirable in itself but creating

a potentially very unpleasant weakness on e6) then White should be able to reach a favourable accommodation on the kingside which will guarantee him a clear advantage. But in his notes in *Informator 53*, Lautier doesn't show any suitable way for Black to get going, in which case the whole line with 7...0-0 seems slightly doubtful.

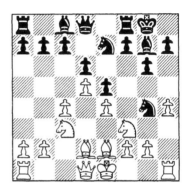

10...c6

Black has a wide choice here:

a) If 10...f5?! 11 h5!, opening the h-file, leaves the black king somewhat exposed.

b) Black can pre-empt this with 10...h5 himself, but then 11 ♘g5 ♘h6 12 f3 (preparing 13 g4) 12...f5 is far from pleasant for Black. Lautier also gives 10...h5 11 ♘g5 f6 12 ♘e6 ♗xe6 13 dxe6 f5 14 f3 ♘f6 15 g4 with a large plus and 11...f5 12 f3 ♘f6 13 ♕b3, which he considers better for White but only marginally so – so if he's right then that is Black's best.

c) Dautov has suggested the very pragmatic 10...♘f6!? – of course the bishop is better on d2 than c1, but the more important point is the future shape of the kingside and at least White can't get in ♗e3 and ♘d2.

11 ♘g5 h5

If 11...f5!? White has a choice:

a) 12 ♘e6 ♗xe6 13 dxe6 ♕c8 14 ♗xg4 fxg4 15 ♕xg4 ♖f6 16 ♗g5 ♕xe6 and White has a clear edge.

b) 12 h5 ♕b6 13 ♗xg4 fxg4 14 ♕e2 ♕xb2 15 ♖b1 ♕a3 16 hxg6 hxg6 17 ♘e6 ♗xe6 18 dxe6 (18 ♖xb7!?) 18...g3! 19 fxg3 b6 is very unclear – White has a ready-made attack on the h-file, but if Black can defend then he may emerge with a good game.

12 f3 ♘h6

He probably really ought to retreat to f6 since after White's next move the position finally clarifies.

13 g4!

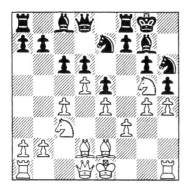

Were the knight on f6 then this wouldn't threaten g4xh5 at a suitably unpleasant moment.

13...♔h8

If 13...f5 14 exf5 gxf5 15 gxh5.

14 ♕c1

14 ♗e3 was also good.

14...♘eg8

Certainly not 14...hxg4? 15 h5 but 14...♘hg8 15 gxh5 gxh5 16 f4 exf4 17 ♗xh5 was also bad.

15 ♕c2?!

Lautier says that White should first have exchanged on h5, since now Black could have defended with 15...♘f6!

15...♕e8?! 16 gxh5 gxh5 17 0-0-0 f6 18 ♗e3! c5

Since Black can't shift the g5-knight his position is already absolutely critical. Of course, 18...fxg5? 19 hxg5 would be murder.

19 ♘b5

19 ♕d2! (Lautier) was even stronger, intending 19...a6 20 ♘e6 ♗xe6 21 dxe6 ♖d8 22 ♖hg1 ♕xe6 23 ♖g6 ♔h7 24 ♖dg1 ♖d7 25 ♘d5 to be followed by f3-f4-f5 etc.

19...♕e7 20 ♘e6 ♗xe6 21 dxe6 ♖ad8 22 f4 a6?

He should have offered the exchange with 22...f5! 23 fxe5 ♗xe5 24 ♗g5 ♕xe6! (24...♗f6 25 ♕d2! is terrible) 25 ♗xd8 ♖xd8 with some sort of blockade.

23 ♘c3 ♕xe6?

And 23...f5! was better here too.

24 f5 ♕f7 25 ♕d2

25...b5

White is now winning. If instead 25...♘g4 26 ♗xg4 hxg4 27 h5 ♖fe8 28 h6 ♗f8 29 ♖dg1 etc.

26 ♖dg1 ♘g4 27 ♗xg4 hxg4 28 h5 ♔h7 29 h6 ♗h8 30 ♖xg4 ♘e7 31 ♕g2

In view of the unanswerable threat of 32 ♖g7+, Yusupov resigned. A very powerful display by Lautier.

Game 46
Van Wely-Shahade
New York open 1996

---

1 d4 g6 2 c4 ♗g7 3 ♘c3 d6 4 ♘f3 ♘d7 5 e4 e5 6 ♗e2 ♘e7 7 0-0

In *Winning with the Modern*, Norwood says that what worries him most about this whole line for Black is that White will simply 'castle kingside and slowly consolidate the central space advantage.' While he has a potentially very good position, Black must certainly negotiate many dangers here since with the knight on e7, he is much less eager to play ...c7-c6, as the d6-square can easily become a very serious problem. The only really logical plan is, therefore, with or without ...h7-h6, to play the very sharp ...f7-f5. White can't stop this break but must aim to exploit the temporary looseness of Black's position when it's played.

7...0-0 8 ♗e3 f5!?

Of course if this is possible, then Black would prefer to dispense with the preparatory 8...h6 (see the next main game). But this is extremely risky and although there are possible improvements Van Wely shot the line out of the water in this present game.

9 ♘g5

The obvious attempt at refutation, though it might be more accurate to insert 9 dxe5 dxe5 first, since now 9...♘b8 10 dxe5 ♗xe5 isn't too clear after either 11 c5 f4 12 ♗d4 ♘bc6 13 ♗xe5 dxe5 or 11 f4 ♗xc3 12 bxc3 h6 13 ♘f3 fxe4.

9...♘f6 10 dxe5 dxe5 11 ♕xd8! ♖xd8 12 ♘b5 ♘e8 13 ♖fd1

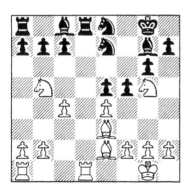

13...♗d7

Although White's play has been extremely crude, Black is under intense pressure. 13...♖xd1+ 14 ♖xd1 ♘c6 may be somewhat better when:

a) 15 c5 h6 16 ♗c4+ ♔f8 17 ♘e6+ ♗xe6 18 ♗xe6 f4 is perfectly reasonable for Black.

b) 15 exf5 is much more demanding since if:

b1) 15...gxf5 16 ♗h5! wins material immediately.

b2) 15...♗xf5 16 ♗f3!? e4! is quite playable, but 16 g4! is more challenging when:

b21) Not 16...♗c2? 17 ♖d2, when the bishop eventually gets trapped after 17...a6 (17...♗b1 18 ♘c3) 18 ♘a3! (not 18 ♘c3? ♘d4) 18...h6 (18...♗a4 19 b3) 19 ♘e6 ♗e4 20 f3.

b22) But the calm 16...♗c8 is still quite unclear. Probably White should continue 17 ♗f3 h6 18 ♘d5+ ♔h8 19 ♘f7+ ♔h7 20 g5 h5 (it's important that 20...♗g4? can be met by 21 f3 – that's why White chose ♗f3-d5+ rather than the apparently more appealing 17 c5 and 18 ♗c4+) and now maybe 21 f3. This may represent the best that Black can achieve but White still looks better since, vitally, 21...a6 22 ♘c3 ♘d4?, which Black would of course like to play, fails to 23 ♘xe5!

b3) 15...a6! is also possible to try and remove the knight before recapturing with the g-pawn, so that the e8-knight if attacked can then move without allowing ♘xc7. There are then possible piece sacrifices such as 16 fxg6!? but simply 16 ♘c3 gxf5 (16...h6 17 ♘e6) 17 ♘d5 is pretty good – for example, the innocent looking 17...h6? still runs into 18 ♗h5!, when if ♘f6 19 ♗f7+ ♔h8 (19...♔f8? 20 ♗c5+ ♘e7 21 ♗xe7 mate!) 20 ♘xc7 wins the house.

14 c5 ♗xb5

If 14...♗f6 15 ♗c4+ ♔g7 16 ♘f7! ♗xb5 17 ♗h6+ ♔g8 18 ♗xb5 ♖xd1+ 19 ♖xd1 the knight is of course indirectly protected due to 19...♔xf7 20 ♗c4+ and if 19...♗g7 20 ♗xg7 ♔xg7 21 ♘xe5 fxe4, when White has a very strong initiative which should certainly net some material gain.

15 ♗xb5 ♖xd1+ 16 ♖xd1 ♗f6 17 ♘c4+ ♚g7 18 ♖d7!

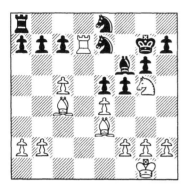

With the rook's penetration, the game is already all but decided.

18...f4 19 ♘e6+ ♚h8 20 ♗d2 ♖c8 21 ♗c3 ♘g8 22 ♚f1 g5 23 f3 a6 24 a4 ♘h6 25 ♗d5 b5 26 axb5 1-0

After 26...axb5 27 ♗b7 ♖b8 28 c6 the c-pawn falls and Black will soon lose at least a piece.

Game 47
Cebalo-Minic
Yugoslavia 1986

---

1 d4 g6 2 c4 ♗g7 3 ♘c3 d6 4 e4 ♘d7 5 ♘f3 e5 6 ♗e2 ♘e7 7 0-0 0-0 8 ♗e3 h6

Much more sensible than 8...f5 in the previous game.

9 ♕c2!?

They often play 9 ♕d2 ♚h7, but it's not clear that this helps White particularly except inasmuch that in some lines the king may become exposed to action down the c2-h7 diagonal later.

9...f5!?

The logical follow-up. The rather repulsive 9...g5 was played in a game Shestakov-Tsarev, Belgorod 1989. After 10 dxe5 dxe5 11 ♖ad1 ♘g6 12 g3 c6 13 c5 ♕e7 14 b4 ♘f6 15 ♘d2 ♘f4 16 ♘c4 ♘xe2+ 17

♕xe2 ♘e8 18 ♗c1 ♘c7 19 ♘d6 ♘e6 20 ♘f5 ♕f6 21 ♗e3 ♖e8 White played 22 ♖d2? and after 22...♚h7 23 f3? (23 ♖fd1 ♘f4!) 23...♘d4! 24 ♘xd4 exd4 25 ♗xd4 ♕xd4+ 26 ♖xd4 ♗xd4+ 27 ♚g2 ♗xc3 28 ♕c4 ♗g7 29 ♕xf7 Black won, but White could have improved not with 22 ♖d3 b6, threatening ...♗a6, but rather 22 ♚g2 getting the king off the d4-g1 diagonal and intending f2-f3 next move when the tactic with ...♘d4 now won't work.

10 dxe5 dxe5

10...f4!? was interesting when if:

a) 11 exd6 fxe3 12 dxe7 exf2+ 13 ♖xf2 ♕xe7 14 ♖af1 and despite the pawn deficit Black will be doing fairly well as long as he doesn't get hit by some combination of e4-e5 and pressure down the f-file immediately.

b) 11 ♗c1!? ♘xe5!? (11...dxe5 12 b3 gives White some edge). Now 12 c5 is critical but 12...dxc5 13 ♖d1 ♕e8 14 ♘d5 ♘xd5 15 ♖xd5 ♘xf3+ 16 ♗xf3 ♗d4! looks fairly good for Black. White should sacrifice the exchange at once with 17 ♖xc5 (he doesn't want to block the long dark diagonal with 17 e5 ♗e6 18 ♖xc5 ♗xc5 19 ♕xc5) but after 17...♗xc5 18 ♕xc5 ♕f7 19 ♗d2 ♗e6 20 ♗c3 while White has compensation for the exchange, it certainly doesn't look like more than enough.

11 ♖ad1 f4

12 ♗c5!?

12 ♗c1 again offered a safe edge, but as long as Black can't profitably sacrifice his queen then 12 ♗c5 is clearly better.

12...♖f7

The queen sacrifice with 12...♘xc5 was critical, but 13 ♖xd8 ♖xd8 14 ♘d5 is assessed by Cebalo in *Informator 42* as clearly favourable for White and I think he's right, e.g. 14...♖d7 15 ♖d1 and now:

a) 15...c6 16 ♘xe7+ ♖xe7 17 ♖d8+ ♔h7 18 b4 (not 18 ♕d1?! ♘xe4 19 ♗d3, hoping for 19...♘c5?? 20 ♘g5+!, but Black can defend with 19...♘f6!) 18...♘e6 19 ♖d6 ♗d7 20 ♕d1 ♗e8 21 c5 looks very good for White.

b) 15...♘c6 16 b4 ♘e6 17 c5 when if:

b1) 17...♘cd4?! 18 ♘xd4 ♘xd4 19 ♖xd4 exd4 20 ♘xf4 (if 20 c6! ♖f7!).

b2) 17...♖f7 18 ♗c4.

b3) 17...♔h7 18 ♗b5.

The latter two lines look better for Black than the first but all are certainly pretty good for White.

13 ♗a3

Cebalo assesses this as just an edge for White but it looks bigger than that to me.

13...♗f6 14 c5 ♖g7

If 14...c6 15 ♘d2 en route via c4 to d6.

15 ♘d5 ♘c6

After 15...♘xd5 16 exd5 the centre pawns give White a large advantage.

16 b4 a6

Not 16...♘d4 17 ♘xd4 exd4 18 ♗b2 and the d4-pawn will drop off.

17 ♗b2 g5 18 h3 h5 19 ♘h2! ♖h7 20 ♖d3

see following diagram

20...♖b8?

After this passive move White takes control. He had to try 20...♘d4, when 21 ♗xd4 exd4 22 ♘xf6+ ♕xf6 23 ♖fd1 ♘e5 24 ♖xd4 g4 yields quite serious counterplay. Instead Cebalo recommends simply 21 ♕d1!

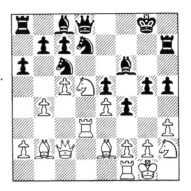

21 ♖fd1 ♘d4 22 ♗xd4 exd4 23 ♘xf6+ ♕xf6 24 ♖xd4 g4?

A mistake but if 24...♘e5 White can choose between 25 ♗c4+ ♘xc4 26 ♕xc4+ ♗e6 27 ♕c2 and the more incisive 25 ♘f3! ♘xf3+ (25...g4 26 ♘xe5 ♕xe5 27 ♗c4+ etc) 26 gxf3!, which looks stronger as after 26...♗xh3 27 e5! White gets a huge attack.

25 hxg4 hxg4 26 ♗xg4 ♘f8 27 ♕b3+ ♔g7

Or 27...♗e6 28 ♗xe6+ ♘xe6 29 ♘g4.

28 ♕c3!

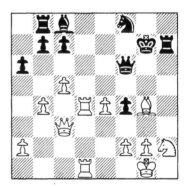

28...♗e6?

Losing, but if 28...♔g8 White can win simply with 29 ♖4d3! ♕xc3 (if 29...♕h4 30 ♖h3!) 30 ♖xc3 etc.

29 ♗xe6 ♘xe6 30 ♖d7+ 1-0

Although Black lost disastrously in this game, there are plenty of interesting potential improvements along the way.

Summary

In contrast to the previous two chapters, 4...♘d7 leads to apparently much more amorphous lines in the opening at least, and so could well be a better choice for a stronger player trying to defeat a weaker one as Black; the more so since there's no 'forced draw'. White's space advantage should give him some edge. But despite his apparent breadth of choice, he has to react very precisely to keep much so that I would view 8 c5! in Game 40, for example, as in a higher sense an 'only move' – and if Black can really get a good game after 11...♕b6 then White faces a real problem.

Unwilling to believe that Game 40 is playable, Black players have instead indulged in various contortions to develop the knight on h6, notably in the unappealing Game 41. So unless Game 40 does work I suppose Black should resign him or herself to developing the knight on e7. My feeling is that if possible White should then maintain the central tension as long as possible so Game 47 is the most critical and Black needs at least a small improvement,

1 d4 g6 2 c4 ♗g7 3 e4 d6 4 ♘c3 ♘d7

5 ♘f3 e5 6 ♗e2 *(D)* **♘e7**
      6...♘h6 – *Game 39*
      6...c6 7 0-0
            7...♘h6 – *Game 40*
            7...f6 – *Game 41*
7 0-0
      7 h4 *(D)*
            7...exd4 – *Game 42*
            7...h6
                  8 ♗e3 – *Game 43*
                  8 h5 – *Game 44*
      7 d5 – *Game 45*
7...0-0 8 ♗e3 *(D)* **h6**
      8...f5 – *Game 46*
9 ♕c2 – *Game 47*

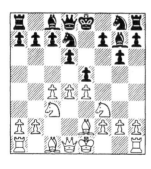

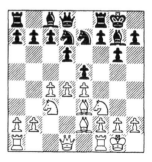

      6 ♗e2   *7 h4*   *8 ♗e3*

CHAPTER EIGHT

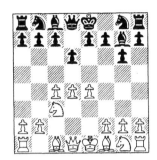

Averbakh Variation: Other Lines

1 d4 g6 2 c4 ♗g7 3 e4 d6 4 ♘c3

In this chapter, we examine other lines of the Averbakh apart from 4...♘c6 and 4...♘d7. There are three main alternatives:

a) 4...c6

This usually transposes to lines in the 4...♘d7 chapter unless White plays 5 f4 (Game 48).

b) 4...e5 5 dxe5 dxe5 6 ♕xd8+ ♔xd8

This is quite an important line. Black hopes to soak up the white initiative and then eventually generate his own play, often, though certainly not necessarily, on the dark squares. Personally, I don't go for this line much, but if you don't mind deliberately aiming for a defensive position at the start then it may suit you (see Game 49). Note that White is not obliged to enter the ending and may also try 5 ♘f3/5 ♘ge2, when the main line goes 5...exd4 6 ♘xd4 ♘c6 7 ♗e3 ♘ge7. But again I'm not too impressed and you can see why in my two defeats by Kasparov and Azmaiparashvili (Game 50).

c) 4...f5

This has been pioneered almost single-handedly by Hungarian Grandmaster Istvan Bilek, and although theory frowns somewhat, he still played a game with this line just two years ago (Game 51).

Game 48
Uhlmann-F.Olafsson
Reykjavik 1968

1 d4 g6 2 c4 ♗g7 3 e4 d6 4 ♘c3 c6 5 f4!?

This is supposedly somewhat better against 4...♘d7, though even in that case Black gets counterplay. The nice game Hjartarson-Berg, Akureyri 1994, continued (with the knight on d7 and pawn on c7): 5 f4 e5 6 fxe5 dxe5 7 d5 ♘gf6 8 ♘f3 0-0 9 ♗d3 c6 10 0-0 ♕b6+ 11 ♔h1 ♘g4 12 ♕e2 ♘c5 13 ♗c2 f5 14 exf5 ♗xf5 15 ♗xf5 gxf5 16 h3 ♘f6 17 ♗e3 ♘fe4 18 ♘xe4 ♘xe4! 19 ♗xb6 ♘g3+ 20 ♔h2 ♘xe2 21 ♗c7 e4 22 ♘g5 cxd5 23 ♘e6 d4 24 ♖f2 d3 25 ♖af1 ♗xb2 26 ♖b1 ♗c3 27 ♘xf8 ♖xf8 28 ♖xb7 e3 29 ♖f1 d2 30 ♖b3 ♖c8 31 ♗d6 ♖xc4 32 ♖b8+ ♔g7 33 ♖e8 ♖e4 34 ♗f8+ ♔g6 35 ♖xe4 fxe4 0-1.

5...♕b6 6 ♘f3

White can play 6 ♗e3, though after 6...♕xb2 he has nothing obviously better than to force an immediate repetition with 7 ♘a4 ♕b4+ 8 ♗d2 ♕a3 9 ♗c1. Instead in Smirin-Smyslov Biel Interzonal 1993, the ex-world champion gamely tried 6...e5. After 7 ♘f3 exd4 8 ♗xd4 ♗xd4 9 ♕xd4

♕xd4 10 ♘xd4 ♘a6 11 0-0-0 ♘f6 12 ♗e2 ♗g4 13 ♘f3 0-0-0 14 h3 ♗xf3 15 ♗xf3 ♖he8 White has an edge but the game was drawn in 39 moves.

White can also try to avoid the pin with 6 e5?!, but after 6...♘h6 he can't develop 7 ♗e3 in view of 7...♘f5 and if 7 ♘f3 ♗g4 comes anyway.

6...♗g4 7 d5 ♘f6 8 h3 ♗xf3 9 ♕xf3 ♘a6 10 ♖b1 ♘d7 11 ♗d2 ♘dc5 12 ♗e2 0-0

Black's lead in development and dark-square pressure already make the white position quite uncomfortable. If now 13 b4? ♘xb4 14 a3 ♘c2+ 15 ♔d1 ♘d4 is simply bad for White; or 13 ♕e3 ♘b4 14 0-0 (14 ♖c1 ♘cd3+) 14...♘c2 15 ♕f2 ♗d4; or 13 ♕f2 ♗xc3 14 ♗xc3 ♘xe4.

So despite the notes in *Informator 5* which award White's next move a ?, it doesn't seem so foolish; though perhaps the pawn should have rather gone to g3.

13 g4 ♘b4 14 ♔f1 e6 15 ♔g2 exd5 16 exd5 ♖fe8 17 ♗d1 cxd5 18 cxd5 ♕a6 19 ♗e2 ♘bd3 20 ♔h2

Certainly not 20 b4? ♗xc3 21 ♗xc3 ♖xe2+!

20...♕c4 21 b3 ♕d4 22 ♘b5

---

see following diagram

White seems to have emerged with an advantage but Olafsson was ready with:

22...♘e5! 23 ♘xd4

Not 23 fxe5? ♗xe5+ 24 ♔g2 ♕xd2; and of course he can't move the queen since if 23 ♕c3?? ♕f2 is mate.

23...♘xf3+ 24 ♗xf3 ♗xd4 25 ♖he1 ♘d3 26 ♖e4 ♖xe4 27 ♗xe4 ♘c5 28 ♗f3 ♖e8 29 ♔g2?

A bad mistake. After 29 ♖e1 ♖xe1 30 ♗xe1 ♗e3 (30...♘d3 31 ♗d2) 31 f5 if Black could exchange dark-squared bishops he would emerge with a great advantage (unless the white king somehow became active). But of course White will resist this exchange with reasonable chances.

29...♘d3 30 ♖f1 ♗e3 31 ♗xe3 ♖xe3 32 ♗d1 f6 33 a3 ♔g7 34 b4 g5 35 fxg5 fxg5 36 ♗f3?

The final blunder, though Black would win at least a pawn – to start with – while keeping complete control in any case.

36...♘e1+ 37 ♔f2 ♖xf3+ 38 ♔xe1 ♖xf1+ 39 ♔xf1 ♔f6 0-1

1 d4 g6 2 e4 ♗g7 3 c4 d6 4 ♘c3 e5 5 dxe5 dxe5 6 ♕xd8+ ♔xd8 7 f4!

The most critical since, although White risks isolating his e-pawn in return he develops an immediate initiative.

I ought, though, to provide an example

of what Black's aiming at: 7 ♗e3 c6 8 0-0-0+ ♚e8 9 h4 h5 10 ♘h3 ♗h6 11 ♗xh6 ♘xh6 12 f3 ♗xh3! 13 ♖xh3 ♘d7 14 g3 ♘c5 15 ♖h2 a5 16 ♗h3 ♚e7 17 ♚c2 ♖hd8 18 ♖hd2 ♖xd2+ 19 ♚xd2 f6 20 ♚e3 ♘f7 21 b3 ♘d6 22 ♗f1 f5!

The superb knights give Black a decided advantage. After the further 23 ♗e2 ♖f8 24 ♖g1 ♖d8 25 ♖d1 ♘e6 26 ♘a4 f4+! 27 gxf4 exf4+ 28 ♚f2 ♘f7 29 ♖xd8 ♚xd8 30 ♘b2 ♘e5 he had an ideal endgame, the more so after White exchanged off his only possible source of counterplay, the knight: 31 ♘d3 ♘xd3+ 32 ♗xd3 ♘c5 33 ♗c2 ♘d7 34 a3 c5 35 ♗d3 ♚e7 36 ♗f1 ♘e5 37 ♚e2 ♘c6 38 ♗h3 ♘d4+ and White had had enough in Durao-Robatsch, Leipzig Olympiad 1960.

Returning to the main game, Black now faces a vital choice:

7...♘c6

The most immediately active reply, though following the present game, Black needs improvements.

a) 7...♘d7 8 ♘f3 c6 is somewhat more passive. Crouch-Norwood, 4NCL 1998, became something of a cautionary tale after 9 ♗e2 f6 10 0-0 ♘h6 (10...♚e8 first is safer) 11 fxe5 ♘xe5 12 ♘xe5 fxe5 13 b4 ♗e6 14 b5 ♘f7 (if 14...♘c7 15 bxc6 bxc6 16 ♘a4 en route to c5)

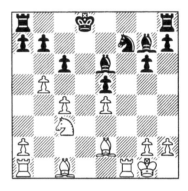

15 ♗g4! and now:

a1) 15...♗xc4 16 ♖d1+ ♚e7 (16...♚e8 17 bxc6 bxc6 18 ♗d7+ ♚e7 19 ♗a3+ ♚f6 20 ♖f1+ is simpler because the bishop doesn't hang after ...♚g5) 17 bxc6 bxc6 18 ♗a3+ ♚f6 (18...c5 19 ♗xc5+ ♚f6 20 ♖f1+ ♗xf1 21 ♖xf1+ ♚g5 22 ♖xf7 ♚xg4 23 ♖xg7 ♖ac8 24 ♗b4 ♖c4 25 a3 doesn't help) 19 ♖f1+ ♗xf1 (not 19...♚g5? 20 ♗e2 ♗xe2 21 ♖xf7) 20 ♖xf1+ ♚g5 21 ♗e2! (21 h3! is also very strong, but not the obvious 21 ♖xf7? ♗f8! 22 ♗xf8 ♖hxf8 and Black fights on) 21...♖hf8 (if 21...♘h6? 22 ♗e7+ and mate next move) 22 ♗c1+ ♚h4 23 ♖f3 ♘g5 24 ♖g3 and wins.

a2) The game continued 15...♗xg4 16 ♖xf7 ♗f8 17 ♗g5+ ♚c8 18 ♗e7!, when White's rook is far too strong, i.e. 18...♗h6 19 ♗d6 ♗e3+ 20 ♚h1 ♗b6 21 c5 ♗a5 22 ♗xe5 ♖e8 23 ♗f6 ♗xc3 24 ♗xc3 cxb5 25 ♖xh7 a5 26 ♖f1 ♗e6 27 ♗e5 ♗c4 28 c6 bxc6 29 ♖c7+ ♚d8 30 ♖d1+ ♗d5 31

♗g3 1-0.

b) 7...♗e6 lends the game a quite different character. Relying on this powerful bishop, Black will now even sometimes be happy to exchange off ...♗g7xc3 to cripple White's pawns, after which Black will try to play on the light squares. Play might run 8 ♘f3 ♘d7 9 ♗e2 h6 and now:

b1) Rogozenko-Badea, Ciocaltea memorial 1998, continued 10 g3?! (to recapture on f4 with the g-pawn, but this turns out to be a bad plan) 10...♘e7 11 0-0 ♖e8 12 ♗e3 exf4 13 gxf4 (13 ♗xf4 doesn't make sense after playing 10 g3 and indeed 13...g5 looks fine for Black) 13...♗xc3! 14 bxc3 ♘c6 15 ♗d3 ♘a5 16 ♘d2 f5! 17 e5 ♔e7 and Black had a good game, though the game was eventually drawn.

b2) Instead it's better simply to castle 10 0-0 ♘e7 when:

b21) 11 ♗e3 exf4 12 ♗xf4 g5 13 ♗g3 g4 14 ♘h4 ♗d4+ 15 ♔h1 ♗e5 16 ♖ad1 ♗xg3 17 hxg3 h5 18 ♘d5 ♘c6 ½-½ Adorjan-Todorcevic, Szirak Interzonal 1987.

b22) 11 ♖d1! is better to prepare to put the knight on d4 if it gets hit later by ...g5-g4. After 11...exf4 12 ♗xf4 g5 13 ♗g3 ♘g6 14 ♖d2 c6 15 ♘d4 ♗xd4+ 16 ♖xd4 ♔e7 17 ♗d6+ ♔f6 18 ♖f1+ ♔g7 19 c5 b6 20 cxb6 axb6 21 a3 ♘de5 22 ♖b4 b5 23 ♖d1 ♖hc8 24 a4 bxa4 25 ♘xa4 ♖xa4 26 ♖xa4 White had an edge in Suba-Azmaiparashvili, Reykjavik 1990, which he later converted to victory.

8 ♘f3 ♘d4!? 9 ♔f2 exf4

Opening the bishop's diagonal. 9...♘xf3 10 gxf3 is a possible alternative, when Black has plenty of dubious moves, such as 10...c6 or the rather repulsive 10...f6, but 10...♗e6 seems consequent and Estremera Panos-Sutovsky, European Team Championship, Pula 1997, continued 11 ♗e3 exf4! 12 ♖d1+ ♔c8 13 ♗xf4 ♗xc3 14 bxc3 ♘e7 15 ♗g5 ♘c6 16 ♗f6 ♖e8 17 ♖d2 b6 18 c5 ♔b7 19 ♗e2 ♘a5 20 ♖hd1 ♖ab8 21 ♗b5 c6 22 ♗e2 b6 23 ♗d8

♘c4 24 ♗xc4 ♗xc4 25 a3 ½-½.

10 ♗xf4 ♘e6 11 ♗g3!?

Here the bishop controls c7 and so prevents ...c7-c6 followed by ...♔c7 getting organised. Instead in Petursson-Ehlvest, Yerevan Olympiad 1996, the bishop retreated to the more passive d2-square and Black quickly obtained the advantage: 11 ♗d2?! ♘f6 12 h3 ♘d7 13 ♗d3 ♘e5 14 ♗e2 c6 15 ♘a4 ♘xf3 16 ♗xf3?! (16 gxf3! was better though far from inspiring)16...♔c7 17 ♗c3 ♗xc3 18 ♘xc3 ♘c5 19 ♖hd1 a5 and Black won on move 86.

11...♗d7

It's quite possible that with 11 ♗d2?! Petursson was trying to avoid Ehlvest's supposed improvement on one of his own (i.e. Petursson's) previous games against I.Nikolaidis at the Athens open 1993 which had gone 11...♘h6 12 ♗d3 ♗xc3 13 bxc3 f6 14 ♖he1 ♗d7 15 ♖ad1 ♔e8 16 ♔g1 ♘f7 17 e5 f5 18 c5 ♘fd8 19 ♗f2 ♖g8 20 ♗c4 ♖g7 21 ♖d2 ♗c6 22 ♘d4 ♖d7? 23 ♗xe6 ♘xe6 24 ♘xe6 ♖xd2 25 ♘xc7+ ♔d7 26 ♘xa8 ♗e4 27 e6+ ♔xe6 28 ♘c7+ ♔d7 29 ♘b5 ♖xa2 30 ♘xa7 ♖b2 31 c4 1-0.

12 ♖d1 ♔c8 13 ♗d3

If 13 ♘d5 at once then Black might well take the pawn with 13...♗xb2.

13...♘e7 14 ♘d5 ♖e8

Not 14...♘xd5 15 cxd5 ♘c5 16 b4 ♘xd3+ 17 ♖xd3 when the pressure along the c-file will be most unpleasant.

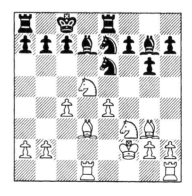

15 e5

Attacking the dark-square weaknesses. This is much better than 15 ♗h4?, when 15...♘xd5 16 cxd5 ♘c5 is hugely better for Black than the previous note, since he effectively has two extra tempi – the bishop which moved to h4 needs to go back to g3 if it is to pressure c7.

15...♘c5

15...c6 16 ♘f6 ♗xf6 17 exf6 is also nasty.

16 ♘f6

Even without being pushed, the knight goes into f6. If instead 16 ♗c2 ♗f5! 17 ♘xe7+ ♖xe7 18 ♗xf5+ gxf5 Black has counterplay based on playing ...♘e4(+).

16...♗xf6 17 exf6

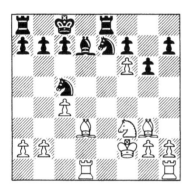

White's lead in development and the annoying pawn on f6 give him some advantage, though exactly how much is difficult to say since Black has a perfectly good structure. The size of White's advantage depends upon exact assessments at the end of various lines in which Black tries to wriggle out.

17...♘f5

Gaining time by threatening at some point to take the bishop. 17...♘c6 18 ♗c2 ♘e4+ 19 ♗xe4 ♖xe4 20 b3 gives White a clear safe edge.

18 ♗f4 ♘e4+

18...♘xd3+?! 19 ♖xd3 looks more serious for Black. White's lead in develop-

ment is becoming very pronounced and g2-g4 is in the air.

19 ♗xe4 ♖xe4 20 g3 ♗c6

Not 20...♖xc4? 21 ♖xd7 ♖c2+ (or 21...♔xd7 22 ♘e5+) 22 ♖d2!

21 ♖he1 ♖xc4!?

Correctly snatching a pawn. Instead both 21...♖xe1 22 ♖xe1 ♗xf3 23 ♖e8+ and 21...b6 22 ♖xe4 ♗xe4 23 ♘g5 are awful.

22 ♘e5 ♖c2+ 23 ♔g1 b6 24 ♖c1!

Certainly not 24 ♘xc6 ♖xc6 25 ♖e8+ ♔b7 26 ♖xa8 ♔xa8 27 ♖d7 ♖xf6; while 24 ♘xf7 ♖g2+ 25 ♔f1 ♖xh2 is very unclear.

24...♖xc1

Now 24...♖g2+? 25 ♔f1 ♗d5 26 ♖cd1 ♗b7 27 ♘xf7 would be disastrous.

25 ♖xc1 ♗d5 26 ♘xf7 c5 27 ♘e5 ♔b7 28 ♖d1

28...♘d4

Now Sadler forced a simple clear advantage. If 28...♖d8!? White has a variety of ways to go wrong – for instance in, *Chess-Base magazine* Ribli notes that if 29 ♘f7 ♖f8 30 ♘d6+? ♘xd6 31 ♗xd6 ♖xf6 32 ♖xd5 ♔c6! But he also gives the simple clear 29 ♖xd5! ♖xd5 30 f7 ♖d8 31 ♘d7! winning a piece.

29 ♗e3 ♘f3+

If 29...♘e8? 30 f7 ♗xf7 (or 30...♖f8 31 ♗h6 ♖xf7 32 ♘xf7 ♗xf7 33 ♗e3 etc.) 31 ♗xd4 cxd4 32 ♘xf7 ♖e2 White must win, while if 29...♖xa2 30 ♗xd4 cxd4 31 ♖xd4 the f-pawn is much too strong, e.g.

31...♖f8 32 ♖d7+ ♔a6 33 f7 and the only way to salvage the exchange is 33...♗b3 34 ♖e7 ♗a4, which leaves Black hopelessly passive.

30 ♘xf3 ♗xf3 31 ♖d7+ ♔c6 32 ♖xh7

Despite the opposite-coloured bishops, the extra f-pawn gives White excellent winning chances.

32...♖f8 33 ♗g5 a5 34 ♔f2 ♗d5 35 a3

Not 35 b3?! a4 with some counterplay.

35...♖f7?!

The rook is passive here so 35...a4 looks better.

36 ♖h6 ♗e4 37 ♔e3 ♗b1 38 ♖h8 ♖d7 39 ♖g8 b5 40 h4

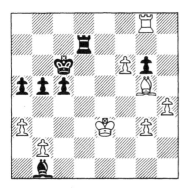

40...♔d5?

Losing at once, since it blocks the a2-g8 diagonal, but I imagine that 40...b4 41 ♖g7!? bxa3 42 bxa3 ♖xg7 43 fxg7 ♗a2 44 g4 should also be sufficient for White.

41 ♖g7! ♔e6

Or 41...♖d8 42 f7 ♖f8 43 ♗e7.

42 ♖xd7 ♔xd7 43 f7 1-0

Game 50
M.Gurevich-Speelman
Antwerp 1993

1 d4 g6 2 c4 ♗g7 3 e4 d6 4 ♘c3 e5 5 ♘ge2 exd4 6 ♘xd4 ♘c6

The actual move order in the game was 1 d4 d6 2 c4 e5 3 ♘f3 exd4 4 ♘xd4 g6 5 ♘c3 ♗g7 6 e4 ♘c6.

7 ♗e3 ♘ge7 8 h4!?

The most critical response, though of course White can also simply play to castle. After 8 ♗e2 0-0 9 0-0 f5 White has:

a) 10 ♘xc6 and now:

a1) 10...bxc6 and:

a11) 11 ♗d4 ♗xd4 12 ♕xd4 c4 13 ♕d2 ♗b7 is very playable for Black.

a12) 11 ♗f3 ♗e6 seems safest rather than 11...♖b8 12 ♕d2 c5 13 ♗g5 ♕d7, when 14 e5! would have been most unpleasant in Lputian-Azmaiparashvili, Yerevan 1989.

a2) 10 ♘xc6 ♘xc6 is also quite playable. Shulman-Rogers, New York open 1998, continued 11 ♕d2 ♕f6 12 exf5 ♗xf5 13 ♗f3?! (13 ♖ad1 seems better at once in view of the next note) 13...♔h8 14 ♖ad1 and here in their notes in *Informator 72*, Shulman and Kapengut recommend 14...♘e5!, when if 15 ♗xb7?! ♘xc4 16 ♕d5 (not 16 ♗g5? ♘xd2 17 ♗xf6 ♘xf1 18 ♗xg7+ ♔xg7 19 ♗xa8 ♘xh2!) 16...♗e6! 17 ♕c6 ♖ab8 18 ♕xc7 ♘xe3 19 fxe3 ♕e5 20 ♖xf8+ (20 ♕xd6? ♖xf1+) 20...♖xf8 21 ♕xd6 ♕xe3+ 22 ♔h1 ♗g4 with a strong initiative, while 15 ♗e2 obviously loses two tempi.

Instead Rogers continued 14...♖ae8 and after 15 ♗g5 ♕d4 16 ♘b5 ♕xd2 (16...♕xc4?! 17 ♘xc7 ♖c8 18 ♗d5 is excellent for White) 17 ♖xd2 ♘e5 18 ♗e2 a6 (18...♖f7) 19 ♘xc7 (19 ♘d4!?) 19...♖c8 20 f4 ♘xc4 21 ♗xc4 ♖xc7 White had some advantage, though they drew fifteen moves later.

b) 10 exf5 is what Black is hoping for due to 10...♗xd4 11 ♗xd4 ♘xf5 12 ♗e3 (12 ♘b5 a6 13 ♗c3 axb5 14 cxb5 ♘ce7 15 g4 ♘g7 has been tried a few times but seems quite unsound and Black has won all four games in my database) 12...♘xe3 13 fxe3. At the cost of a small lag in development, Black has inflicted quite serious damage on White's pawn structure. In fact, this position is reasonably playable for White and White even won a few games in the eighties after 13...♖xf1+ 14 ♕xf1 ♗e6 15 ♕f4 ♕e7 16 ♖f1.

But if you reach this position as Black, it will almost certainly be as a result of White falling into the 'trap' rather than by his design. And 13...♗e6 immediately may be better, e.g. 14 ♕d2 ♕g5 15 b3 ♘e5 16 ♖f4 b6 17 ♖af1 ♕e7 18 ♗f3 ♖ae8 19 ♗d5 g5 20 ♖f5 ♖xf5 21 ♖xf5 h6 22 ♕f2 ♘g4 23 ♕f3 c6! 24 ♗xe6+ ♕xe6 25 e4 ♘e5 26 ♕f2 ♕e7 27 h3 ♘d3 28 ♕g3 ♘c5 29 ♕f3 ♕g7 30 ♔h1 ♘e6 31 ♖f6 ♘d4 32 ♕f2 ♖e6 33 ♖xe6 ♘xe6 and Black went on to win in Peng Zhaoqin-Rogers Sonnevanck 1995.

8...f5

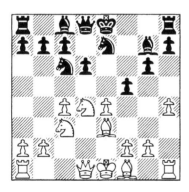

Faced with 8 h4 in the Barcelona World Cup as Black against Kasparov, I chose the weaker 8...h6!? and was murdered after 9 ♗e2 f5 (if 9...0-0 10 ♕d2 ♔h7 11 g4!) 10 exf5 ♘xf5 11 ♘xf5 ♗xf5 12 ♕d2 ♕d7? (12...♕f6!? was better) 13 0-0! 0-0-0?! (Kasparov recommends 13...h5, preparing to castle short) 14 b4! ♘xb4?! (but 14...♔b8!? 15 b5 ♘e5 16 ♘d5 ♘g4 17 ♗xg4 ♗xg4 18 ♖ab1 is also good for White)

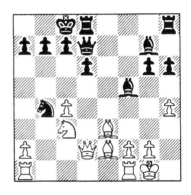

15 ♘b5! ♘c2 (if 15...♗xa1 16 ♕xb4 ♗e5 17 ♘xa7+ ♔b8 18 ♗f3 c5 19 ♕a3 ♕c7 20 g4 ♗c2 21 ♖c1 ♖hf8 22 ♗d5 ♕b6 23 ♘b5 etc., while 15...c5 16 ♖ad1 is repulsive) 16 ♗f3! d5 (if 16...♗xa1 17 ♘xa7+ ♔b8 18 ♖b1! c5 19 ♘c6+ ♔c8 20 ♕a5 ♘b4 21 ♖xb4 cxb4 22 ♕a8+ ♔c7 23 ♗b6+! ♔xb6 24 ♕a5 mate!; or 16...♘xe3 17 ♕xe3 ♗xa1 18 ♕xa7 ♕g7 19 ♕xb7+ ♔d7 20 ♖e1! ♖c8 21 ♘xd6 winning; or 16...♘xa1 17 ♘xa7+ ♔b8 18 ♕a5 c6 19 ♘b5!; so 16...c5 17 ♖ad1 ♗e5 18 ♘xa7+ ♔b8 19 ♘b5 looks relatively best – or rather least bad) 17 ♗xd5 ♘xa1 18 ♘xa7+ ♔b8 19 ♕b4 ♕xd5 (or 19...c5 20 ♗f4+! ♔a8 21 ♕a5) 20 cxd5 ♘c2 21 ♕a5 ♘xe3 22 fxe3 ♖he8 23 ♘b5 ♖xd5 24 ♕xc7+ ♔a8 25 ♕a5+ 1-0.

9 h5 fxe4 10 hxg6 hxg6

10...♘xg6 has been tried but in Bönsch-Azmaiparashvili, Dortmund 1990, White quickly got a very good game with simple moves: 11 ♕d2 ♘xd4 12 ♗xd4 ♘e5 13 ♘xe4 ♕e7 14 0-0-0 ♗e6 15 f4 ♘c6 16 ♗xg7 ♕xg7 17 ♘g5 ♗f5 18 ♖e1+ ♔d7 19 ♗d3 ♖af8 20 ♗xf5+ ♖xf5 21 ♕d3 and Black sacrificed the exchange with

21...Rxg5 22 fxg5 Wxg5+ 23 ⌖b1 h5 but lost 30 moves later.

11 Rxh8+ ⌖xh8 12 ⌖xe4 ⌖f5

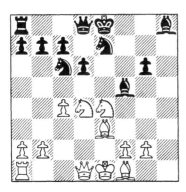

13 ⌖xf5!

This looks better than 13 ⌖g3, which Zsuzsa Polgar played against Seirawan in the blindfold discipline of the Melody Amber tournament 1993: 13...⌖xd4 14 ⌖xd4 ⌖d7 15 ⌖e2 ⌖c6 16 ⌖e3 ⌖xb2 17 Rb1 ⌖c3+ 18 ⌖f1 Wh4 19 Rxb7 Rh8 20 ⌖f3.

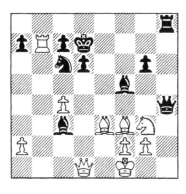

And here Yasser missed the opportunity to deliver a quite beautiful mate with 20...⌖d3+!! 21 Wxd3 Wh1+ 22 ⌖xh1 Rxh1+ 23 ⌖e2 Re1. Instead he lost on time four moves later in a bad but still not entirely hopeless position after 20...Wxc4+ 21 ⌖g1 ⌖e5 22 ⌖e2 Wh4 23 ⌖b5+ ⌖c8 24 Rxa7.

13...gxf5

13...⌖xf5 14 ⌖g5 Wd7 15 Wd2 ⌖f7 is reasonably playable, though Black's king is rather shaky.

14 Wh5+ ⌖d7 15 0-0-0! Wg8!

Not 15...fxe4? 16 Wh3+ ⌖e8 17 Wxh8+ ⌖d7 18 Wh3+ ⌖e8 19 ⌖e2 winning.

16 ⌖c5+ ⌖c8 17 ⌖e6!? ⌖d7 18 ⌖f4 ⌖e5

The attempt to create counterplay with 18...b5?! is merely weakening after 19 ⌖d5 bxc4 20 ⌖xc4

19 ⌖d5 Wg4! 20 Wh7!

20 Wxg4 ⌖xg4 21 ⌖g5 ⌖xd5 22 Rxd5 Rf8! 23 f3 ⌖e5 is fine for Black.

20...Wg7 21 Wxg7 ⌖xg7 22 ⌖xe7 ⌖xe7 23 c5!

Breaking up Black's structure.

23...⌖g4

Not 23...dxc5 24 ⌖xc5+ ⌖e6 25 f4.

24 cxd6+ cxd6 25 ⌖g5+ ⌖f6 26 ⌖xf6+

26...⌖xf6?

Mistakenly aiming for 'activity' which turns out to be merely temporary. Instead 26...⌖xf6 27 ⌖d3 is a little uncomfortable but after 27...Rg8! (not 27...f4 28 ⌖f5 Rg8 29 Re1+ ⌖f8 30 ⌖h3 and White will soon win material) 28 g3 f4! 29 gxf4 Rg4 30 f5 Rf4 31 Re1+ ⌖f7 32 Re6 d5 Black is fine, so unless White can improve earlier this line is theoretically perfectly playable for Black.

27 Rxd6+ ⌖e5 28 Rd2 Rh8 29 ⌖c2!

29 ⌖d1?! Rh1 30 ⌖e2 ⌖h2 31 Rd1 f4

gives some counterplay, though whether Black gets anything worthwhile after f2-f3 followed by ♔f2 isn't at all clear to me now.

29...f4

Or 29...♖h1 30 ♗c4 ♖h2 31 ♗d5 with a sound extra pawn.

30 ♗e2! ♘xf2 31 ♗f3 ♖c8+ 32 ♔b3 ♘h1 33 ♖d5+

33 ♖d7 ♖b8 34 ♖xb7 ♖xb7+ 35 ♗xb7 also won.

33...♔f6 34 ♖a5 ♘g3

34...♘f2 was slightly better, though presumably White should win after 35 ♗xb7 ♖c7 36 ♗f3 (not 36 ♖xa7? ♘d3) 36...♘d3 37 a4.

35 ♖xa7 ♘f1 36 ♖xb7 ♘d2+ 37 ♔b4 ♖c4+ 38 ♔b5

Of course not 38 ♔a3?? when Black replies 38...♘b1+ and escapes with perpetual check.

38...♖c2 39 ♔a6 ♘c4 40 ♖c7 1-0

Game 51
Polugayevsky-Bilek
Lipeck 1968

---

1 c4 g6 2 d4 ♗g7 3 e4 d6 4 ♘c3 f5!?

Although I don't really believe this, it could certainly be employed for shock value alone.

5 exf5

Obvious, but in his several outings with 4...f5!? which I have on my database, Bilek faced most difficulties in his game with Gufeld at Kecskemet 1968 in which White simply developed: 5 ♘f3 ♘h6 6 ♗e2 (for the record, the amusing game Thang Trang-Bilek, Budapest 1997, ended in perpetual check after 6 exf5 ♘xf5 7 g4 ♘h6 8 h3 0-0 9 ♗g2 ♘f7 10 0-0 ♘d7 11 ♗e3 e5 12 d5 ♘f6 13 ♕d2 e4 14 ♘d4 ♘e5 15 b3 ♘f3+ 16 ♘xf3 exf3 17 ♗xf3 ♘xg4 18 ♗xg4 ♗xg4 19 hxg4 ♕h4 20 ♖fc1 ♕xg4+ 21 ♔f1 ♕h3+ 22 ♔e1 ♕h1+ 23 ♔e2 ♕f3+ 24 ♔e1 ♕h1+ 25 ♔e2 ♕f3+) 6...0-0 7 0-0

fxe4 8 ♘xe4 ♘f5 9 d5 and now:

a) 9...e5 runs into 10 dxe6 ♗xe6 11 ♘eg5 which was given as slightly better for White many years ago by Fridstein and is at least that since White can play 11...♕f6 12 ♘xe6 ♕xe6 13 ♘g5 ♕e5 14 ♗f3 c6 (if 14...♘c6 15 ♗d5+ ♔h8 16 ♘f7+ ♖xf7 17 ♗xf7 Black surely doesn't have enough for the exchange) 15 ♖e1 ♕f6 16 ♘e6.

b) Of course Bilek played 9...c5, when play continued 10 ♖e1 ♘a6 11 ♖b1 ♘c7?! (this seems wrong since it helps White to play 12 b4 – perhaps 11...♗d7 was better first) 12 b4 b6?! (and I also don't like this, though after 12...cxb4 White must be a bit better) 13 bxc5 bxc5 14 ♗b2! ♖b8 15 ♗xg7 ♖xb1 16 ♕xb1 ♘xg7 17 ♕b2 ♗f5 18 ♗d3 ♗g4 19 ♘ed2.

The exchange of dark-squared bishops

took most of the dynamism out of Black's game. He now decided to rid himself of the potentially weak e7-pawn and gain some space but created serious light-square weaknesses as a result: 19...e5!? 20 dxe6 ♘cxe6 21 ♗e4 ♔h8 22 h3 ♗xf3 23 ♘xf3 ♘f4 24 ♖e3 ♔g8 25 ♖b3 ♘e8 26 ♖b7 ♕f6 27 ♕d2 ♖f7 28 ♖xf7 ♔xf7 29 g3 ♘e6 30 ♗d5 ♘8c7 31 ♘g5+ ♔g7 32 ♘xe6+ ♘xe6 33 ♕a5! (White is winning now) 33...♕e7 34 ♗xe6 ♕xe6 35 ♕xa7+ ♔f6 36 ♕xh7 ♕xc4 37 ♕h4+! ♕xh4 38 gxh4 ♔e5 39 a4 c4 40 ♔f1 d5 41 a5 ♔d6 42 a6 ♔c6 43 h5! 1-0.

Not terribly encouraging, though of course there were various possible improvements for Black along the way.

5...♗xf5 6 ♘f3

In the stem game, Portisch-Bilek, Sousse Interzonal 1967, Portisch reacted to the surprise with 6 ♗d3!?, but this really helps Black since although his king has to run, he gets a good structure: 6...♗xd4 7 ♗xf5 ♗xc3+ 8 bxc3 gxf5 9 ♕h5+ ♔d7 10 ♕xf5+ e6 11 ♕d3 (Black achieved an excellent position after 11 ♕h3 ♕f6 12 ♘e2 ♘e7 13 0-0 ♘bc6 14 c5 ♕f5 15 ♕xf5 ♘xf5 16 ♖b1 b6 17 cxd6 cxd6 in Comas Fabrego-Bilek, Palma de Mallorca 1989, and won in the end) 11...♕f6 12 ♘f3 ♘c6 13 c5 ♕g6 and now:

a) The game continued 14 ♕d1 ♕e4+ 15 ♗e3 ♘ge7 16 cxd6 cxd6 17 ♕b3 ♘a5

18 ♕b5+ ♘ec6 19 0-0-0 a6 20 ♕c5 d5 21 ♘g5 ♕c4 and with his attack broken, Portisch, who was at that time one of the very top players in the world, acceded to a draw.

b) In his notes in *Informator* 4, Portisch recommends the exchange of queens 14 ♕xg6 hxg6. assessing this as slightly better for White. Keene and Botterill continued the analysis in their excellent *The Modern Defence* (sadly now long out of print) with 15 ♗f4 when:

b1) 15...e5 16 ♗e3 (16 ♗g3) 16...d5 17 0-0-0 ♘ge7 18 c4 d4 19 ♘xe5+! ♘xe5 20 ♗xd4 is certainly disastrous for Black.

b2) 15...♘ge7 16 cxd6 cxd6 17 ♖d1 ♘d5 18 ♗xd6 (not 18 ♗g3 b5!) ♔xd6 19 c4 which they assess as slightly in White's favour in view of Black's weak pawns. But his centralised king could also turn out to be a powerful asset and I think – though it's almost impossible to know without trying it – that I'd be reasonably happy to play Black here.

6...♘h6

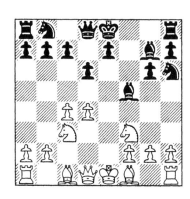

7 ♗e2

Yet another Bilek game, this time as Black against Dutchman Kick Langeweg in the Lugano Olympiad 1968, continued 7 h3 0-0 8 ♗e3 ♘a6 9 ♕d2 ♘f7 10 ♗e2 c5 11 0-0 b6 12 ♖fe1 ♘b4 13 ♖ac1 e5 14 d5 ♘a6 15 a3 ♘c7 16 b4 ♘e8 17 g4 ♗d7 18 ♘e4 ♘f6 19 ♗d3 h5 20 gxh5 ♘xh5 21

♔h2 ♘h8 22 ♗g5 ♕c7 23 ♘h4 ♘f4 24
♖e3 ♖f7 25 ♖g1 ♖af8 26 ♖eg3 ½-½.
**7...0-0 8 0-0 ♘a6 9 d5 c5 10 ♘g5 ♘c7
11 ♗d3 ♗d7 12 ♘e2 ♘f7 13 ♘xf7 ♖xf7
14 a4 ♕f8**

14...e6!? was possible at once.

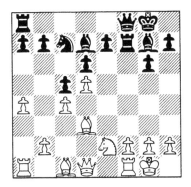

15 ♖a3?!

Since he soon blocks the third rank,
this is wrong. Instead 15 ♗e3! e6 16 dxe6
♘xe6 17 ♕d2 offered White a slight edge.

15...e6 16 dxe6 ♗xe6 17 ♘c3 ♗d4!

With White's pieces in a muddle Black
is now better and Polugayevsky had to
make a serious concession to stem the
enemy activity.

**18 ♗e3 ♗xe3 19 fxe3 d5 20 cxd5 ♘xd5
21 ♘xd5 ♗xd5 22 ♗e2 ♖xf1+ 23 ♗xf1
♕f5 24 ♖c3! b6**

After 24...♖f8 25 ♕xd5+! ♕xd5 26 ♗c4
♕xc4 27 ♖xc4 b6 the ending should end in
a draw.

25 a5 ♖e8 26 axb6 axb6 27 ♕d3

27...♕e5

27...♗e4! would have kept the edge.
Now White succeeds in exchanging bishops, after which Black has very little.

**28 ♕b5 ♖f8 29 ♗c4 ♗xc4 30 ♕xc4+
♔g7 31 ♖b3 ♕f5 32 h3 ½-½**

Summary

4...c6 usually transposes back into the previous chapter though Black has committed himself a little early. I'm not hugely struck on 4...f5 though it's certainly good for an occasional outing against an unprepared opponent.

4...e5 is much more important. The most critical question is how good Game 49 is for White and the decision as to whether you're happy to play this with Black is up to the individual. If you are, then when White replies 5 ♘f3 or 5 ♘ge2 you've 'achieved' something since you can play the Black side of Game 50. But as my defeat there shows the achievement is a highly double-edged one when White quite correctly hits out with 8 h4.

1 d4 g6 2 c4 ♗g7 3 e4 d6 4 ♘c3 *(D)*

4...c6

    4...e5 *(D)*

        5 dxe5 – *Game 49*

        5 ♘ge2 – *Game 50*

    4...f5 – *Game 51*

5 f4*(D)* – *Game 48*

4 ♘c3

4...e5

5 f4

CHAPTER NINE

1 d4 g6 2 c4 ♗g7: Odds and Ends

1 d4 g6 2 c4 ♗g7

One of the problems with the Modern is that because Black's initial moves are not at all forcing, White can adopt a number of different move orders to try to stamp his own ideas on the game. In this chapter, we examine the most significant of these early deviations, where Black avoids transposing to the King's Indian Defence with an early ...♘f6.

Black's first significant decision actually takes on his first move. Since we are sticking to the Modern move order with 1...g6, I'm not going to get involved in the details but I really should point out that, particularly if he's happy playing a Pirc rather than a Modern, Black can play 1 d4 d6, when:

a) 2 c4 e5 leads to a complex of variations:

a1) 3 dxe5 dxe5 4 ♕xd8+ ♔xd8 isn't supposed to be particularly good for White since c2-c4 weakens the d4-square while all of Black's moves are useful.

a2) 3 ♘c3 exd4 4 ♕xd4 gives White some space advantage but in return for a significant Black lead in development. With very accurate play White may be able to consolidate, but there are plenty of opportunities for Black on the way.

a3) 3 ♘f3 e4 (of course 3...exd4 is also playable, but Black generally plays 3...e4 since it gains quite a lot of space) 4 ♘g5 (other knight moves are possible as well of course) when:

a31) 4...♘f6 5 ♘c3 ♗f5 6 g4 ♗xg4 7 ♗g2 is somewhat better for White, though I did draw this against Kasparov in Belfort 1988.

a32) 4...f5 5 ♘c3 c6 is a main line which is quite playable for Black.

b) In order to avoid these lines, White often plays 2 ♘f3 (2 g3 is a third important alternative – see 2...g6 3 ♗g2 ♗g7 4 c4 e5 5 ♘f3 ♘d7 6 ♘c3 in Games 52 and 53) when if Black wants to avoid the position after 1 d4 d6 2 ♘f3 g6 3 c4 ♗g7 then he should play 2...♗g4, though there's a lot of theory on that too. Otherwise 2 ♘f3 g6 3 c4 ♗g7 4 ♘c3 leads to 'normal' Modern lines considered below.

Our preferred move order, however, goes 1 d4 g6 2 c4 ♗g7. Now if he's aiming for the position after 1 d4 d6 2 ♘f3 g6 3 c4 ♗g7 then White is well advised to play 3 ♘f3 rather than 3 ♘c3 which gives Black a further opportunity, albeit a somewhat dubious one, of playing 3...c5!? and if 4 d5 capturing now or possibly next move on c3 as in Game 59.

Therefore it seems more accurate to play 3 ♘f3 when of course 3...d6 4 ♘c3 leads again to our normal Modern position (White can also try the odd-looking 4 e4, see Game 57). Black can still play 3...c5 here too but there are two significant drawbacks associated with this:

a) 4 d5 is much more of a problem here since after 4...d6 5 e4 Black has more or less run out of waiting moves and must accede to a normal Benoni rather than the line with ...♝xc3+!?

b) White can also play 4 e4 when 4...cxd4 5 ♘xd4 leads to a Sicilian Maroczy Bind, a line that many players dislike as Black, though there is an opportunity to put a spoke in the works with 4...♛a5+ – see Game 58.

By far the most common position that arises through these various move orders is the one after 1 d4 g6 2 c4 ♝g7 3 ♘c3 d6 4 ♘f3. Here Black has a choice between 4...♘d7 and 4...♝g4 (Games 54-56). The former is particularly important as it can arise in so many different ways, for example 1 d4 g6 2 c4 ♝g7 3 ♘c3 d6 4 ♘f3 ♘d7 5 g3 e5 6 ♝g2 or 1 d4 g6 2 ♘f3 ♝g7 3 c4 d6 4 g3 ♘d7 5 ♝g2 e5 6 ♘c3. Now 6...♘f6 of course transposes back into a King's Indian, but Black can reach somewhat different positions by playing his knight to either h6 or e7 (see Games 52 and 53).

Game 52
Makarov-Todorcevic
Yugoslav Team Ch., Cetinje 1993

---

1 ♘f3 g6 2 d4 ♝g7 3 c4 d6 4 g3 ♘d7 5 ♝g2 e5 6 ♘c3 ♘e7

This seems preferable to 6...♘h6 since the plan associated with the latter of ...f7-f6 and ...♘f7 is somewhat passive. In the game Wojtkiewicz-Gaprindashvili, Tallinn rapidplay 1998, White obtained excellent queenside play, while Black never got going on the kingside at all after 7 0-0 0-0 8 e4 f6 9 ♖e1 ♘f7 10 ♖b1 c6 11 ♕c2 ♕e7 12 b4 ♖d8 13 d5 c5 14 a3 ♘b6 15 ♘a4 ♘xa4 16 ♕xa4 ♝d7 17 ♕b3 b6 18 a4 ♖dc8 19 a5 bxa5 20 bxc5 ♖xc5 21 ♝a3 ♖c7 22 ♘d2 ♝h6 23 ♖ed1 ♝g4 24 f3 ♝c8 25 c5 ♖b7 26 ♕c3 ♖xb1 27 ♖xb1 dxc5 28 ♘c4 a4 29 ♕a5 ♕d8 30 ♕xa4 ♝d7 31 ♕b3 ♝f8 32 ♝f1 ♕c7 33 ♕b7 ♖c8 34 ♕xc7 ♖xc7 35 ♖b8 ♔g7 36 ♝b2 ♘d6? (allowing a crushing retort, though White had more than enough for the pawn in any case) 37 ♘xe5! ♝c8 (if 37...fxe5 38 ♝xe5+ ♔f7 39 ♖xf8+! Etc.) 38 ♘c4 ♖b7 39 ♖xb7+ ♝xb7 40 ♘xd6 ♖xd6 41 f4 ♝c7 42 ♝c4 g5 43 e5 gxf4 44 gxf4 ♔g6 45 d6 ♝b8 46 d7 ♝c7 47 exf6 1-0.

7 0-0

7 h4?! h6 helps Black more than his opponent since the g4-square has become very inviting. In Bareev-Azmaiparashvili, USSR 1986, Black got the advantage after 8 e4 exd4 9 ♘xd4 ♘e5 10 0-0 0-0 11 b3 ♘7c6 12 ♘de2 f5 13 ♘f4?! g5 14 hxg5 hxg5 15 ♘h5 f4! and eventually won.

7...0-0

8 e4

8 e3 is perfectly sensible but Zurab Azmaiparashvili, who has played many games in this line, demonstrated a good way to meet this against L.Basin in Minsk 1985 with 8...exd4! (improving on 8...f5 which he had played against Yuri Razu-

vayev the previous year; that game went 9 b3 e4 10 ♘g5 ♘f6 11 f3 c6 12 fxe4 h6 13 e5! dxe5 14 ♘f3 e4 15 ♘e5 h5 16 h3!, when White had a very good game and won rather quickly – it's sufficiently gory that I'm reproducing it here in full: 16...♘d7 17 ♘xd7 ♕xd7 18 ♗a3 b6 19 ♘e2 g5 20 h4 f4 21 ♗xe4 ♗b7 22 hxg5 fxe3 23 ♕d3 c5 24 d5 ♗xa1 25 ♖xa1 ♘f5 26 ♗b2 ♘d6 27 ♗g6 ♘f5 28 ♗f6 ♘d6 29 ♖f1 h4 30 ♖f4 ♖xf6 31 gxf6 ♖f8 32 ♕xe3 hxg3 33 ♕xg3 1-0) 9 ♘xd4 ♘b6 10 b3 c5 11 ♘de2 d5 12 ♗a3 dxc4 13 ♕xd8 ♖xd8 14 ♗xc5 ♘c6

15 ♖ac1 ♘d7 16 ♗d4 ♘xd4 17 ♘xd4 cxb3 18 ♘xb3 ('Azmai' gives 18 axb3 as equal in his notes in *Informator 40*) ♘e5 19 ♘d5 ♔f8 20 ♘c5 ♖b8 21 ♘c7 ♖d2 22 ♖fd1 ♖xd1+ 23 ♖xd1 ♗g4 24 ♖c1 b6 25 ♘5a6 ♖d8 26 h3 ♗e2 27 ♘b4 ♘f3+ 28 ♔h1 ♖d2 29 ♘cd5 ♗b2 30 ♖b1 g5 31 e4 a5 32 ♘c6 ♗d3 0-1.

8...exd4

If 8...♘c6 White can reply not 9 ♗e3 exd4 10 ♘xd4 ♘de5! transposing into the next note but 9 ♗g5! f6 10 ♗e3, though this is also far from bad for Black.

9 ♘xd4 ♘c6

9...♘e5 is also playable but this is most challenging. Given that exchanging on c6 isn't particularly strong, Black must already have a good position. In the next game, we examine a line in which White

instead moves his knight back to e2, which is also quite pleasant for Black.

10 ♘xc6

Of course, White would like to play 10 ♗e3, but then 10...♘de5 threatening both the c4-pawn and ...♘g4 is most annoying. If 11 ♘xc6 bxc6 12 ♕a4 ♗e6 13 b3 c5 or 13...♕d7 leaves the queen rather stranded on a4.

10 ♘c2 is also playable but not terribly threatening. Black became active very quickly with 10...♘c5 11 ♘e3 ♘d4 12 b4 ♘ce6 13 ♖b1 f5 14 exf5 gxf5 15 ♘ed5 c6 16 ♘f4 ♘xf4 17 ♗xf4 ♘e6 18 ♗d2 f4 in Rechlis-McNab, Thessaloniki Olympiad 1988, and subsequently won.

10 ♘de2 is the subject of the next main game.

10...bxc6 11 f4?!

To prevent 11...♘e5, but this puts rather too much strain on White's position and Black immediately slightly more than equalises.

11 ♕c2 is normal when:

a) 11...♘e5 is an attempt to equalise immediately. Play continues 12 b3 and:

a1) 12...♘f3+!? tries to short circuit White's play completely. Kirov-Azmaiparashvili, Baku 1983, was agreed drawn after just six more moves, 13 ♗xf3 ♕f6 14 ♗f4 ♕xc3 15 ♕xc3 ♗xc3 16 ♖ac1 ♗e5 17 c5 ♗xf4 18 gxf4 ♗b7 ½-½, though I feel that in the final position Black's pawn structure is even more damaged than White's.

a2) The calmer 12...♛f6 was played in Co.Ionescu-McNab, Thessaloniki Olympiad 1988. That game continued 13 ♗b2 ♘f3+ 14 ♔h1 ♗g4 15 ♕d3 ♘e5 16 ♕e3 ♗f3 17 ♘a4 ♖fe8 18 ♖ae1 ♗xg2+ 19 ♔xg2 ♕e6 20 ♕c3 ♗f6 21 f4 ♘d7 22 ♕d2 ♗xb2 23 ♕xb2 f5 24 exf5 ♕xf5 25 ♕d4 ♘f6 26 ♘c3 a5 27 h3 h5 28 ♕d2 ♘e4 29 ♕d4 ♘f6 30 ♕d2 ½-½. However, White's structure looked a little better during this and even a move before the end he might have tried to continue with 29 ♘xe4 ♖xe4 30 ♖xe4 ♕xe4+ 31 ♔f2, though 3l...h4 32 ♖e1 hxg3+ 33 ♔xg3 ♕f5 34 ♖e7 ♖f8 35 ♖xc7 g5! looks very messy and the queen ending after 35...♖f7 36 ♖e8+ ♖f8 37 ♖xf8+ ♔xf8 must be fine for Black.

b) 11...♕f6 12 ♘e2 ♖e8 13 ♖b1 ♕e7 has been played a few times and seems eminently playable for Black, e.g. 14 ♗e3 c5 15 ♖be1 ♖b8 16 b3 ♕e5 17 ♗d2 ♗b7 18 ♘c3 ♕e7 19 h3 ♘f8 20 ♘d5 ♕d8 21 ♘f4 ♘e6 22 ♘xe6 ♖xe6 23 h4 ♕e7 24 ♗g5 ♕e8 ½-½ Dorfman-Azmaiparashvili, European Club Cup Lyon 1994.

11...♗a6! 12 ♖e1

If 12 ♕e2? ♘b6! simply wins the pawn and 12 ♕d3 ♘c5 13 ♕e2 ♕b8! is also better for Black, if less starkly.

12...♗xc4 13 ♕a4 ♗e6 14 ♕xc6 ♘c5 15 ♕b5 ♖b8 16 ♕e2 ♗c8!

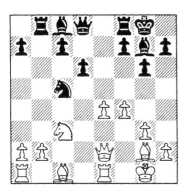

Black's excellent minor pieces and pressure down the b-file give him a good game, but he must still play very accurately since if White can get out then his structural advantage may take over as the dominant factor.

17 ♗e3 ♗a6 18 ♕d2 ♘d3 19 ♖eb1 c5! 20 b3!?

20 ♗f1!? c4 21 ♗xd3 cxd3 was possible if somewhat unpleasant.

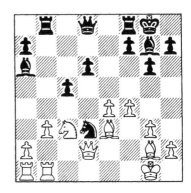

20...♖e8?!

It's natural to try and increase the pressure but Black could have cashed in with 20...♕a5 21 ♘d5 ♕xd2 22 ♗xd2, and now certainly not 22...♗xa1 23 ♖xa1 f6 24 ♗c3 ♔g7 25 g4 ♘b4 26 ♘xf6! but 22...♘b4! at once with a big advantage.

21 ♘d5! ♘b4

21...♗xa1 22 ♖xa1 ♘b4 23 ♘xb4 ♖xb4 24 ♖d1! gives reasonable compensation for the exchange.

22 ♘xb4 cxb4?!

Todorcevic's problem was that if 22...♖xb4 23 e5 dxe5 24 ♕xd8 ♖xd8 25 ♗xc5 ♖b5 26 ♗xa7 exf4 27 ♖d1! is rather dangerous, but now White gets the advantage.

23 ♗d4 ♗xd4+ 24 ♕xd4 ♕b6 25 ♖d1 ♖e6 26 ♖ac1

Of course not 26 ♗h3? ♖xe4!

26...♕xd4+ 27 ♖xd4 ♖b6 28 ♖c7 ♗b7 29 ♖d7 ♔f8 30 ♖d8+?!

Dissipating the pressure, though 30

♔f2!? ♔e8 31 ♖c7 ♖e7 32 ♖dc4 isn't very clear.

30...♖e8 31 ♖4xd6 ♖xd6 32 ♖xd6 ♗xe4 33 ♗xe4 ♖xe4 34 ♔f2 ♖e7 35 ♖d8+

Now Black manages to equalise. White could still have maintained winning chances by playing 35 ♖a6, intending after ♖a4 to force the enemy rook to the rather passive b7-square, though I imagine that Black is okay, e.g. if 35...♖c7 36 h4!? h5!? 37 ♖a4 ♖b7 38 ♔e3 ♔e7 39 ♔d4 ♔e6 40 ♔c4 ♔f5 is already very good for Black (of course White could have drawn earlier) since if 41 ♖xb4 ♖xb4+ 42 ♔xb4 ♔g4 Black wins the pawn ending!

35...♔g7 36 ♖b8 ♖c7 37 ♖xb4 ♖c2+ 38 ♔f3 ♖xa2 39 ♖b7 ½-½

Game 53
Ki.Georgiev-Azmaiparashvili
Groningen 1994

---

1 d4 d6 2 ♘f3 g6 3 c4 ♗g7 4 ♘c3 e5 5 g3 ♘d7 6 ♗g2 ♘e7 7 0-0 0-0 8 e4 exd4 9 ♘xd4 ♘c6 10 ♘de2

10...a5

If Black intends to play ...♘c5 then it's more flexible to play this necessary move first, keeping White guessing as to whether the horse will emerge on c5 or e5.

10...♘de5 is also quite playable, but against an opponent as well prepared as Kiril Georgiev, 'Azmai' here decided to

vary from his game with R.Tomaszewski in Moscow 1986, which went 11 b3 f5 12 f4 ♘g4!? (rather than the older 12...♘f7) 13 exf5 ♗xf5 14 h3 ♘f6 15 ♗e3 (in his notes , 'Azmai' states that 15 g4?! ♘xg4! 16 hxg4 ♗xg4 is very dangerous for White here) 15...♕d7 and now:

a) Tomaszewski played the submissive 16 ♔h2? and after 15...♖ae8 17 ♕d2 ♖e7 18 ♖ae1 ♖fe8 19 ♘c1 ♘e4 20 ♘xe4 ♗xe4 21 ♗f2 d5!! 22 ♗xe4 (if 22 cxd5 ♗xg2 23 ♔xg2 ♘d4! 24 ♗xd4 ♕xd5+ 25 ♔h2 ♕xd4 is most unpleasant) 22...dxe4 23 ♕xd7 ♖xd7 Black was better and later won.

b) But 16 g4! is critical, e.g. ♖ae8 17 ♗f2 and now:

b1) Here 'Azmai' gives 17...♘e4 18 ♕d5+ ♕f7 19 gxf5! ♘xc3 20 ♘xc3 ♗xc3 21 ♖ac1 ♗g7 22 fxg6 hxg6 23 c5, when it's certainly true that White's a bit better at least.

b2) He also quite rightly asserts that 17...♘xg4 18 hxg4 ♗xg4 19 ♕d5+ ♔h8 20 ♖ae1 is clearly better for White. This was tested in Wojtkiewicz-Djurkovic, Nova Gorica open 1997, which lasted just half a dozen more moves: 20...♗h3 21 ♕f3 ♗xg2 22 ♔xg2 ♘e5 23 ♕g3 ♘g4 24 ♗d4 ♘h6 25 ♗xg7+ ♔xg7 26 ♘d5 ♖f5 1-0.

11 h3 ♘c5 12 ♗e3 ♗e6

12...a4 was also possible at once.

13 b3 a4 14 ♖b1 axb3 15 axb3 f5!

Exploiting the fact that after 16 exf5 ♗xf5 the b1-rook is embarrassed.

16 ♔h2 fxe4 17 ♘xe4 ♘xe4 18 ♗xe4 ♗f5 19 ♕d5+

19 ♗xf5 ♖xf5 20 ♕d2 was about equal.

19...♔h8 20 ♗xf5 ♖xf5 21 ♕d2 ♕f6

Black's very active play has yielded him fairly easy equality.

22 ♘f4 ♖fa5 23 ♘d5 ♕f7 24 ♗h6 ♗e5

Quite ambitious. The ending after 24...♗xh6 25 ♕xh6 ♖a2 26 ♕f4 ♕xf4 27 gxf4 ♖c8 28 ♔g2 is roughly level.

25 ♕d3 ♖a2 26 ♔g2 ♗d4 27 ♕f3?!

27 ♗e3 ♗xe3 28 ♕xe3 ♘e5 was still about equal. Now though, Black gets an edge.

27...♕xf3+ 28 ♔xf3 ♘e5+ 29 ♔g2

And not 29 ♔e4? ♗xf2 30 ♘xc7 ♖e2+ 31 ♔d5 ♘f7 32 ♗f4 ♖c8 33 ♘e6 ♖e8, when the knight can't move in view of 34 ♘c7 ♖8e5+ 35 ♗xe5 ♖xe5 mate!

29...♘f7

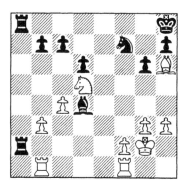

30 ♘xc7?!

Now Black gains a material advantage. Instead 30 ♗e3 ♗xe3 31 ♘xe3 is better for Black in view of his control of the a-file but he has nothing special as yet.

30...♘xh6 31 ♘xa8 ♖xa8 32 ♖fd1 ♘f5 33 g4?

Weakening the kingside; 33 ♖d2 was correct.

33...♘h4+ 34 ♔g3 ♗f6

Of course the d-pawn can't now be cap-

tured in view of 35 ♖xd6 ♗e5+.

35 f4 ♖a2 36 g5 ♘f5+ 37 ♔f3 ♗d4 38 ♖d3 ♔g7 39 ♖bd1?!

39 b4 was better since now the bishop gets anchored on c5. In near desperation White immediately sacrifices before Black can get completely co-ordinated.

39...♗c5

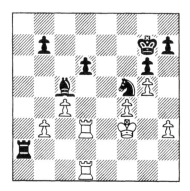

40 b4!? ♗xb4 41 ♖b3 ♖a4 42 c5 ♔f8 43 cxd6 ♗xd6 44 ♖xb7 ♖xf4+ 45 ♔e2 ♗e7

And Black slowly converted his advantage:

46 ♖d3 ♖h4 47 ♖c3 ♖h5 48 ♔f2 ♖xg5 49 ♖cc7 ♖h5 50 ♖c3 ♖h4 51 ♔g2 ♔f7 52 ♖a7 ♖b4 53 ♖a2 h5 54 ♖d3 ♗d6 55 ♖a7+ ♔e6 56 ♖a2 ♘h4+ 57 ♔f2 ♖f4+ 58 ♔e2 ♘f5 59 ♖a6 ♖b4 60 ♖a2 ♖b1 61 ♔f2 ♗c5+ 62 ♔g2 ♖g1+ 63 ♔h2 ♖g5 64 ♖e2+ ♔f6 65 ♖ed2 ♗g1+ 66 ♔h1 ♗e3 67 ♖g2 ♘g3+ 68 ♔h2 h4 69 ♖d1 ♖a5 70 ♖b2 ♘h5 71 ♖d3 ♗f4+ 72 ♔g2 ♗g3 73 ♖b6+ ♔g5 74 ♔f3 ♖f5+ 0-1

Game 54
Pomar-T.Petrosian
Siegen Olympiad 1970

1 d4 g6 2 c4 ♗g7 3 ♘c3 d6 4 ♘f3 ♗g4 5 g3 ♕c8!?

This classic game shows Petrosian at his provocative best. But I suppose that in theory Black should really carry out his threat with 5...♗xf3 6 gxf3 when:

a) 6...&c6 7 d5 &d4 8 &e3 c5 9 dxc6 &xc6 gives White a pleasant edge.

b) 6...c6 7 &g2 &f6 8 f4 0-0 9 0-0 &bd7 10 &e3 (10 &e1 is also very playable of course) 10...e6 11 d5! exd5 12 cxd5 c5 gave White a nice space advantage in Mikhalevski-Davies, Hogeschool, Zeeland open 1998. White now hurried with 13 f5!?, but in his notes recommended 13 &d3, intending either &ab1, a2-a3 and b2-b4 or &fe1 and f4-f5.

c) In order to avoid the necessity to play ...c7-c5, Krasenkov as Black against Robert Kempinski in the Polish Championship 1996, chose instead to develop his king's knight on e7: 6...e6 7 &g2 &e7 8 0-0 0-0 9 f4 c6 (9...d5!? is possible here, so White perhaps should have played 9 d5 himself first) 10 d5 exd5 11 cxd5 &a6! (possible since the c6-pawn is protected) 12 dxc6 bxc6 13 &d2 d5 14 b3 &f5 15 &b2 &c5 16 &ac1 &e6 17 &fd1 &c8 18 &a4 &xb2 19 &xb2 and although Krasenkov himself assesses this as slightly better for White in his notes, it can't be too terrible for Black.

6 &g2 &h6!?

An idea of the great Canadian eccentric (on the chessboard that is) Duncan Suttles.

7 h3

Of course 7 0-0 is also perfectly playable.

7...&d7 8 e4 f6 9 &e3 &f7 10 &d2 c5

Further provocation. 10...0-0 was the 'normal' alternative but would be miserable to play once Black had struck out for the unknown with his previous few moves.

11 dxc5!?

Aiming to refute Black's play. Instead the more conservative 11 d5 would have offered a positional edge.

11...dxc5 12 0-0-0 &c6

13 &b1

13 &xc5 was critical though very hard to play in such a nice position. The main line goes 13...&ce5 (13...&a5 14 b3 is good for White, as if then 14...&xh3 15 &xh3 &xc5 16 &d7+ &f8 17 &d4 is very bad for Black) 14 &xe5 &xe5 when:

a) 15 f4 &xc5 (&xc4 16 &d4 is easier for White) 16 fxe5 0-0-0 17 &d5 is very unclear.

b) 15 &d4! looks better, though hard to judge in a game, e.g. 15...b6 16 &xe7.

b1) 16...&xe7? 17 &d6+ &e8 (or 17...&f7 18 f4 &f8 19 &d4 &c5 20 &d2 &xc4 21 &xd7+ &xd7 22 &xd7+) 18 &d5.

b2) 16...&c6! 17 &xd7+ &xd7 18 &xd7 &xd7 19 &a3 leaves White with two pawns for the exchange and the initiative.

13...b6 14 g4

If 14 e5 fxe5 15 &g5 &f5+ 16 &a1 &d4!; while 14 &h4 e5! is reasonably playable for Black. but of course not 14...g5? 15 &f5 &xf5 16 exf5 &xf5+ 17

♗e4 ♕c8 18 ♕d5 when he gets slaughtered.

14...♖b8 15 ♖he1 ♖b7 16 e5!? fxe5 17 ♘g5 0-0

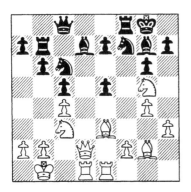

18 ♘d5?

Obvious but wrong. Instead he should have induced a further weakness with 18 ♗d5! e6 19 ♗g2 when:

a) For some reason Maric in *Informator* suggested 19...a6, which indeed prevents 19 ♘b5 but does nothing against the move 20 ♘ce4.

b) In their excellent analysis in *The Modern Defence*, Keene and Botterill suggest the much saner 19....♘xg5 20 ♗xg5 ♘d4, though 21 ♗xb7 ♕xb7 22 ♗h6! still leaves White with the advantage.

18...♘xg5 19 ♗xg5 ♗e8!

Certainly not 19...♖f7?/19...♖e8? 20 ♘xe7+, while if 19...♗e6 20 ♘xe7+ ♘xe7 21 ♗xb7 ♕xb7 22 ♕d6 ♔f7! defends both pieces, though White can and presumably should force a draw with 23 ♖xe5 ♗xe5 24 ♕xe5 ♘g8 when he has an immediate perpetual with 25 ♕f4+ ♔g7 26 ♕e5+ ♔f7, but I don't think he can do any better.

20 ♗h6

Not now 20 ♘xe7+ ♘xe7 21 ♗xb7 ♕xb7 22 ♕d8 ♘c6 etc.

20...e6! 21 ♗xg7 ♖xg7 22 ♘c3 ♘d4 23 ♖xe5 ♖gf7

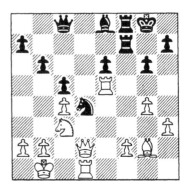

24 ♘e4?

Getting his rook in a fatal tangle. 24 ♖f1 was correct, though after 24...♗c6 (or 24...♕c7 25 ♕e3 ♗c6) the powerful knight combined with pressure down the f-file give Black the advantage.

24...♕c7 25 ♖g5

If 25 ♕g5 ♖f4 26 ♖xd4 cxd4 27 ♖xe6 ♕xc4 28 ♘f6+ ♖4xf6 29 ♖xf6 ♕d3+ 30 ♔c1 ♗f7 will win and 26...h6! 27 ♕xh6 ♕xe5 is even cleaner, since 28 ♘g5 gets mated at once after 28...♕e1+ 29 ♔c2 ♖xf2+ 30 ♔b3 ♕e3+ 31 ♖d3 ♕xd3.

25...♖f4! 26 ♕d3 h6! 27 ♘d6 hxg5 28 ♘xe8 ♖xe8 29 ♕xg6+ ♔f8 30 ♕xg5 ♕h7+ 0-1

Game 55
Prakash-Speelman
Calcutta 1999

1 d4 d6 2 ♘f3 ♗g4 3 c4 ♘d7 4 ♘c3 e5 5 e3 g6!? 6 ♗e2 ♗g7

Obviously, you could also reach this position via a more 'standard' move order: 1 d4 g6 2 c4 ♗g7 3 ♘c3 d6 4 ♘f3 ♗g4 5 e3 ♘d7 6 ♗e2 e5. Although Black's play aiming for pressure against d4 is positionally well founded, I can't recommend the line since it seems to lose too much time if White reacts sufficiently vigorously.

7 0-0 ♘e7

8 b3

The forcing 8 h3! is annoying, since if 8...exd4?! (maybe 8...♗xf3 9 ♗xf3 ♖b8) 9 exd4 ♗xf3 10 ♗xf3 both:

a) 10...c6 11 ♘e4 ♘b6 (11...♘f5 12 ♗g4!) 12 c5! and

b) 10...♖b8 11 ♗g5 0-0 12 ♘d5 f6 13 ♘xe7+ ♕xe7 14 ♖e1 ♕d8 are unpalatable for Black.

8...0-0 9 ♗b2 ♗xf3!?

Forcing the change of structure, since if 9...c6 White can and should exchange on e5: 10 dxe5 dxe5 with an edge.

10 ♗xf3 exd4 11 exd4 c6

11...♖b8 looks better to keep c6 free for the horse.

12 ♗g4 ♘f6 13 ♗h3 d5 14 ♖e1 ♖e8 15 g3

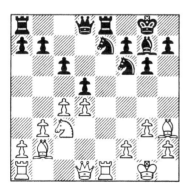

If Black could only activate the e7-knight then he would get a fine game with

pressure against d4. I now initiated a tactical operation to achieve this, but while he was thinking about his 17th move, I realised that it was unsound.

15...dxc4?! 16 bxc4 b5? 17 ♗a3??

17 cxb5 cxb5 18 ♘xb5! was correct (18 ♗a3 en route to c5 is also quite good) 18...♖b8 19 ♕a4 ♕b6 and now 20 ♗a3!! was the move that he missed altogether and I saw too late:

a) 20...♕xb5 21 ♕xb5 ♖xb5 22 ♗xe7! with a big advantage – but certainly not 22 ♖xe7? ♖xe7 23 ♗xe7 ♘d5 with equality.

b) 20...♘ed5 21 ♘d6 leaves White with a good extra pawn but at least keeps more tension in the position.

17...bxc4 18 ♗xe7?

After this further concession, things rapidly turn extremely nasty for White.

18...♖xe7 19 ♖xe7 ♕xe7 20 ♕a4 c5! 21 ♕c6

If 21 ♕xc4 cxd4 with a good extra pawn and the initiative.

21...♖d8

22 dxc5? ♘e8!

Here White resigned in view of 23 ♖c1 (or 23 ♕f3 ♖d3) 23...♗xc3 24 ♖xc3 ♕e1+.

Going back to the diagram he could still have fought hard with 22 ♕xc5! ♕xc5 23 dxc5 when:

a) If 23...♘d5? 24 ♖d1 ♗xc3 25 ♗g2 ♗b4 White has at least 26 ♖xd5 ♖xd5 (if 26...♖c8 27 c6 c3 28 ♖d4!) 27 ♗xd5 c3 28

$\mathbf{\hat{\perp}}$b3 $\mathbf{\hat{\perp}}$xc5, when despite the pawn deficit he will surely draw.

b) 23...♘e4! and now:

b1) 24 ♖d1 (which I'd totally missed) happens to lose to 24...♖xd1+ 25 ♘xd1 c3 26 ♘e3 ♗d4 27 c6 (or 27 ♗g2 ♘xf2 28 c6 ♗xe3 29 c7 ♘e4+ 30 ♔f1 ♘d6) 27...♗xe3 28 c7 ♘d6.

b2) 24 c6 and:

b21) 24...f5? 25 ♖d1!

b22) 24...♘xc3! is much the simplest, though it depends on whether the ending after 25 c7 ♖f8 26 c8♕ (26 ♖e1 f5 27 ♖e7 ♘d5 28 ♖d7 ♘b6 29 ♖d8 ♗f6 wins for Black) 26...♖xc8 27 ♗xc8 ♘e2+ 28 ♔f1 ♘xg3+ 29 hxg3 ♗xa1 is winning or not.

b23) If not then 24...♘g5 (suggested by Fritz) might be tried. It looks very odd, and of course the consequences go way beyond the machine's horizon, but it may be a good move anyway, e.g. 25 ♗g4 (not 25 c7? ♘xh3+ 26 ♔g2 ♖c8 27 ♘d5 ♖xc7!) 25...f5 26 ♖d1! ♖c8 (26...♖f8) 27 ♘d5 ♔f7 28 ♗e2 ♖xc6 29 ♘b4! ♖c7 (29...♖c8 30 ♖d7+ ♔f8) 30 ♘a6 ♖c8 with good winning chances.

Game 56
Udovcic-Ivkov
Maribor 1967

---

1 c4 g6 2 d4 ♗g7 3 ♘c3 d6 4 ♘f3 ♗g4 5 e3 ♘c6 6 ♗e2 e5

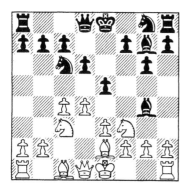

7 d5

Gaining space in the obvious way. 7 dxe5 dxe5 is pretty harmless but there is quite a lot to be said for 7 ♘xe5 when:

a) 7...♗xe2? 8 ♘xc6 ♗xd1 9 ♘xd8 ♗g4 10 ♘xb7 seems good for White. Landenbergue-D'Amore, Biel 1990, continued 10...a5 'trapping the knight', but after 11 ♘b5! ♔d7 12 f3 ♗e6 13 d5 ♗xd5 14 cxd5 ♖b8 15 ♘7xd6 cxd6 16 a4 White was already easily winning.

b) So Black should play 7...dxe5! 8 ♗xg4 exd4 9 exd4 (Ivkov gave 9 ♘d5!? ♘f6 as nice for Black but this is much more testing) and now:

b1) 9...♘xd4 10 0-0 ♘e7 11 ♖e1 (11 ♗g5 h6! 12 ♗xe7 ♔xe7 looks fine for Black) 11...0-0 12 ♗g5 f6 13 ♗e3 ♘ec6 (13...f5 14 ♗g5 ♗f6 15 ♗xf6 ♖xf6 16 ♖xe7! wins for White) 14 ♘b5 f5 15 ♗f3 ♘xf3+ 16 ♕xf3 ♖f7 17 ♖ad1 ♕f8 must be somewhat better for White, though Black did subsequently draw in Stohl-Tibensky, Stary Smokovec 1988.

b2) The more adventurous 9...♕xd4 may also be playable, i.e. 10 0-0 ♕xc4!? 11 ♖e1+ ♘ge7!? (11...♔f8 isn't absurd) 12 ♕d7+ ♔f8 13 ♗e2 ♕b4 14 ♕xc7 ♘d5! 15 a3 ♘xc7 16 axb4 and now 16...♘xb4 should be reasonably playable, though White does have a strong initiative for the pawn. Instead Black played 16...♘e6 in Blees-Dedes, Athens open 1992, and eventually lost rather horribly: 17 b5 ♘cd4 18 ♗d1 ♘c5 19 ♗f4 ♘d3 20 ♗d6+ ♔g8 21 ♖xa7! ♖d8 22 ♗c7 ♖c8 23 ♖e3 ♘xb2 24 b6 ♘f5 25 ♗g4 ♘c4 26 ♗xf5 gxf5 27 ♘d5 ♔f8 28 ♖e1 ♖e8 29 ♖xe8+ ♔xe8 30 ♖xb7 ♗b2 31 ♗f4 ♘a5 32 ♖e7+ ♔d8 33 b7 1-0.

7...♘ce7 8 0-0

Now 8 ♘xe5? loses to 8...♗xe2 9 ♕a4+ c6 10 dxc6 bxc6 11 ♘xc6 ♕d7.

Of course 8 e4 is also possible first, when the consequent line is 8...♗xf3 9 ♗xf3 h5. Instead I played 8...♘f6 against Tony Miles at the British Championship,

Torquay 1998. After 9 ♗e3 ♗xf3 10 ♗xf3 h5 11 0-0 ♔f8 (not 11...♘h6 12 ♗xh6 ♖xh6 13 ♕d2 ♖h8 14 ♗d1 with f2-f4! coming) 12 ♕d2 ♘eg8 13 h3 ♗h6 14 ♗d1 ♘d7 15 ♗a4! ♘b6 16 c5! ♗xe3 17 ♕xe3 dxc5 18 ♕xc5+ ♕d6 19 ♕e3 a6 White has a serious structural advantage and Tony later won.

8...♗xf3 9 ♗xf3 f5

9...h5 also looks possible here – Black was well advised to exchange on f3 first since otherwise there are many lines in which the knight moves, offering the advantageous exchange of light-squared bishops.

10 e4 ♘f6 11 g3

In his notes in *Informator 4*, Ivkov assesses this position as greatly in White's favour in view of his potential light-square pressure.

11...0-0 12 ♗g2 ♔h8 13 f3 c5 14 ♗h3 a6 15 ♕c2 ♖b8 16 ♗d2 ♘fg8 17 ♘e2 b5 18 b3 fxe4

Quite a serious concession but presumably if 18...♘h6 at once he feared 19 f4.

19 fxe4 ♗h6 20 ♖xf8 ♕xf8 21 ♖f1 ♕g7 22 cxb5 axb5 23 ♗e6

At the moment the bishop is very impressive here, though much later it ends up hitting empty air.

23...♗xd2 24 ♕xd2 ♘f6 25 g4!

Ivkov assesses this as already being winning for White.

25...♖f8 26 ♘g3?

But here he rightly suggests 26 a4! setting up a powerful outside passed pawn.

26...b4! 27 g5 ♘h5 28 ♕e2 ♘xg3 29 hxg3 ♘g8 30 ♕a6?

The wrong direction. Interestingly, White could have headed straight for a pure minor piece endgame in which it turns out that the bishop dominates the knight with 30 ♖xf8 ♕xf8 31 ♕f1 ♕g7 32 ♕f7 ♕xf7 33 ♗xf7 ♘e7 34 ♔f2 ♔g7 35 ♗e6 h6 (or 35..♔f8 36 ♗d7!, cutting the

king off) 36 ♔e3 hxg5 37 g4! ♔f8 38 ♔d3 ♔e8 39 ♔c4 ♔d8 40 ♔b5 ♔c7 41 ♔a6 and White wins.

30...♖xf1+ 31 ♔xf1?

31 ♕xf1 was still strong and if 31...h6 32 ♕h3 c4 33 ♗xg8! (not 33 bxc4 ♕a7+ 34 ♔h1 ♕xa2) 33...c3 (or 33...cxb3 34 axb3 ♕a7+ 35 ♔h1 ♕a1+ 36 ♔h2 ♕b2+ 37 ♕g2 ♕xg2+ 38 ♔xg2 ♔xg8 39 ♔f3 hxg5 40 ♔e3 en route to the b4-pawn and victory) 34 ♗e6 c2 35 ♕f1 ♕a7+ 36 ♔g2! ♔h7 37 ♕f8! hxg5 (or 37...♕g7 38 ♕c8) 38 ♗g8+ ♔h8 39 ♗f7+ ♔h7 40 ♕g8+ ♔h6 41 ♕h8 mate.

31...♕f8+ 32 ♔e2 h6 33 gxh6?

33 ♗xg8 was still equal.

33...♘f6!

For all its imperfections, this game does provide a classic example of the sort of endgame which Black is aiming for from the start in which his queen and knight overrun the enemy queen and light-squared bishop. The rest was slaughter.

34 ♕d3 ♕xh6 35 ♕f3 ♔g7 36 ♔d3 ♕c1 37 ♕e3 ♕c3+ 38 ♔e2 ♕c2+ 39 ♔f3 ♕xa2 40 g4? ♕h2 41 g5 ♘h5 42 ♗d7 ♕g3+ 43 ♔e2 ♘f4+ 44 ♔d2 ♕xg5 0-1

Game 57
Epishin-Gulko
World Open, Philadelphia 1998

---

1 d4 d6 2 ♘f3 g6 3 c4 ♗g7 4 e4!?

This looks rather strange since Black is encouraged to pin the f3-knight immediately, but Epishin has scored several successes with 4 e4 and it certainly shouldn't be underestimated.

4...♗g4

The only consequent reply, unless Black is happy to go into a King's Indian now that the knight is committed to f3 so precluding, among others, the Sämisch variation.

5 ♗e2 ♘c6

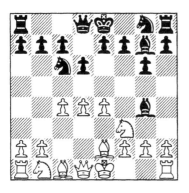

6 ♗e3

6 ♘bd2 is a reasonable alternative, since while the knight isn't very well placed on d2 nor is the bishop on g4. My game with Helgi Olafsson at Reykjavik 1990 continued 6...♘f6 7 d5 ♘b8 8 0-0 (in my notes at the time I recommended 8 ♕c2!, aiming to recapture on f3 with the knight, but 8...♘bd7 9 h3 ♗xf3 10 ♘xf3 ♘c5 looks fine) 8...♘bd7 9 h3 (again 9 ♕c2 is possible, but 9...♘c5!? puts a spoke in the works, when if 10 b4?! ♘cxe4 11 ♘xe4 ♘xe4 12 ♕xe4 ♗xf3 13 ♗xf3 ♗xa1 14 ♗h6 White's compensation is rather strained) 9...♗xf3 10 ♗xf3 0-0 11 ♖e1 ♖e8 12 ♖b1 e6 13 b3 ♘c5 14 ♗a3! (not 14 ♕c2? exd5 15 cxd5 ♘xd5) 14...♘d3 15 ♖f1? (15 ♗e3 ♘e5 16 ♗b2 was equal – but not 16 ♗e2? ♗h6) 15...a5! with an excellent position which I later won. The knight on d2 gave a very bad impression

throughout: 16 dxe6 ♖xe6 17 e5 dxe5 18 ♗xb7 ♖b8 19 ♗e4 (19 ♕f3!?) 19...♘b4 20 ♗xb4? (20 ♕e2 ♘xa2 21 ♗b2 is less bad) 20...axb4 21 ♕e2 ♖d6! 22 ♖b2 (not 22 ♖bd1? ♗h6 or 22 ♘f3 ♘xe4 23 ♕xe4 f5) 22...♖d4! 23 ♗b1 e4!

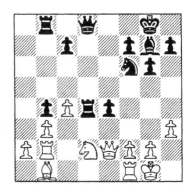

24 c5?! (24 ♖e1 or 24 f3 were tougher) 24...♘d5 with a winning advantage. The game finished 25 ♘xe4 ♖xe4 26 ♗xe4 ♘c3 27 ♕a6?! (or 27 ♕e3 ♘xe4 28 ♖e2 ♘c3 29 ♖d2 ♘d5!) 27...♘xe4 28 ♖e2 ♘xc5 29 ♕c6 ♘e6 30 ♖fe1?! ♗c3 0-1.

6...e5 7 d5 ♗xf3 8 ♗xf3 ♘d4 9 ♗xd4 exd4

10 ♘d2

In the fifth game of their Candidates match in 1989 – a game which Timman really had to win – Portisch (White) played 10 ♘a3. After 10...♘e7 11 0-0 c6 12 ♖b1 0-0 13 ♘c2 c5 14 b4 ♘c8?! (Timman gives 14...b6 as equal) 15 ♕d3 ♕c7 16 ♗e2 ♖e8?! (again he recommends 16...b6) 17 bxc5 dxc5 18 f4 b5 19 ♖xb5! ♘d6 20 e5 ♘xb5 21 cxb5 White had enormous compensation for the exchange, though in fact Timman did wriggle out and even won in the end.

10...♘e7

Attempting to improve on their game in the Yerevan Olympiad 1996, where Gulko had played 10...c5 and after 11 dxc6 bxc6 12 b4 ♘e7 13 0-0 0-0 14 ♘b3 ♕b6 15 a3 ♖ab8 16 c5 dxc5 17 ♘xc5 ♖fd8 18 ♘d3 Epishin had a big edge, though Gulko did hold that one in the end.

11 ♗e2 0-0 12 0-0 c6

12...c5 was played in Epishin-D.Hennig, Hamburg open 1997. Now that the knight is committed to e7 - it wants to be on the circuit en route to e5 and could have gone there via f6 and d7 if White had ignored 10...c5 in the note above - Epishin simply ignored this and built up a strong centre and potential dangerous pressure on the light squares, culminating in a central breakthrough in the endgame which won a piece: 13 f4 a6 14 ♗d3 ♖b8 15 h4 b5 16 h5 ♘c8 17 hxg6 fxg6 18 ♕g4 ♔h8 19 b3 ♘b6 20 ♘f3 ♕d7 21 ♕xd7 ♘xd7 22 g3 bxc4 23 bxc4 ♖b2 24 ♖f2 ♖xf2 25 ♔xf2 ♖b8 26 ♖e1 ♖b2+ 27 ♖e2 ♖xe2+ 28 ♔xe2 ♗f6 29 ♗c2 ♔g7 30 ♔d3 g5 31 ♗a4 ♘b6 32 ♗e8 ♔f8 33 ♗h5 gxf4 34 gxf4 ♘a4 35 e5 ♗e7 36 ♘d2 ♘c3 37 ♘e4 dxe5 38 d6 ♗xd6 39 ♘xd6 exf4 40 ♘e4 ♘a4 41 ♔c2 1-0.

13 ♘f3 ♕b6 14 ♕d2 f5

Black is very active but if White can quell the uprising then his better structure will be highly significant. Not now 15 ♕c2 fxe4 16 ♕xe4 ♖ae8 17 ♕e6+ ♔h8 18 ♘g5 ♘xd5 19 ♘f7+ ♖xf7 20 ♕xe8+ ♖f8 21 ♕e4 ♘f4 with excellent compensation for the exchange. But by calmer, less ambitious play, Epishin does succeed in asserting his control.

15 ♗d3 fxe4 16 ♗xe4 cxd5 17 cxd5 ♖ac8 18 ♕e2!

Much better than 18 ♖ad1 ♖c5! 19 ♕e2 (19 ♘xd4 ♖c4) 19...♕b5 20 ♗d3 ♕d7 21 ♘g5 ♘xd5 22 ♕e6+ ♕xe6 23 ♘xe6 ♖e8 24 ♘xc5 dxc5 25 ♗c4 ♖d8 26 ♖fe1 ♗f6! 27 g3 ♔g7.

18...♗f6

Against ♘g5.

19 ♘e1! ♗g7 20 ♘d3

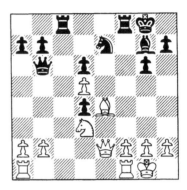

This powerful blockader gives White a clear advantage.

20...♖ce8 21 ♖fe1 ♕b5?

Initiating tactics which backfire. He should have curled up into a ball with 21...♔h8 22 ♗f3 ♕d8, but after 23 ♕d1 White is much better.

22 g3! ♘xd5

22...♔h8 23 ♘f4 ♕xe2 24 ♖xe2 is foul but this is worse.

23 ♘f4

This simple move wins the exchange. Epishin chose not to win material with 23 a4 ♕a5 24 b4 ♘xb4 25 ♘xb4 ♕xb4 26 ♗d5+ ♔h8 27 ♕xe8 ♖xe8 28 ♖xe8+ ♗f8 29 ♖xf8+ ♔g7 30 ♖f7+ ♔h6, since he presumably didn't want (possibly in time trouble) to have to cope with the passed d-pawn. But this must be a clear win, e.g. 31 ♖c1 d3 32 ♖cc7 d2 33 ♗f3 d1♕+ 34 ♗xd1 ♕e1+ 35 ♔g2 ♕xd1 36 h4 ♔h5 37 ♖xh7+ ♔g4 38 ♖cf7 etc.

23...♘c7 24 ♕xb5 ♘xb5

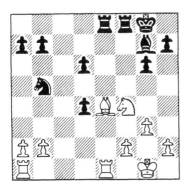

25 ♘e6! ♖xe6

Both 25...♖f6 26 ♗d5 ♔h8 27 a4 and 25...♖f7 26 ♗d5 ♔h8 27 a4 are also both winning for White.

26 ♗d5 ♔h8 27 ♖xe6 d3 28 ♖d1 ♗d4 29 ♖xd3 ♗xf2+ 30 ♔g2 ♘d4 31 ♖e4 ♘c2 32 ♖f3 ♘e1+ 33 ♖xe1 ♖xf3 34 ♖e8+ 1-0

Game 58
M.Pavlovic-Vaulin
Podgorica 1993

---

1 c4 c5 2 ♘f3 g6 3 d4 ♗g7 4 e4 ♕a5+

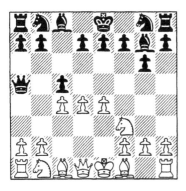

5 ♗d2

Probably the most critical. Of course 5 ♘c3 is perfectly reasonable as well, and after 5...♘c6 (5...♘f6 is also quite playable, though one sensible line is 6 ♗d2 cxd4 7 ♘xd4 ♘c6 8 ♘b3 ♕d8 giving White quite

a pleasant Maroczy Bind; and 5...d6 can also be played) play might go:

a) 6 ♗e3?! ♘f6! causes a serious problem since if 7 ♕d2 ♘g4!, while if 7 d5 ♘xe4 8 dxc6 ♘xc3 9 ♕d2 b6 10 ♗d3 dxc6 11 0-0 ♘a4 12 ♕xa5 bxa5 and Black was doing well in L.Schmid-Gheorghiu, Nice Olympiad 1974.

b) 6 d5 ♘d4 7 ♗d2 d6 and now:

b1) 8 ♘b5 ♘xf3+ (8...♕d8 9 ♗c3 ♗g4 10 ♘bxd4 cxd4 11 ♗xd4 ♗xf3 12 gxf3 ♕a5+ 13 ♔e2 ♘f6 was also playable in Urday-Verduga, Carlos Torre memorial, Mexico 1997) 9 ♕xf3 ♕d8 10 ♗c3 ♘f6 and here, crucially, 11 e5 dxe5 12 ♗xe5 0-0 13 ♘c7 ♗g4! is nice for Black. So White played the more modest 11 ♗e2 in Malich-Savon, Halle 1974, and after 11...a6 12 ♘a3 0-0 13 0-0 e5 14 dxe6 ♗xe6 15 ♖ad1 ♕e7 Black had a good position.

b2) So 8 ♘xd4 is normal but after 8...cxd4 9 ♘a4 we've transposed into one of the main lines of the Averbakh variation: 1 d4 g6 2 c4 ♗g7 3 e4 d6 4 ♘c3 ♘c6!? 5 d5 ♘d4 6 ♗e3 c5 7 ♘ge2 ♕b6 8 ♘xd4 cxd4 9 ♘a4 ♕a5+ 10 ♗d2 which is currently (especially after 10...♕c7) doing quite well for Black see Chapter 5.

5...♕b6 6 ♗c3

Instead 6 ♘c3 cxd4 7 ♘d5 ♕d8 8 ♗f4 d6 9 ♘xd4 is also critical when:

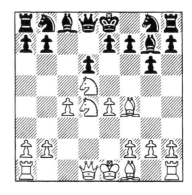

a) 9...e5!? 10 ♘b5 exf4 and:

a1) 11 ♘bc7+?! led to disaster in

Christiansen-Beliavsky, Teesside 1973: 11...♗f8 12 ♘xa8 ♘a6 13 ♕d2 ♘f6 14 ♘xf6 ♗xf6 15 ♗e2 ♗e6 16 ♕xf4 ♗xb2 17 ♖d1 ♕a5+ 18 ♔f1 ♔g7 19 h4 ♗e5 20 ♕e3 ♕c5 21 ♕b3 ♖xa8 and Black soon won.

a2) But 11 ♘dc7+ ♔e7 12 c5 dxc5 13 ♕xd8+ ♔xd8 14 0-0-0+ ♗d7 15 ♘xa8 seems to be good for White, since it's not possible to exploit the knight on a8. Wl.Schmidt-R.Nicevski, Polanica Zdroj 1974, continued 15...♘c6 16 ♘d6 ♘h6 17 ♘xb7+ ♔e7 18 ♘c7 ♖b8 19 ♘d5+ ♔f8 20 ♘xc5 ♗xb2+ 21 ♔d2 ♗e8 22 ♖b1 ♘e5 23 ♔c2 ♖c8 24 ♔xb2 ♖xc5 25 ♗e2 and White went on to win.

b) So Black should probably ignore the bait with 9...♘f6! Darga-Hartmann, German Bundesliga 1981/82, continued 10 ♘xf6+ (if 10 ♘b5 ♘xd5 11 cxd5 ♗xb2 12 ♖b1 ♗g7 White has some development for the pawn but nothing very clear) 10...♗xf6 11 ♗e3 ♕a5+ 12 ♕d2 ♕xd2+ 13 ♔xd2 ♘c6, when Black is pretty comfortable and in fact drew just a few moves later: 14 ♘b5 0-0 15 ♖b1 b6 16 ♗e2 ♗b7 17 ♖hd1 ♖fd8 18 ♔e1 ♘b4 19 f3 ♘c2+ 20 ♔d2 ♘xe3 21 ♔xe3 ♗g5+ 22 f4 ♗h6 23 g3 ♗c6 ½-½.

6...♘c6!?

If he likes that kind of thing, then Black can simply chop off wood with 6...cxd4 7 ♗xd4 ♗xd4 8 ♕xd4 ♕xd4 9 ♘xd4; while 6...♘f6!? is playable, intending after 7 d5 to follow up with a later ...e7-e5 to claim that the bishop is misplaced on c3.

7 dxc5!?

7 d5 is also very sharp, e.g. 7...♘d4 (not 7...♗xc3+ 8 ♘xc3 ♘d4 9 ♘xd4 cxd4 10 ♘b5 a6 11 ♕xd4!) 8 e5 ♘xf3+ 9 ♕xf3 and now Titov-Nesterov, Tiraspol 1994, continued 9...f6!? 10 ♕e2 (10 exf6 ♘xf6 11 ♗d3 0-0 12 0-0 d6 13 ♕e2 ♗g4 is equal) 10...fxe5 11 f4 (11 ♗xe5 ♘f6 12 ♘c3 0-0 13 0-0-0 d6 14 ♗g3 ♗f5 is also level) 11...d6 12 fxe5 dxe5 13 ♗xe5 and here Black played 13...♘f6 14 ♘c3 0-0 15 h3 e6! with

an unclear position which was eventually drawn; Belov's suggestion of 13...♗xe5 14 ♕xe5 ♕f6 15 ♕e2 ♘h6 16 ♘c3 ♘f5 also looks very playable.

7...♗xc3+ 8 ♘xc3 ♕xb2

If 8...♕xc5 9 ♘d5! gives White a safe edge.

9 ♘d5

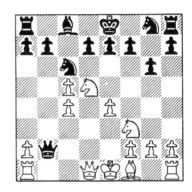

9...♔f8?!

In his notes in *Informator 57*, Pavlovic suggests instead 9...♘f6 when:

a) 10 ♗d3 0-0 11 0-0 is the only line given in *Informator*. He assesses it as slightly better for White, though it looks perfectly reasonable for Black unless something bad happens quickly.

b) 10 ♘c7+? ♔d8 11 ♘xa8 ♘xe4 12 ♕c1 ♕xf2+ 13 ♔d1 ♘d4! is very strong.

c) 10 ♖b1 ♕xa2! 11 ♘c7+ (of course, if he wanted White could force a draw by repetition with 11 ♖a1) 11...♔d8 12 ♘xa8 ♘xe4! 13 ♕c1 ♕xf2+ 14 ♔d1 gives Black a lot of compensation but needs proper testing, of course.

10 ♗e2 ♕a3

Vaulin suggests 10...e6!?, which also looks like an improvement on the game.

11 0-0 ♕xc5 12 ♕d2 ♔g7

If Black wants to play 12...d6!? he could do so at once since after

13 ♖ab1!

13...d6 is now prevented by 14 ♕c3+ followed by 15 ♖b5, trapping the queen.

13...♕a5 14 ♕b2+ f6

14...♘f6 15 ♖fd1 is also very strong.

15 e5 fxe5?

15...♕d8 was forced, though 16 ♖fe1 maintains huge pressure.

16 ♘xe5 ♘f6 17 ♗f3 ♕c5! 18 ♖fe1 ♕d4 19 ♘c7! ♕xb2 20 ♖xb2 ♘xe5!

Not 20...♖b8 21 ♗xc6 dxc6 22 ♘xc6.

21 ♖xe5! ♖b8 22 ♖xe7+ ♔h6

It has to run since 22...♔f8 23 ♖be2 is terrible, but now the king gets caught in a mating net.

23 ♖f7! ♘e8 24 ♘xe8 ♖xe8 25 h4 b6 26 g4!

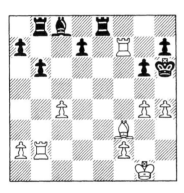

26...g5 27 ♖b5 ♔g6 28 ♖bf5 gxh4 29 ♗d5! d6 30 ♖5f6+ ♔g5 31 f4+ ♔xg4 32 ♖g7+ 1-0

Game 59
Bacrot-Speelman
Elista Olympiad 1998

1 d4 g6 2 c4 ♗g7 3 ♘c3 c5 4 d5 f5!?

I plucked this line straight out of the then England team captain David Norwood's *Winning with the Modern*. Although it is very playable at a club level, one would have to be something between extremely brave and recklessly foolhardy to repeat it internationally. There's something to be said for playing 4...♗xc3+!? 5 bxc3 and then 5...f5 to forestall 5 ♕c2 next move, but with the game move order

White has at least been induced by his opponent's structural profligacy with ...f7-f5 to spend – or if Black is grossly optimistic 'waste' – a tempo to preserve his own.

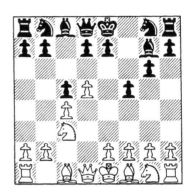

5 h4!?

5 ♕c2 is very prudent.

5...♗xc3+ 6 bxc3 ♘f6 7 h5 ♖g8!

Essential. 7...♘xh5 8 e4 ♕a5 9 exf5 ♕xc3+ 10 ♗d2 ♕e5+ 11 ♗e2 0-0 12 fxg6 would be a slaughter.

8 hxg6 hxg6

In my notes in *New in Chess* I wrote: 'Having played quite energetically over the last few moves, White now sank into something of a torpor with some listless play which surrendered the initiative to me. Without wishing to commit infanticide on Grandmaster Norwood's baby, I can say that there were improvements which would have made my life most uncomfortable...'

I suppose that, this being an opening book, I should be more specific. 9 ♕a4! is very annoying here, though not necessarily fatal.

9 ♕c2 d6 10 ♘f3 ♘bd7 11 ♗f4 ♕a5 12 ♘g5

If 12 ♘d2 g5 is excellent.

12...♘b6 13 e3 ♘a4 14 ♖c1 b5!?

This seemed obvious to me at the time, but as pointed out by my team-mates later, the less demanding 14...♗d7 15 ♗e2 0-0-0 was simple and strong.

15 ♕d2!

15 cxb5 ♘xd5 16 ♗c4 ♘ab6 would be fine for Black.

15...bxc4 16 f3! ♖b8 17 e4 ♖b2!?

I didn't want to free his pieces by exchanging on e4. This seems to be correct for after 17...fxe4 18 ♘xe4 (18 fxe4 ♖b2 19 ♕e3 ♘b6 20 ♗e2 ♕xa2 is less good) 18...♘xe4 19 fxe4 ♖b2 20 ♕e3 ♘b6 21 ♖h7! White creates serious threats.

18 ♕e3 ♘b6

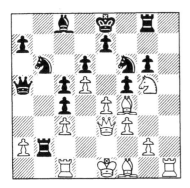

19 ♘h7!

I had foreseen this but could find no way to avoid it and was surprised by just how strong it turned out to be – presumably it demonstrates that 14...b5 was incorrect. Instead 19 ♗xd6 exd6 20 exf5+ ♔d8 (conceivably 20...♔f8 – Hiarcs) 21 ♘f7+ ♔c7 22 ♕e7+ ♘bd7 23 ♕xd6+ ♔b7 24 ♗xc4 yields insufficient compensation for the piece.

19...♘h5

After a long think though I still remained ahead on time.

The main point of 19 ♘h7 was that if 19...♘fxd5 20 exd5 ♘xd5 White has the deflection 21 ♘f6+! ♘xf6 22 ♗xd6 ♘d5 23 ♕e5 with a real mess which I didn't care for at all, since my structure has been smashed.

20 ♗xd6! exd6 21 ♖xh5! gxh5 22 ♘f6+ ♔d8 23 ♘xg8 ♕xa2

More or less forced since if 23...fxe4 24

♕xe4 ♗d7 25 ♕e7+ ♔c7 26 ♘f6 sets up the gigantic threat of ♘e8+, e.g. 26...♕xa2 27 ♘e8+ ♔b7 28 ♘xd6+ ♔a6 29 ♘xc4! winning.

24 exf5?

Quite short of time, Bacrot rather made the wrong choice. Instead, 24 ♕f4 ♔c7 25 ♘f6 was good for him since his king looks much the safer after 25...♖b1 26 ♖xb1 ♕xb1+ 27 ♔f2; while if 25...♗d7 26 e5 is unpleasant.

24...♘xd5 25 ♕e4 ♖d2

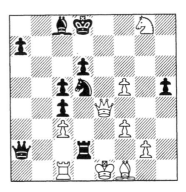

26 f6?

The fatal error. He had to control b2 with 26 ♖b1 when:

a) 26...♖c2? 27 ♖d1 ♕b2 28 ♕xd5 ♕xc3+ 29 ♖d2 gives Black insufficient play for the piece.

b) 26...♖c2 27 ♖xc2 (not 27 f6 ♕xc3) 27...♖xc2 is most rational, though it's such a mess that I was far from certain what was going on after, e.g. 28 g4.

c) In *New In Chess* I suggested that 'The fun move is 26...♖d4!?!' 27 cxd4 c3' and gave interesting lines starting 28 ♖d1 (not 28 ♕d3 c4) 28...c2. But unfortunately, as pointed out in a subsequent reader's letter, 28 ♗e2! avoids losing a tempo with the rook and is very strong, e.g. 28...♕d2+ 29 ♔f2 c2 30 ♖a1 ♗b7 (if 30...♗a6 31 ♕xd5!) 31. dxc5 dxc5 32 f6 wins.

26...♕b2 27 ♕b1 ♗e6 28 f7 ♗xf7 29 ♘h6 ♗e6 0-1

Summary

The 'pseudo g3 King's Indian' lines where Black develops his knights on d7 and e7 are quite attractively disorientating to the opponent if, as a Modern player should, that's the sort of thing he likes as Black.

Game 54 is poetry but I'm not sure about the metre. Game 55 turned out very well for me but felt excessively dodgy at the time. Game 56 is a model example of Black's dark-square strategy but in the opening the bishop isn't terribly well placed at g4 so White starts out a bit better.

The line in Game 57 looks fun for Black but unfortunately Epishin seems to have sat on it. There are many different lines stemming form Game 58 and they give excellent practical value though their theoretical value is open to doubt. And as for Game 59 of course I enjoyed it a lot at the time but the doubt in the case of this line is a looming thunder cloud.

1 d4 g6 2 c4 ♗g7

3 ♘c3
       3 ♘f3 *(D)*
             3...d6 4 e4 – *Game 57*
             3...c5 – *Game 58*
3...d6
       3...c5 – *Game 59*
4 ♘f3 ♘d7
       4...♗g4 *(D)*
             5 g3 – *Game 54*
             5 e3
                   5...♘d7 – *Game 55*
                   5...♘c6 – *Game 56*
5 g3 e5 6 ♗g2 ♘e7 7 0-0 0-0 8 e4 exd4 9 ♘xd4 ♘c6 *(D)* 10 ♘xc6
       10 ♘de2 – *Game 53*
10...bxc6 – *Game 52*

       3 ♘f3   *4...♗g4*   *9...♘c6*

INDEX OF COMPLETE GAMES